Classical and Christian Ideas in English Renaissance Poetry

Since its first publication Isabel Rivers' sourcebook has established itself as the essential student guide to English Renaissance Poetry. It

- provides an account of the main classical and Christian ideas, outlining their meaning, their origins and their transmission to the Renaissance;
- illustrates the ways in which Renaissance poetry drew on classical and Christian ideas;
- contains extracts from key classical and Christian texts and relates these to the extracts of the English poems which draw on them;
- includes suggestions for further reading, and an invaluable bibliographical appendix. In this new edition, the bibliographies have been updated to take account of important recent publications in philosophy, religion and Renaissance studies.

Dr Isabel Rivers is a Fellow and Tutor in English of St Hugh's College, Oxford.

By the same author

The Poetry of Conservatism 1600–1745: A Study of Poets and Public Affairs from Jonson to Pope (1973)

Books and their Readers in Eighteenth-Century England (editor) (1982)

Reason, Grace, and Sentiment: A Study of the Language of Religion and Ethics in England, 1660–1780, volume I: *Whichcote to Wesley* (1991)

Classical and Christian Ideas in English Renaissance Poetry

A Students' Guide

Second Edition

ISABEL RIVERS

London and New York

First published in 1979 by George Allen & Unwin (Publishers) Ltd

Reprinted 1992
by Routledge
11 New Fetter Lane, London EC4P 4EE
29 West 35th Street, New York, NY 10001

Second edition 1994

Reprinted 1996, 1999

Routledge is an imprint of the Taylor & Francis Group

© George Allen & Unwin (Publishers) Ltd 1994

Typeset in Times by Solidus (Bristol) Limited
Printed and bound in Great Britain by
Biddles Ltd, Guildford and King's Lynn

British Library Cataloguing in Publication Data

Rivers, Isabel
    Classical and Christian Ideas in English
Renaissance Poetry
  1. English poetry – Early modern, 1500-1700 –
History and criticism. 2. Christianity and literature
3. Literature and history
I. Title
821.´3´093   PR538.C/   78–40853

Library of Congress Cataloguing in Publication Data

Rivers, Isabel
    Classical and Christian Ideas in English Renaissance Poetry: A
students' guide / Isabel Rivers. – 2nd ed.
    p. cm.
Includes bibliographical references and index.
  1. English poetry – Early modern, 1500-1700 – History and criticism.
2. Christian poetry, English – History and criticism. 3. English
poetry – Classical influences. 4. Christianity and literature.
5. Renaissance – England. 6. Classicism – England. I. Title.
PR535.R4R58   1994
821´.3´093–dc20   94– 12710

ISBN 0–415–10646–X (hbk)
ISBN 0–415–10647–8 (pbk)

Contents

(Note: numbers in parentheses in the introductory sections refer to the extracts at the end of each chapter.)

Preface to the Second Edition

This handbook has been in print continuously since its first publication in 1979, and I am pleased that several generations of undergraduate and graduate students and their teachers have found it useful. Since I wrote it there has been an explosion of research and publication in many areas of Renaissance studies, and in order for the book to retain its usefulness as a bibliographical guide I thought it necessary to bring the bibliographical sections up to date. I have partly rewritten the Introduction, but otherwise the structure, the introductory chapters, and the collections of extracts remain unchanged, except for some minor corrections. I have added a new paragraph to each of the sections under Further Reading, taking account of significant publications since 1977 (when I completed the first edition); in a few cases I have included earlier books which I was unaware of or unable to consult. Bibliographical Appendix A and the introductory section to B have been comprehensively revised; further titles have been added to the majority of the authors under B, and thirteen new authors have been included. I am very grateful to Julia Griffin of St John's College, Oxford, who has helped me with the work for the Bibliographical Appendix.

There have been important developments in scholarly research in two of the principal subjects with which this book is concerned: religion and philosophy. First, many historians of the sixteenth and seventeenth centuries have become much more interested in ideas and beliefs and what these meant to those who held them, and much less willing to translate these ideas and beliefs into modern secular or socio-economic terms. One consequence of this valuable new emphasis is a continuing debate among historians of the English Reformation and Revolution as to the meaning of key terms such as Reformed and Catholic, Calvinist and Arminian, and Puritan and Anglican. Much important new work has been done by literary historians on Spenser, Donne, Herbert, Milton, and other poets in the light of this development. Second, the vitality and variousness of Renaissance philosophy is now increasingly recognised, and our knowledge has been significantly extended, for example in the study of humanism and rhetoric and of the continuing strength of Aristotelianism in the sixteenth century. There is now much more material available to help modern readers set English Renaissance poetry in its intellectual contexts. If this revised, second edition

encourages students to follow up some of this new material it will have
succeeded in its purpose.

ISABEL RIVERS
OXFORD, SEPTEMBER 1993

Preface to the First Edition

I conceived the idea of a book that would make Renaissance poetry more accessible to the student reader when I first began undergraduate teaching, and throughout the preparation and writing of this book I have had the needs of the student reader foremost in my mind. In my attempt to synthesise and clarify large and often complex areas of knowledge I have drawn freely on the work of scholars in a number of fields relevant to Renaissance studies. The way in which I have chosen to organise the book, with the interests of the student, not the scholar, in mind, means that I have not distinguished the original from the borrowed parts of my argument. However, although I have not acknowledged specific debts, the more important of these are indicated in the lists of Further Reading at the end of the book. I can only hope that my wish to see the intellectual context of Renaissance literature more widely understood will justify my dependence on the work of others.

I owe more immediate debts to former teachers and colleagues. My supervisors at Columbia University, especially Professor E.W. Tayler, taught me the need to explore the intellectual context of Renaissance literature. Colleagues at Leicester have given me help of different kinds: Professor A.D. Fitton Brown has provided me with some classical sources; J.C. Hilson has had many conversations with me about the nature of literary contexts; in particular, R.K. Biswas has discussed the planning of the book at all stages and patiently read and criticised the first draft in detail. T.M. Rivers has helped correct the proofs.

I wish to thank Penguin Books Ltd for permission to quote from the following copyright material: Augustine, *Concerning the City of God against the Pagans*, translated by Henry Bettenson, and Ovid, *Metamorphoses*, translated by Mary M. Innes.

ISABEL RIVERS
LEICESTER, DECEMBER 1977

Introduction: Renaissance Poetry and Modern Readers

Modern readers approach Renaissance poetry severely handicapped. They do not share the intellectual preconceptions of Renaissance authors; they have not read the books that formed their minds; they do not ask the same metaphysical or moral or aesthetic questions; though they may use the same vocabulary, they do not assign it the same meaning. These handicaps exist, but they can be surmounted. One solution is to attempt to ignore such differences and concentrate instead on those aspects of the poetry that modern readers can regard as perennial and interpret in the light of their own interests. This approach seems to me mistaken. It is arrogant, in that it supposes that the habits of mind of the present are fundamentally more important than the habits of mind of the past; it is limiting, in that it restricts the amount of a work that modern readers can grasp; by ignoring difficulties in effect it hinders their capacity to reach and hence enjoy the literature of the past. I have written this guide in the belief that the precondition for enjoyment is understanding, that Renaissance poetry is in many ways alien to modern readers and difficult for them to understand, but that the necessary understanding can be achieved by the recovery of the context within which the poetry was written.

By context I mean the intellectual assumptions, the literary conventions, and the terminology which Renaissance poets shared with their contemporary readers, and which their poetry might in many different ways appraise, explore or question. I am concerned in this book with a range of assumptions about the nature and function of man which derive from fifteen hundred years of blending of the classical and Christian traditions. How did these traditions affect the educated English poet of the period 1580 to 1670? First, he was a Christian. He had a thorough knowledge of the Bible, and of the language and arguments of theology. He was probably fairly widely read in works of religious controversy, both of his own day and (in fewer cases) of the early centuries of the Church. Second, he was a classical scholar. Latin was the basis of his education. He was widely read in Latin poetry, history and moral philosophy; he had some acquaintance with Greek, though he usually read Greek literature in Latin or English translations – only the exceptionally learned read Greek in the original. His knowledge of the classical and Christian traditions came not only from first-hand reading of the texts – the Bible, the Fathers of the Church, the Latin and Greek classics – but also from popular handbooks and encyclopedias which digested the traditions for him. He perhaps consulted these handbooks more often than the original texts. He did not regard the traditions as separate; he read classical literature in the light of his Christian beliefs. However, the blending of these traditions did not create one uniform world picture; rather, it provided a range of sometimes complementary, sometimes contradictory assumptions about and explanations of the nature of the physical universe, man's relationship with God, his moral stature, and the purpose of his earthly activities.

Most of the assumptions that Renaissance poets shared with their contemporaries are unfamiliar to modern readers. I have written this book for students who wish to read and enjoy Renaissance literature, but who have no knowledge of Greek, probably none of Latin, only a hazy acquaintance with the contents of the Bible and the tenets of Christianity, and who are thus unlikely to be aware of the difficulties confronting them. My intention is to show them the means by which they can in part recover the intellectual context of Renaissance poetry. It seems to me that illustration of what is likely to be unfamiliar material is as important as explication. I have therefore organised this guide according to the following method. Each chapter is concerned with one important group of ideas. Chapters 1 to 6 deal mainly with classical ideas and their assimilation by Christianity; Chapters 7 and 8 deal with Christian ideas; and Chapters 9 to 13 deal with ideas about education and the interpretation and writing of literary works. In a book of restricted length I have chosen to exclude certain subjects, notably political thought, psychology, rhetoric and most aspects of the occult, but I hope that this decision has allowed me to give adequate representation to those subjects I have considered most important. Each chapter is divided into three parts: (1) an introductory account outlining the nature of the ideas in question, their origins and their transmission to the Renaissance, and suggesting how they were taken up by poets; (2) a collection of extracts from original sources, illustrating the genesis and development of these ideas, followed by extracts from English poetry of the period 1580 to 1670 incorporating aspects of these ideas and their terminology; (3) suggestions for further secondary reading, which are collected under chapter headings at the end of the book. The extracts are numbered and keyed to the introductory account, so that students can use them in two different ways: when reading the introduction they can turn to the relevant numbered extract which illustrates a particular point in the argument; or they can read and compare the group of extracts as a whole, thus themselves placing the poems within a part of their intellectual context. The Bibliographical Appendix provides as concisely as possible further information about the authors from whom the extracts are taken.

Most of the extracts are translations from Latin (classical, medieval and Renaissance); some are translations from Greek, Italian, French and German; there are several extracts from the Bible. Many of the works represented were translated into English in the Renaissance, but with a few exceptions (for example Harington's Ariosto, Hoby's Castiglione, Florio's Montaigne and Fairfax's Tasso) I have decided against using these translations. Instead I have used readily available modern translations (Penguin Classics or the Loeb Classical Library whenever possible), so that students may easily locate an extract and read further. For the sake of consistency I have taken all extracts from the Bible from the Authorised Version, though in some cases (for example, extracts from Augustine which include biblical quotations) this has meant anachronistically substituting it for other versions. Extracts from English Renaissance poetry are taken from standard modern editions, though I have modernised the spelling throughout. The poets represented by the greatest number of extracts are Spenser, Jonson, Donne, Herbert, Marvell and Milton, though I have included examples of other poets. I have deliberately excluded dramatic poetry. I have provided brief references to book, chapter and line numbers, etc. below each extract, and full bibliographical references, arranged alphabetically, at the end of the book.

The organisation of material in terms of specific groups of ideas has seemed to me the best way of illustrating the problems, but I am aware that this approach has its dangers. In the interest of clarity I have simplified complex concepts, and my account of their historical modification is cursory. A greater danger is that of systematisation. I am not attempting to fit Renaissance poets within particular systems of thought, nor do I believe that it can be done. Ideas expressed in works of literature are not the same as ideas tested for their own sake. Renaissance poets freely explored and amalgamated ideas which in themselves are contradictory. Thus many of the assumptions of classical ethics are strictly incompatible with Christian belief, yet we find them coexisting in Renaissance literature. The same group of ideas can be treated in very different ways by different poets; students need to consider not simply the presence of certain ideas in a specific poem, but, more important, the use to which they are put.

The groups of extracts are intended to provide a fairly broad range of illustration for students to draw on in their reading of Renaissance poetry. However, this book is intended as a guide to the classical and Christian traditions; it is not a substitute for first-hand knowledge of them. Establishing the context of Renaissance poetry means reading at least the more important of the books Renaissance authors read. I suggest that students should make themselves familiar with the following works:

Classical poetry: Homer's *Iliad*; Virgil's *Aeneid*; Ovid's *Metamorphoses*.
Classical philosophy: Plato's *Symposium* and *Republic*; Aristotle's *Nicomachean Ethics*; Cicero's *Of Duties*.
Christian literature: the Bible in the Authorised Version, especially the Pauline Epistles; Augustine's *City of God*, Books XI–XXII.

In addition, students should read Sir Thomas Browne's *Religio Medici*, which provides an invaluable example of how a certain kind of Renaissance mind worked.

In order to illustrate ways in which this book may be of use, I give below four examples of well-known passages from Renaissance poems which require some knowledge of their intellectual context to make them comprehensible to modern readers; I have chosen some of these passages because I have seen them misread by my own students, who were not aware of the difficulties. I am not suggesting that Renaissance poems are never ambiguous, or that one correct meaning is always there to be unlocked by those in possession of the proper key. I do believe, however, that some apparent ambiguities are simply misreadings, and that knowledge of a poem's context reveals aspects of the poem that are closed to the ignorant. In some cases allusions which would have clarified and enriched meaning for Renaissance readers simply bewilder modern readers who are unfamiliar with them; in other cases the problem is one of the correct definition of a single word, which is superficially comprehensible to modern readers but which is used by the Renaissance poet in a technical sense which would have been familiar to his contemporaries.

1   Not that great champion of the antique world,
     Whom famous poets' verse so much doth vaunt,
     And hath for twelve huge labours high extolled,
     So many furies and sharp fits did haunt,
     When him the poisoned garment did enchant,
     When Centaur's blood and bloody verses charmed;
     As did this knight twelve thousand dolours daunt,
     Whom fiery steel now burnt, that erst him armed;
     That erst him goodly armed, now most of all him harmed.
                    Spenser *The Faerie Queene* I xi stanza 27

Canto xi narrates the battle between Red Cross Knight and the dragon. Up to this point the narrative has been conducted at the literal level, stressing the physical conflict. Spenser here introduces an allusion to Hercules: Red Cross is burnt through his armour by the dragon's fiery breath, just as Hercules was tortured by the poisoned garment sent him by his wife, who was tricked by the Centaur Nessus into believing that his blood would act as a love potion. The armour that should protect Red Cross torments him; the garment that was intended as a charm to win back love becomes an instrument of destruction. Modern readers unfamiliar with the tradition may see in this allusion simply an attempt to magnify the sufferings of Red Cross, which are greater than those of Hercules. But much more is implied. Spenser would expect his readers to complete the story. In his agony Hercules burns himself alive on a funeral pyre on Mount Oeta; his mortal flesh is consumed, but his divine form is transmuted, and he goes to join the gods. For Renaissance readers the hero who is greater than Hercules is Christ. In the remainder of the canto the allusions are largely Christian: to baptism, the tree of life, regeneration, the three days from crucifixion to resurrection. The comparison of the burning armour of Red Cross to the poisoned garment of Hercules is thus a reference to the passion of Christ, which is a necessary prelude to his triumphant conquest of sin and the devil. The armour which both protects and torments Red Cross, and which he tries to put off, is the armour of faith of every Christian (Ephesians 6: 10–18; see **4** below), which brings him both salvation and persecution. By means of a classical allusion Spenser moves from literal narrative to Christian allegory. (On the Christianisation of classical myth see Chapter 2.)

2   Having been tenant long to a rich Lord,
       Not thriving, I resolvèd to be bold,
       And make a suit unto him, to afford
    A new small-rented lease, and cancel the old.

    In heaven at his manor I him sought:
       They told me there, that he was lately gone
       About some land, which he had dearly bought
    Long since on earth, to take possession.

Herbert 'Redemption' ll. 1–8

Herbert's sonnet is a parable, a deceptively simple narrative based on commonplace experience yet containing a religious meaning. The imagery used – the tenant who complains of his inability to make a success of the old property leased to him, and who asks his Lord of the Manor for a new one on more favourable terms – both recalls the parables of Christ, in which the relationship between God and man is often cast in the similar but not identical terms of the contractual relationship between master and servant (see e.g. Matthew 18:23–34; 20:1–16; 21:33–41), and embodies the principles of covenant theology, in which the law, or the old covenant of works, under which man cannot 'thrive' because he cannot achieve righteousness through his own efforts, is replaced by the gospel, the new covenant of grace which is the free gift of God. Man's redemption is literally a 'buying back': a debt paid by Christ on his behalf, so that he can exchange one contract for another, better one. I have heard this beautiful sonnet condemned by a student unfamiliar with its context for its commercial view of religion. (On Law and Gospel see Chapter 8; on parables see Chapter 12.)

3   Happy those early days! when I
     Shined in my angel-infancy.
     Before I understood this place
     Appointed for my second race,
     Or taught my soul to fancy aught
     But a white, celestial thought,
     When yet I had not walked above
     A mile, or two, from my first love,
     And looking back (at that short space),
     Could see a glimpse of his bright face;
     When on some gilded cloud, or flower
     My gazing soul would dwell an hour,
     And in those weaker glories spy
     Some *shadows* of eternity.

                    Vaughan 'The Retreat' ll. 1–14 (italics mine)

Vaughan's most famous poem usually has an immediate attraction for modern readers. To a large extent it is self-explanatory; the Christian–Platonic doctrine of the recollection of a first, better state of existence may be unfamiliar but in Vaughan's treatment it is not obscure. However, the technical term 'shadows' will not mean very much to readers unfamiliar with its typological sense. Vaughan is using the term here not so much in its Platonic sense as in the sense employed in Biblical exegesis. 'Shadows' in the Platonic sense (as in the Allegory of the Cave) would mean the world of the senses, deceptively real, but in fact insubstantial, and incomparable to the real world of Ideas. 'Shadows' in its exegetical sense means 'foreshadowings'. A flower is a weaker glory than God, yet such glory as it has foreshadows for man in this life the greater glory he will perceive in the next. The brightness of God's face is veiled for man by his corporeal existence, yet through the shadows of the physical world he can perceive glimpses of brightness which otherwise would be unbearable. The best gloss on 'shadows' is a passage from Browne's *Garden of Cyrus*, ch. iv:

Light that makes things seen, makes some things invisible; were it not for darkness and the shadow of the earth, the noblest part of the Creation had remained unseen, and the stars in heaven as invisible as on the fourth day, when they were created above the horizon, with the sun, or there was not an eye to behold them. The greatest mystery of religion is expressed by adumbration [i.e. foreshadowing], and in the noblest part of Jewish types, we find the Cherubims shadowing the mercy-seat: Life itself is but the shadow of death; and souls departed but the shadows of the living: All things fall under this name. The sun itself is but the dark simulacrum [i.e. image], and light but the shadow of God.

(For Platonism see Chapter 3, for Biblical exegesis Chapter 10, for allegory Chapter 12.)

4   And opportunity I here have had
To try thee, sift thee, and confess have found thee
Proof against all temptation as a rock
Of adamant, and as a *centre*, firm
To the utmost of mere man both wise and good ...
....
There on the highest pinnacle he set
The Son of God; and added thus in scorn:
    There *stand*, if thou wilt *stand*; to *stand* upright
Will ask thee skill; I to thy Father's house
Have brought thee, and highest placed, highest is best,
Now show thy progeny; if not to *stand*
Cast thyself down; safely if Son of God:
For it is written, He will give command
Concerning thee to his angels, in their hands
They shall uplift thee, lest at any time
Thou chance to dash thy foot against a stone.
    To whom thus Jesus: Also it is written,
Tempt not the Lord thy God, he said and *stood*.
But Satan smitten with amazement fell.
          Milton *Paradise Regained* IV ll. 531–5, 549–62 (italics mine)

Satan presents the Son of God with his last temptation, that of the pinnacle of the temple. (Milton follows the order of the temptations in Luke 4:1–13; Matthew 4:1–11 puts this temptation second.) In neither of the gospel versions is there any question of the temptation being one of standing on the pinnacle; Jesus is set there by Satan, and tempted to cast himself down. The word 'stand' does not appear in the gospel temptations, yet Milton places great stress on it. It is used in two senses. Satan uses it in the false sense of Stoic self-sufficiency; he admires in the Son the perfect Stoic sage, immovable, complete in himself 'as a centre'. This terminology is repeatedly used by Jonson, who urges himself and his moral heroes to stand, to rely on their own completion and circular perfection, to rest on their own centre. These terms appear in 'An Epistle Answering to One that Asked to be Sealed of the Tribe of Ben':

> Live to that point I will, for which I am man,
> And dwell as in my centre, as I can . . .
> . . . . . . Now stand, and then
> Sir, you are sealèd of the tribe of Ben.

ll. 59–60, 77–8

Satan erroneously believes that man is capable of this self-sufficiency, but morally, not where it is physically impossible. He expects Jesus either, as man, to fall and die, or, as God, to be rescued in falling by angels. But neither happens; refusing to tempt God, but instead putting his trust in him, Jesus stands, and Satan falls. The episode demonstrates both the Son's divinity and the true meaning of 'stand'. With God's grace man can stand, not like the Stoic in opposition to the world, but like the armed Christian, in preparation for action:

> Wherefore take unto you the whole armour of God, that ye may be able to withstand in the evil day, and having done all, to stand.

Ephesians 6:13

(For Stoicism see Chapter 4.)

1 The Golden Age and the Garden of Eden

Both classical and Christian cultures shared a belief in an original state of human perfection, in which man lived effortlessly and in complete harmony with nature, free from time, change and death. In classical culture this period was known as the golden age. The idea goes back to a very early Greek poem, Hesiod's *Works and Days*, which describes five races of men succeeding one another chronologically: golden (ideal), silver (impious), brazen (warlike and cruel), the race of heroes (demigods who approached the perfection of the golden race), and iron (the present race, who lead a miserable and laborious life). In some later versions there are only two races, the golden and the iron. Cronos (later identified with the Roman Saturn) ruled during the golden age; when his son Zeus (the Roman Jupiter) deposed him the golden age ended and man's troubles began (**1, 5**). The goddess of justice, Astraea, has a significant part in the story; in one version she flees to the mountains during the silver age, and finally abandons mankind during the age of bronze.

This myth of the ages of mankind locates the ideal in the distant past and implies the progressive degeneration of the species. But classical myth also describes two other kinds of ideal existence, one present, but distant in space, one future, to be attained after death. In Hesiod's story the race of heroes did not entirely die out; a few live on in the Isles of the Blest, somewhere in the Atlantic. Similarly in Homer some of the heroes are promised an immortal and happy life on earth; Menelaus is told that he will join others favoured by the gods in the Elysian plain, also situated in the west (*Odyssey* IV) (**2**). The garden of the Hesperides (whose trees bore golden fruit which were stolen by Hercules as one of his labours) was sometimes linked in the Renaissance with these islands. In classical literature after Homer Elysium becomes the reward for the souls of the just after death. The best-known classical account is in *Aeneid* VI; Aeneas, led through the underworld by the Sibyl, comes to the Elysian fields where he observes the Blest, dancing and singing, still taking pride in their chariots and horses, and meets his dead father Anchises. These states of existence, whether conceived of as past, present or future, are both physically and morally perfect.

In Christian myth there are similar temporal distinctions. The ideal existence in the past is that of Adam in paradise, the garden made by God in Eden (**6, 9**). The word 'paradise' goes back to Old Persian via Greek, and means an enclosed park or garden; Eden means pleasure in Hebrew. Christian commentators (with a few exceptions) were certain that Eden had a real historical existence; in *The City of God* XIV xi Augustine argues that its pleasures were as much physical as spiritual. Eden was traditionally located in Mesopotamia; in his *History of the World* (1614) Ralegh provides a map of the Middle East with the exact spot marked.

In Jewish and, later, Christian tradition there is a recurrent contrast between garden and wilderness. The history of Israel is seen as a journey through the wilderness and back to the garden, the promised land of Canaan (**7**). The earthly paradise is thus set in the present as well as the past; it can be recovered. In the seventeenth century America comes to have the connotations of the promised land for Puritans fleeing religious persecution in the Old World (indicated by the names of New England towns: Salem, New Canaan). In Christian thought, though both kinds of earthly paradise, past and present, Eden and the promised land, are good in themselves, they are ultimately foreshadowings of the future heavenly paradise, which in spite of its name is usually envisaged as a city rather than a garden. (For the idea of the two cities see Chapter 5.)

The classical and Christian earthly paradises have certain important characteristics in common. There are no seasons; the time is perpetual spring. Man does not work to survive; the earth gives up its produce spontaneously. The land flows with wine, milk and honey. Agriculture, trade and travel are unknown. There is abundance of vegetation and water. There is no conflict between man and man or man and nature; there is no decay (**3, 5, 9**).

Christian writers found various ways of explaining these common characteristics and of assimilating the idea of the golden age to Eden. One version was that the golden age was the period when the pagans had worshipped the true God; subsequently (as indicated by the usurpation by Zeus/Jupiter of the throne of Cronos/Saturn) they had lost this knowledge. Another, much repeated, was that the pagans had obtained a rough account of Moses' description of Eden, so that their fables were faint shadows of the truth. Thus when Dante and Virgil reach the earthly paradise in *Purgatorio* xxviii, Virgil recognises that this is the original of the golden age of which he once wrote. In his commentary on Ovid's *Metamorphoses* (1632) George Sandys makes a neat parallel between the classical and Christian accounts: 'Saturn was the first that invented tillage, the first that ever reigned; and so was Adam: Saturn was thrown out of heaven, and Adam out of paradise', and so on. Sandys assumes that Ovid must have read the Books of Moses or at least heard of them;

Ralegh makes the same point spitefully when he says (*History of the World* I iii 3) that the pagans 'did greatly enrich their inventions, by venting the stolen treasures of divine letters, altered by profane additions, and disguised by poetical conversions, as if they had been conceived out of their own speculations and contemplations'.

Although there are important similarities between the traditions, and although Christian authors deliberately drew the two together, one must not make the mistake of assuming that literary use of the theme of paradise is uniform. Renaissance poetry abounds with references to the golden age and Eden, to earthly and heavenly paradises, past, present and future. It is important to define the way in which the theme is being used. Some of the chief kinds of literary allusion are indicated below.

The attempt to recover paradise is sometimes used as a metaphor for the struggle for individual moral perfection (**21**). In Dante's *Purgatorio* the attainment of the earthly paradise, situated at the top of a mountain up which the pilgrims must climb, appears to represent this struggle. Virgil, Dante's guide, can take him as far as the earthly paradise but no further; he cannot give him knowledge of the true heavenly paradise, which Beatrice and St Bernard will reveal. In Spenser's *Faerie Queene* I xi the quest of the Red Cross Knight takes the form of a journey back to Eden, with the defeat of the Satanic dragon, the freeing of the besieged inhabitants of the country, and a temporary recovery of original innocence. The betrothal of Red Cross to Una has political and theological as well as moral connotations (Eden is protestant England), but Red Cross's victory over the dragon is achieved largely because he has conquered himself. On one level of meaning, therefore, paradise is the good Christian life. This meaning is explicit in Milton. The paradise that is lost in Milton's epic is both a physical place (**10**) and a state of mind; the paradise that is regained is only the latter. The mount of paradise is washed away in the Flood, never to be found again; the new earthly paradise, as Michael explains to Adam, is to be an inner one (**11, 12**). Christ creates a metaphorical Eden in the wilderness by overcoming Satan's temptations (**13**). Paradise as a physical place, the heavenly paradise, will not be recovered till the end of the world.

The return of the golden age is often used as a political image. A new regime or dynasty may be celebrated as the new reign of Saturn and the return of Astraea to earth. Virgil is the ultimate source for this idea. In *Aeneid* VIII Aeneas learns that Latium, the Italian kingdom where Rome is to be founded, was governed by Saturn after Jupiter had deposed him. Rome under Augustus achieves the new golden age (**4**); history comes full circle. (See Chapter 5.) Virgil's extraordinarily influential *Eclogue* IV, which Christians interpreted as a Messianic prophecy, treats the birth of a child as the occasion for celebrating the return of Astraea and a new social order (3). This political theme is much imitated in the Renaissance; Elizabeth I is frequently praised as Astraea. In *The Faerie Queene* V Artegall, the Knight of Justice, is Astraea's adopted son; but because he moves through a fallen world he administers justice with the help not of Astraea herself but of her iron henchman Talus. In Jonson's masque *The Golden Age Restored* Astraea praises James I as the agent of her return. In literature after the Civil War the political use of paradise is nostalgic rather than celebratory; thus Marvell sees the England of the 1630s as a lost Eden (**18**).

There is also a social use of paradise which emphasises its enclosed, exclusive nature. Many Renaissance poems celebrating country houses or the pleasures of retirement to the country or the pastoral world draw on golden age and paradise motifs. In these works there is usually a contrast between paradise and the world outside, between the contemplative and active life, but the emphasis may vary considerably. In Sidney's *Arcadia* I and *The Faerie Queene* VI the escapism inherent in the idea of Arcadia, the shepherds' paradise, is tested critically; the life celebrated in Jonson's country house poems, which draw on the Horatian tradition of the Sabine farm, is morally superior to and rejects the temptations of the world outside.

In Renaissance epics the nature of paradise is often defined through comparison with a false paradise, the original source of which is the story of Circe and her island in *Odyssey* X. The pattern is repeated many times: the garden is a false retreat; the hero or knight is seduced by the enchantress away from his moral and social duties; in succumbing he is transformed into an animal. The best examples of false paradises are those of Alcina in Ariosto's *Orlando Furioso* VI (**14**), Armida in Tasso's *Jerusalem Delivered* XV–XVI (**15**), Actrasia in *The Faerie Queene* II xii (**16**). Milton's enchanter Comus, himself the son of Circe, belongs to this tradition. These paradises are false not because they are earthly but because they limit man's nature; the true earthly paradise, though its pleasures may be sensual (as in Spenser's Garden of Adonis, *Faerie Queene* III vi) (Ch. **2.10**), reflects the heavenly paradise and is not an end in itself.

Finally there are uses of golden age and paradise motifs which are consciously amoral or mocking or ironic. In Cavalier poetry paradise is sometimes an image of complete sexual freedom (**22**). In 'A Rapture' Carew envisages Elysium as the place where the world's frustrated and unrequited lovers are satisfied, and where the restrictive codes of marriage and honour no longer apply. Readers should try to distinguish poems in which paradise itself is the subject from those in which it is essentially a literary device used to illuminate another subject.

THE CLASSICAL GOLDEN AGE

1   The gods, who live on Mount Olympus, first
     Fashioned a golden race of mortal men;
     These lived in the reign of Cronos, king of heaven.
     And like the gods they lived with happy hearts
     Untouched by work or sorrow. Vile old age
     Never appeared, but always lively-limbed,
     Far from all ills, they feasted happily.
     Death came to them as sleep, and all good things
     Were theirs: ungrudgingly, the fertile land
     Gave up her fruits unasked. Happy to be
     At peace, they lived with every want supplied,
     Rich in their flocks, dear to the blessed gods.
                                Hesiod *Works and Days*, ll. 109–20

2   Proteus prophesies to Menelaus:
     And now, King Menelaus, hear your own destiny. You will not meet your
     fate and die in Argos where the horses graze. Instead, the immortals will
     send you to the Elysian plain at the world's end, to join red-haired
     Rhadamanthus in the land where living is made easiest for mankind,
     where no snow falls, no strong winds blow and there is never any rain,
     but day after day the West Wind's tuneful breeze comes in from Ocean
     to refresh its folk.
                                Homer *Odyssey* IV ll. 561–8

3   We have reached the last era in Sibylline song. Time has conceived and
     the great sequence of the ages starts afresh. Justice, the virgin, comes
     back to dwell with us, and the rule of Saturn is restored. The first-born
     of the new age is already on his way from high heaven down to earth ...
     Later again, when the strengthening years have made a man of you, even
     the trader will forsake the sea, and pine-wood ships will cease to carry
     merchandise for barter, each land producing all it needs. No mattock will
     molest the soil, no pruning-knife the vine; and then at last the sturdy
     ploughman will free his oxen from the yoke. Wool will be taught no more
     to cheat the eye with this tint or that, but the ram himself in his own
     meadows will change the colour of his fleece, now to the soft glow of a
     purple dye, now to a saffron yellow. Lambs at their pastures will find
     themselves in scarlet coats.
                                Virgil *Eclogue* IV ll. 4–7, 37–45

4   Anchises prophesies to Aeneas:
     And there in very truth is he whom you have often heard prophesied,
     Augustus Caesar, son of the Deified, and founder of golden centuries
     once more in Latium, on those same lands where once Saturn reigned.
                                Virgil *Aeneid* VI ll. 791–4

5   In the beginning was the Golden Age, when men of their own accord,
     without threat of punishment, without laws, maintained good faith and

did what was right. There were no penalties to be afraid of, no bronze tablets were erected, carrying threats of legal action, no crowd of wrong-doers, anxious for mercy, trembled before the face of their judge: indeed, there were no judges, men lived securely without them. Never yet had any pine tree, cut down from its home on the mountains, been launched on ocean's waves, to visit foreign lands: men knew only their own shores. Their cities were not yet surrounded by sheer moats, they had no straight brass trumpets, no coiling brass horns, no helmets and no swords. The peoples of the world, untroubled by any fears, enjoyed a leisurely and peaceful existence, and had no use for soldiers. The earth itself, without compulsion, untouched by the hoe, unfurrowed by any share, produced all things spontaneously, and men were content with foods that grew without cultivation.

Ovid *Metamorphoses* I ll. 89–103

EDEN AND THE PROMISED LAND

6   And the Lord God planted a garden eastward in Eden; and there he put the man whom he had formed.

And out of the ground made the Lord God to grow every tree that is pleasant to the sight, and good for food; the tree of life also in the midst of the garden, and the tree of knowledge of good and evil.

And a river went out of Eden to water the garden; and from thence it was parted, and became into four heads.

Genesis 2:8–10

7   And the Lord said, I have surely seen the affliction of my people which are in Egypt, and have heard their cry by reason of their taskmasters; for I know their sorrows;

And I am come down to deliver them out of the hand of the Egyptians, and to bring them up out of that land unto a good land and a large, unto a land flowing with milk and honey.

Exodus 3:7–8

8   The wolf also shall dwell with the lamb, and the leopard shall lie down with the kid; and the calf and the young lion and the fatling together; and a little child shall lead them.

And the cow and the bear shall feed; their young ones shall lie down together: and the lion shall eat straw like the ox.

And the sucking child shall play on the hole of the asp, and the weaned child shall put his hand on the cockatrice' den.

They shall not hurt nor destroy in all my holy mountain: for the earth shall be full of the knowledge of the Lord, as the waters cover the sea.

Isaiah 11:6–9

9   We conclude then that man lived in paradise as long as his wish was at one with God's command. He lived in the enjoyment of God, and derived his own goodness from God's goodness. He lived without any want, and

had it in his power to live like this for ever. Food was available to prevent hunger, drink to prevent thirst, and the tree of life was there to guard against old age and dissolution. There was no trace of decay in the body, or arising from the body, to bring any distress to any of his senses. There was no risk of disease from within or of injury from without. Man enjoyed perfect health in the body, entire tranquillity in the soul. Just as in paradise there was no extreme of heat or of cold, so in its inhabitant no desire or fear intervened to hamper his good will. There was no sadness at all, nor any frivolous jollity. But true joy flowed perpetually from God ... Between man and wife there was a faithful partnership based on love and mutual respect; there was a harmony and a liveliness of mind and body, and an effortless observance of the commandment.

Augustine *City of God* XIV xxvi

10   Thus was this place,
A happy rural seat of various view;
Groves whose rich trees wept odorous gums and balm,
Others whose fruit burnished with golden rind
Hung amiable, Hesperian fables true,
If true, here only, and of delicious taste:
Betwixt them lawns, or level downs, and flocks
Grazing the tender herb, were interposed,
Or palmy hillock, or the flowery lap
Of some irriguous valley spread her store,
Flowers of all hue, and without thorn the rose.
. . . . . .
        Not that fair field
Of Enna, where Prosperine gathering flowers
Her self a fairer flower by gloomy Dis
Was gathered, which cost Ceres all that pain
To seek her through the world; nor that sweet grove
Of Daphne by Orontes, and the inspired
Castalian spring, might with this Paradise
Of Eden strive.

Milton *Paradise Lost* IV ll. 246–56, 268–75

11 Michael prophesies to Adam:
        Then shall this mount
Of Paradise by might of waves be moved
Out of his place, pushed by the hornèd flood,
With all his verdure spoiled, and trees adrift
Down the great river to the opening gulf,
And there take root an island salt and bare,
The haunt of seals and orcs, and sea-mews' clang.
To teach thee that God attributes to place
No sanctity, if none be thither brought
By men who there frequent, or therein dwell.

Paradise Lost XI ll. 829–38

12   Only add
Deeds to thy knowledge answerable, add faith
Add virtue, patience, temperance, add love
By name to come called Charity, the soul
Of all the rest: then wilt thou not be loath
To leave this Paradise, but shalt possess
A paradise within thee, happier far.

Paradise Lost XII ll. 581–7

13 The angels praise Jesus:
For though that seat of earthly bliss be failed.
A fairer Paradise is founded now
For Adam and his chosen sons, whom thou
A Saviour art come down to reinstall.

Paradise Regained IV ll. 612–15

FALSE PARADISES

14 The kingdom of Alcina:
These maids with courteous speech and manners nice
Welcome Rogero to this paradise.

If so I may a paradise it name,
Where love and lust have built their habitation,
Where time well spent is counted as a shame,
No wise staid thought, no care of estimation,
Nor nought but courting, dancing, play, and game,
Disguisèd clothes, each day a sundry fashion:
No virtuous labour doth this people please,
But nice apparel, belly-cheer, and ease.

Ariosto *Orlando Furioso* VI stanzas 72–3

15 Armida's nymph tempts Rinaldo's rescuers:
This is the place wherein you may assuage
Your sorrows past, here is that joy and bliss
That flourished in the antique golden age;
Here needs no law, here none doth aught amiss;
Put off those arms, and fear not Mars his rage,
Your sword, your shield, your helmet needless is;
Then consecrate them here to endless rest,
You shall love's champions be and soldiers blest.

Tasso *Jerusalem Delivered* XV stanza 63

16 Guyon reaches Acrasia's garden:
There the most dainty Paradise on ground
Itself doth offer to his sober eye,
In which all pleasures plenteously abound
And none does other's happiness envy;

The painted flowers, the trees upshooting high,
The dales for shade, the hills for breathing space,
The trembling groves, the crystal running by,
And, that which all fair works doth most aggrace,
The art which all that wrought appearèd in no place.

One would have thought (so cunningly the rude
And scornèd parts were mingled with the fine)
That nature had for wantonness ensued
Art, and that art at nature did repine;
So striving each the other to undermine,
Each did the other's work more beautify;
So differing both in wills agreed in fine:
So all agreed, through sweet diversity,
This garden to adorn with all variety.
                              Spenser *The Faerie Queene* II xii stanzas 58–9

ENGLAND AS THE EARTHLY PARADISE

17   Only the island which we sow,
          (A world without the world) so far
      From present wounds, it cannot show
                  An ancient scar.

      White Peace (the beautifull'st of things)
      Seems here her everlasting rest
      To fix, and spreads her downy wings
                  Over the nest:

      As when great Jove, usurping reign,
      From the plagued world did her exile,
      And tied her with a golden chain
                  To one blest isle:

      Which in a sea of plenty swam
      And turtles sang on every bough,
      A safe retreat to all that came,
                  As ours is now.
                      Fanshawe 'An ode upon occasion of His Majesty's
                                  proclamation' stanzas 9–12

18   Oh thou, that dear and happy isle
      The garden of the world ere while,
      Thou paradise of four seas,
      Which heaven planted us to please,
      But, to exclude the world, did guard
      With watery if not flaming sword;
      What luckless apple did we taste,

To make us mortal, and thee waste?

Marvell 'Upon Appleton House' stanza 41

AMERICA AS THE EARTHLY PARADISE

19 Virginia,
Earth's only paradise.

Where nature hath in store
Fowl, venison, and fish,
     And the fruitfullest soil,
     Without your toil,
Three harvests more,
All greater than you wish.

And the ambitious vine
Crowns with his purple mass,
     The cedar reaching high
     To kiss the sky,
The cypress, pine
And useful sassafras.

To whose, the golden age
Still nature's laws doth give,
     No other cares that tend,
     But them to defend
From winter's age,
That long there doth not live.

Drayton 'Ode to the Virginian voyage' ll. 23–42

20 What should we do but sing his praise
That led us through the watery maze,
Unto an isle so long unknown,
And yet far kinder than our own?
Where he the huge sea-monsters wracks,
That lift the deep upon their backs,
He lands us on a grassy stage,
Safe from the storm's, and prelate's rage.
He gave us this eternal spring,
Which here enamels everything,
And sends the fowl to us in care,
On daily visits through the air.
He hangs in shades the orange bright,
Like golden lamps in a green night,
And does in the pom'granates close
Jewels more rich than Ormus shows.
He makes the figs our mouths to meet,
And throws the melons at our feet,

But apples plants of such a price,
No tree could ever bear them twice.

Marvell 'Bermudas' ll. 5–24

THE GOLDEN AGE AS A MORAL IDEAL

21   If I would wish, for truth, and not for show,
The agèd Saturn's age, and rites to know;
If I would strive to bring back times, and try
The world's pure gold, and wise simplicity;
If I would virtue set, as she was young,
And hear her speak with one, and her first tongue;
If holiest friendship, naked to the touch,
I would restore, and keep it ever such;
I need no other arts, but study thee:
Who prov'st, all these were, and again may be.

Jonson 'To Benjamin Rudyerd' *Epigrams* 122

THE GOLDEN AGE AS SEXUAL FREEDOM

22   Thrice happy was that golden age
When compliment was construed rage,
　　And fine words in the centre hid;
When cursèd No stained no maid's bliss,
And all discourse was summed in Yes,
　　And naught forbad, but to forbid.

Love, then unstinted, love did sip,
And cherries plucked fresh from the lip,
　　On cheeks and roses free he fed;
Lasses like autumn plums did drop,
And lads indifferently did crop
　　A flower and a maidenhead.

Lovelace 'Love made in the first age' ll. 7–18

2 The Pagan Gods

Because Latin and not Greek literature was for so long the basis of Western education, the pagan gods were known in the Renaissance and subsequently under their Latin names. After the conquest of Greece in the second century BC, Rome gradually began to assimilate Greek culture, and local Roman deities became identified where possible with their Greek counterparts. The table lists the principal gods, the Latin preceding the Greek name, with their associations and activities indicated. (The many lesser gods and demigods are not included.)

Saturn	Cronos	father of Jupiter, deposed by him; golden age
Jupiter, Jove	Zeus	king and father of the gods; power, justice; sky, thunderbolt
Juno	Hera	wife of Jupiter; marriage, childbirth, jealousy; enemy of the Trojans
Neptune	Poseidon	brother of Jupiter and Pluto; king of the sea; trident
Dis, Pluto (from Greek)	Hades, Pluto	brother of Jupiter and Neptune; king of the underworld; husband of Proserpina
Venus	Aphrodite	wife of Vulcan; lover of Mars, mother of Cupid; mother of Aeneas by Anchises; love, beauty
Vulcan	Hephaestus	husband of Venus; fire, forging of metal; lame
Mars	Ares	lover of Venus; war, strife
Cupid	Eros	son of Venus; love; bow, wings
Minerva	Athene	wisdom, justice; technical skill
Apollo (from Greek)	Apollo	brother of Diana; sun; oracles; music; lyre
Diana	Artemis	sister of Apollo; moon; chastity; bow, hunting
Mercury	Hermes	messenger of gods; thief; caduceus (snake-entwined staff)
Liber, Bacchus (from Greek)	Dionysus, Bacchus	wine; irrationality; bull
Ceres	Demeter	sister of Jupiter; mother of Proserpina; corn
Proserpina	Persephone	wife of Pluto; spring
Pan (from Greek)	Pan	goatlegged; shepherd; music; nature

The myths of the pagan gods were not enshrined in any sacred canonical books, but were told and retold with many variations in works of literature. In Greek the word myth ($\mu\hat{v}\theta o\varsigma$) simply means a story. The earliest Greek sources are Homer's *Iliad* and *Odyssey,* and Hesiod's *Theogony.* Almost all Greek tragedies take the myths of the gods and their dealings with men for their plots, and in these works we find the most serious theological questions being asked: Why do the gods behave as they do? Is their portrayal by human beings accurate? Are they just? Are humans morally better than gods?

The myths are of various kinds. They describe the behaviour of the gods towards one another, their parentage, battles, squabbles and jealousies, their treatment of humans, in particular their championing or victimising of individuals, and their sexual encounters with them. The myths also narrate the adventures of demigods like Hercules, half human, half divine, or of heroes like Achilles the scourge of Troy or Aeneas the founder of Rome. In spite of their immortality, the gods are anthropomorphic in conception; they exhibit human passions and desires, and sometimes act in ways which by human standards would be at best amoral and at worst criminal. They are adulterous, treacherous and murderous. The essence of the relations of the gods with men and with one another is conflict. Man's place is insecure; he cannot explain why things are as they are. He cannot expect justice. The universe is not ordered morally, or if it is, it is ordered according to a morality he cannot understand.

However, with the growth of philosophic rationalism in Greece from the fifth century BC, the traditional myths came under attack. As the epics of Homer were the basis of Greek education, every Greek was reared on stories of the gods and their immoral activities. Philosophers moving in the direction of monotheism or scientists interested in assigning rational causes to physical phenomena were faced with the problem of the myths. One solution was to attack them outright; in Plato's *Republic* II 377–89 (**1**) Socrates argues that since the gods are neither responsible for evil nor subject to change, poets like Homer who portray them in an unfavourable light should be censored. The philosophical school most hostile to myth was that of Epicurus. The Roman poet Lucretius, who versified Epicurean philosophy for the Latin reading public in his long poem *The Nature of the Universe,* argued that the gods are utterly removed from the affairs of men and take no interest in them (V ll. 146–73). The other solution, by far the more influential, was to interpret the myths allegorically. Three kinds of allegory were possible, physical, historical and moral. Physical allegory assumes that the myths were invented to account for natural phenomena; hence the rape of Proserpina is an allegory of the seasons and the growing of corn. This kind of physical allegory was popular among the Stoics. Historical allegory (also known as Euhemerism, after Euhemerus, a Greek of the third century BC who invented it) assumes that the gods were once earthly rulers whose subjects deified them, or benefactors (such as Aesculapius, the god of healing) who taught particular skills. Moral allegory (which turns the gods into personifications of virtues and vices) allows enormous freedom to the interpreter; ostensibly immoral myths can be shown to have moral meanings. This kind of interpretation, which was to have a very long history, was particularly practised by the Neoplatonists. Plato himself used moralised myth of his own invention, and can thus be accused of inconsistency in his attitude to traditional myth.

It is evident that educated but devout Greeks and Romans were faced with a dilemma. On the one hand they regarded naive acceptance of the myths as superstition; on the other they regarded too much allegory as a rationalising of religion which led to atheism. They were particularly conscious of the political importance of religion; to undermine religion would be to undermine the state. The Roman antiquarian Varro distinguished three kinds of theology: mythical (the fictitious tales of the poets, of no religious importance); physical (the rationalisations of the philosophers, which Varro accepted); and civil (the rites of the state religion, which are necessary for public order, but which are based on poetic fiction). Varro's works do not survive, but are known through Augustine's detailed analysis in *The City of God* VI–VII, where the logical difficulties of this scheme are exposed. Two works which beautifully illustrate the confused scepticism, honesty and religious yearnings of the educated pagan are Cicero's *The Nature of the Gods* and Plutarch's *Isis and Osiris*. *The Nature of the Gods* is in the form of a dialogue between an Epicurean and a Stoic (**2**), with comments by a sceptic; Cicero himself is a silent observer who finally commits himself to a belief in divine intervention in human affairs. *Isis and Osiris* is a detailed examination of the myth of the principal Egyptian gods, its history, cult and meaning (**17**). Plutarch, hostile to merely physical allegory, emphasises the moral meaning and searches for the unity underlying the diverse myths of different nations (**3**).

Christianity became the official religion of the Roman empire under the Emperor Constantine in AD 324 (the Emperor Julian, known to Christians as the Apostate, failed to bring about a pagan revival a few years later), and pagan forms of worship were finally made illegal in 390 by Theodosius. The myths of the pagan gods were particularly vulnerable to Christian attack, as can be seen in Lactantius' *Divine Institutes* I 9–22 and Augustine's *City of God*. Partly in response to Christian criticism of pagan cults and myths allegorical interpretations devised centuries earlier were revived. Neoplatonism, in its religious aspect the most serious rival to Christianity in the third and fourth centuries, tried through allegory to make the myths of the gods consistent with monotheism. *On the Gods and the World*, by Julian's friend Sallustius, is one of the last of such pagan defences of myth (**4**).

However, the triumph of Christianity and the abolition of pagan worship by no means implied the end of the pagan gods. In the hostile view, put forward by Origen in *Against Celsus*, the gods were fallen angels or demons. But every Christian schoolboy in the Roman empire was brought up on classical Latin literature, and hence on the pagan myths. It was impossible for Christianity to ignore pagan culture and pagan educational methods, largely because it could not as yet provide a substitute. Hence some kind of accommodation was necessary. The traditional argument, repeated by Augustine in *Christian Instruction* II 40 but much older, was that the Christians were entitled to appropriate what was valuable in pagan culture, just as the Israelites had robbed the Egyptians (Exodus 12:35–6). The methods which had been devised to protect the myths from the onslaughts of philosophy and science ensured their survival under Christianity. Over the centuries Christianity treated the myths in four ways: in the orthodox view the gods were demons; euhemeristically they were early kings or benefactors, and found their place in Christian chronologies; physically, they were the planets and stars of astrology; and, by far the most important for literature, they were moral allegories of human conduct and fore-shadowings of Christian truth. Thus the vocabulary of biblical typology (see Chapter 10) could be stretched to accommodate the pagan gods. The pagans had shown how Homer and Virgil could be moralised; the Christians managed to moralise even intractable authors like Ovid. Thus the fourteenth-century French *Ovide moralisé* turns the *Metamorphoses* into a Christian conduct book.

A good deal of knowledge of pagan myths in the Middle Ages and the Renaissance derived not so much from classical sources, of which Ovid was the most important (**6, 15**), as from handbooks which supplied ready-made interpretation. Such handbooks were used in antiquity; they ranged from straightforward narrative compilations, such as *The Library* by Apollodorus, to allegorical commentary on particular poets, such as that of Servius on Virgil. The most important early Renaissance handbook was Boccaccio's *Genealogy of the Pagan Gods*. For Boccaccio poetic myth is the shell which encloses the kernel of philosophical and theological truth; it is a view shared by most Renaissance poets who employ myth (see Chapter 12). Boccaccio's work was extremely influential, but it was in part replaced by three sixteenth-century Italian mythological handbooks: Gyraldus' *The Pagan Gods*, Comes' *Mythology* and Cartari's *Images of the Gods*. The handbooks of Boccaccio, Gyraldus and Comes were in Latin, and hence universally available to the educated reader; Cartari's Italian text was soon translated. The format used by Comes was particularly helpful to poets; after narrating a myth he gives a detailed interpretation with a Neoplatonic slant (**11**). These books were widely read and consulted, and in addition the information they provided was drawn on by the authors of popular dictionaries used in schools, such as Thomas Cooper's *Thesaurus of Latin and English*. In the early seventeenth century English authors began to compile mythological handbooks. Bacon's *The Wisdom of the Ancients* is a very idiosyncratic kind of physical allegory: he uses the myths to expound his own scientific theories. Sandys' commentary on the *Metamorphoses* is a more traditional compendium of physical, historical and moral interpretation (**8, 14**). An eccentric but highly illuminating handbook is Alexander Ross's *Mystagogus Poeticus* (a mystagogue is an initiator into religious mysteries). Ross briefly relates each myth, then gives a long list of interpretations, physical, historical, moral, political and religious (**5, 7, 12**). He always concludes with a specifically Christian interpretation; almost all the pagan gods and heroes are seen as types of Christ.

The handbooks were parasitic, each compiler tending to incorporate the work of his predecessor. Since the handbooks ultimately derive from interpretative works of late antiquity in which oriental religion and occult lore were fused with the Greek and Roman tradition, and since Renaissance poets turned to the handbooks more frequently than to the works of classical authors, the gods in Renaissance literature do not necessarily resemble their counterparts in Homer or Virgil or Ovid very closely. But it is not necessary for twentieth-century readers to have recourse to the handbooks to find out why and in what way a Renaissance poet is using myth. The context should tell them. Briefly, five chief uses of myth can be defined. The first is narrative; the story is told for its own sake, unmoralised, as in Shakespeare's *Venus and Adonis* (**9**) and Marlowe's *Hero and Leander*. Marlowe is much truer to the spirit of Ovid than innumerable Christian allegorisers. The second is for embellishment and enrichment of meaning; mythological allusion can serve to aggrandise the subject of a poem (**16**). However, it can at times clog much late Elizabethan poetry. It was partly against this tradition that Donne reacted; Carew in his 'Elegy' on Donne's death refers to the 'goodly exiled train/ Of gods and goddesses, which in thy just reign/Were banished nobler poems'. The third, and most widespread, is allegorical; this is the method of Spenser in *The Faerie Queene* (**10**, Introduction **1**), of Jonson in his masques, and Milton in his early poems. Pagan myth both adorns and reveals Christian truth (**19**). The fourth is mock-heroic; mythological allusion is used to expose the subject of the comparison, though the myth itself is not being criticised. This technique is typical of late seventeenth-century political satire. The final use is negative and hostile; it draws on the orthodox tradition that the pagan gods were fallen angels and hence forces for evil (**18**). This method is particularly important in *Paradise Lost* I and *Paradise Regained* (**13**); Milton uses mythological allusion to define Christian truth by contrast with what is pagan and inferior. Satan and his crew are apparently embellished but in fact belittled by their pagan associations.

SOME CLASSICAL ATTITUDES TO THE PAGAN GODS

1   Stories like those of Hera being bound by her son, or of Hephaestus flung from heaven by his father for taking his mother's part when she was beaten, and all those battles of the gods in Homer, must not be admitted into our state, whether they be allegorical or not. A child cannot distinguish the allegorical sense from the literal, and the ideas he takes in at that age are likely to become indelibly fixed; hence the great importance of seeing that the first stories he hears shall be designed to produce the best possible effect on his character.

Plato *Republic* II 377

2   The Stoic Balbus summarises his position:
We even think we know the appearance of the gods, their age, their costumes and their fashions! We even claim to know their family histories, their marriages and their relationships to one another, and in every way we reduce them to the stature of our human weakness. We represent them as distracted by our own passions. We are told about their lusts, their griefs and their bad temper. According to the legends they are even plagued by strife and war ... These tales are full of frivolous absurdities and both those who tell them and those who listen to them are a pack of fools. But as long as we scorn and reject such fables, we may well believe that a divine power permeates everything in nature, and earth under the name of Ceres, the oceans under the name of Neptune, and so on. So we ought to worship and revere these gods, each in their own person and their own nature, under the names which custom has bestowed upon them. Such worship of the gods is the best of all things, full of purity and holiness and piety, if our reverence is always true and whole and pure in word and thought. It was not only the philosophers but also our own ancestors who thus distinguished between true religion and the follies of superstition.

Cicero *The Nature of the Gods* II 70–1

3   It is impossible to conceive of [natural objects] as being gods in themselves; for God is not senseless nor inanimate nor subject to human

control. As a result of this we have come to regard as gods those who make use of these things and present them to us and provide us with things everlasting and constant. Nor do we think of the gods as different gods among different peoples, nor as barbarian gods and Greek gods, nor as southern and northern gods; but, just as the sun and the moon and the heavens and the earth and the sea are common to all, but are called by different names by different peoples, so for that one rationality which keeps all these things in order and the one providence which watches over them and the ancillary powers that are set over all, there have arisen among different peoples, in accordance with their customs, different honours and appellations. Thus men make use of consecrated symbols, some employing symbols that are obscure, but others those that are clearer, in guiding the intelligence towards things divine, though not without a certain hazard. For some go completely astray and become engulfed in superstition; and others, while they fly from superstition as from a quagmire, on the other hand unwittingly fall, as it were, over a precipice into atheism.

Plutarch *Isis and Osiris* 377–8

4   Why the myths are divine it is the duty of philosophy to inquire. Since all existing things rejoice in that which is like them and reject that which is unlike, the stories about the gods ought to be like the gods, so that they may both be worthy of the divine essence and make the gods well disposed to those who speak to them: which could only be done by means of myths. Now the myths represent the gods themselves and the goodness of the gods – subject always to the distinction of the speakable and the unspeakable, the revealed and the unrevealed, that which is clear and that which is hidden: since, just as the gods have made the goods of sense common to all, but those of intellect only to the wise, so the myths state the existence of gods to all, but who and what they are only to those who can understand. They also represent the activities of the gods. For one may call the world a myth, in which bodies and things are visible, but souls and minds hidden. Besides, to wish to teach the whole truth about the gods to all produces contempt in the foolish, because they cannot understand, and lack of zeal in the good; whereas to conceal the truth by myths prevents the contempt of the foolish, and compels the good to practise philosophy. But why have they put in the myths stories of adultery, robbery, father-binding, and all the other absurdity? Is not that perhaps a thing worthy of admiration, done so that by means of the visible absurdity the soul may immediately feel that the words are veils and believe the truth to be a mystery?

Sallustius *On the Gods and the World* iii

SOME PAGAN GODS IN CLASSICAL AND RENAISSANCE
LITERATURE

(a)   *Venus and Adonis*

5   He was a beautiful youth, with whom Venus was in love; but whilst he
      was hunting, he was killed by a boar, or by Mars in the shape of a boar,
      and by Venus was turned into a red flower called anemone; he was kept
      after death by Ceres and Proserpina, six months under ground, and other
      six months by Venus, above.

                                     Alexander Ross *Mystagogus Poeticus*

6   [Venus] recognised the groans of the dying Adonis from afar, and turned
      her white birds in his direction. As she looked down from on high she saw
      him, lying lifeless, his limbs still writhing in his own blood. Leaping
      down from her car, she tore at her bosom and at her hair, beat her breast
      with hands never meant for such a use, and reproached the fates. 'But
      still,' she cried, 'you will not have everything under your absolute sway!
      There will be an everlasting token of my grief, Adonis. Every year, the
      scene of your death will be staged anew, and lamented with wailing cries,
      in imitation of those cries of mine. But your blood will be changed into
      a flower . . .' With these words, she sprinkled Adonis' blood with sweet-
      smelling nectar and, at the touch of the liquid, the blood swelled up, just
      as clear bubbles rise in yellow mud. Within an hour, a flower sprang up,
      the colour of blood, and in appearance like that of a pomegranate, the
      fruit which conceals its seeds under a leathery skin. But the enjoyment
      of this flower is of brief duration: for it is so fragile, its petals so lightly
      attached, that it quickly falls, shaken from its stem by those same winds
      that give it its name, anemone.

                                     Ovid *Metamorphoses* X ll. 719–39

7   Our resurrection in this may be typed out; for although death kill us, it
      shall not annihilate us, but our beauty shall increase, and we shall spring
      out of the ground again like a beautiful flower in the resurrection.

                                     Ross *Mystagogus Poeticus*

8   Adonis is said to be slain by a boar, because that beast is the image of
      the winter; salvage, horrid, delighting in mire, and feeding on acorns, a
      fruit which is proper to that season. So the winter wounds, as it were, the
      sun to death, by diminishing his heat and lustre: whose loss is lamented
      by Venus, or the widowed earth, then covered with a veil of clouds:
      springs gushing from thence, the tears of her eyes, in greater abundance:
      the fields presenting a sad aspect, as being deprived of their ornament.
      But when the sun returns to the equator, Venus recovers her alacrity; the
      trees invested with leaves, and the earth with her flowery mantle:
      wherefore the ancient[s] did dedicate the month of April unto Venus.

                                     George Sandys *Ovid's Metamorphosis* X

9   'Since thou art dead, lo here I prophesy,
      Sorrow on love hereafter shall attend:

It shall be waited on with jealousy,
Find sweet beginning, but unsavoury end;
　　Ne'er settled equally, but high or low,
　　That all love's pleasure shall not match his woe.

It shall be fickle, false and full of fraud;
Bud, and be blasted, in a breathing while;
The bottom poison, and the top o'erstrawed
With sweets that shall the truest sight beguile;
　　The strongest body shall it make most weak,
　　Strike the wise dumb, and teach the fool to speak.
　. . . . . .
It shall be cause of war and dire events,
And set dissension 'twixt the son and sire;
Subject and servile to all discontents,
As dry combustious matter is to fire.
　　Sith in his prime death doth my love destroy,
　　They that love best, their loves shall not enjoy.'

By this the boy that by her side lay killed
Was melted like a vapour from her sight,
And in his blood that on the ground lay spilled,
A purple flower sprung up, checkered with white,
Resembling well his pale cheeks and the blood
Which in round drops upon their whiteness stood.
　　　　　　Shakespeare *Venus and Adonis* ll. 1135–46, 1159–70

10　The Garden of Adonis:
　　There wont fair Venus often to enjoy
　　Her dead Adonis' joyous company,
　　And reap sweet pleasure of the wanton boy:
　　There yet, some say, in secret he does lie,
　　Lappèd in flowers and precious spicery,
　　By her hid from the world, and from the skill
　　Of Stygian gods, which do her love envy;
　　But she herself, whenever that she will,
　　Possesseth him, and of his sweetness takes her fill.

　　And sooth, it seems, they say; for he may not
　　For ever die, and ever buried be
　　In baleful night, where all things are forgot:
　　All be he subject to mortality,
　　Yet is eterne in mutability,
　　And by succession made perpetual,
　　Transformèd oft, and changèd diversely;
　　For him the father of all forms they call:
　　Therefore needs mote he live, that living gives to all.

　　There now he liveth in eternal bliss,

Joying his goddess, and of her enjoyed;
Ne feareth he henceforth that foe of his,
Which with his cruel tusk him deadly cloyed:
For that wild boar, the which him once annoyed,
She firmly hath emprisonèd for ay,
That her sweet love his malice mote avoid,
In a strong rocky cave, which is, they say,
Hewn underneath that mount, that none him loosen may.

Spenser *The Faerie Queene* III vi stanzas 46–8

(b) *Hercules*

(Hercules, also known as Alcides, was the son of Jupiter and Alcmena, a mortal. Most of the myths are concerned with his twelve labours. He killed the giant Antaeus, the son of Earth, by holding him in the air away from his mother's protection and crushing him. He died by burning himself alive on a funeral pyre on Mount Oeta; he then ascended to Olympus and became a god.)

11   Hercules, who owed his glory to Juno's hatred, is said to have been the son of Jove and Alcmena; in fact he represents probity, fortitude, and superlative strength of mind and body, which drives out all faults from the mind and destroys them.

Comes *Mythologiae* VII i

12   Our blessed Saviour is the true Hercules, who was the true and only Son of God, and of the virgin Mary: who was persecuted out of malice, and exposed to all dangers, which he overcame; he subdued the roaring lion, that red dragon, that tyrant and devourer of mankind, the devil; he subdued the Hydra of sin, the Antaeus of earthly affections; he by his word supporteth the world; Satan is that Cacus . . . that sea monster, from whom by Christ we are delivered; it is he only that went down to hell, and delivered us from thence; he alone travelled through the torrid zone of his Father's wrath; he purged the Augean stable of Jewish superstition, and heathenish profanation; he overcame the world, and all his enemies, and hath killed the eagle of an evil conscience, which continually fed upon the heart of man; he was that only true . . . expeller of all evil from us; who with the club of his power, and chains of his eloquence hath subdued and drawn all men after him; who at last was burned but not consumed by the fire of his Father's wrath.

Ross *Mystagogus Poeticus* (see also Introduction 1)

13   But Satan smitten with amazement fell
As when Earth's son Antaeus (to compare
Small things with greatest) in Irassa strove
With Jove's Alcides, and oft foiled still rose,
Receiving from his mother Earth new strength,
Fresh from his fall, and fiercer grapple joined,
Throttled at length in the air, expired and fell;

So after many a foil the tempter proud,
Renewing fresh assaults, amidst his pride
Fell whence he stood to see his victor fall.

Milton *Paradise Regained* IV ll. 562–71

14   The moral is more fruitful: Hercules being the symbol of the soul and
Antaeus of the body, prudence the essence of the one, and sensual
pleasure of the other; between whom there is a perpetual conflict. For the
appetite always rebels against reason; nor can reason prevail, unless it so
raise the body, and hold it aloft from the contagion of earthly things, that
it recover no more force from the same, till desires and affections thereof,
which are the sons of the Earth, be altogether suffocated.

Sandys *Ovid's Metamorphosis* IX

15   Jupiter addresses the gods:
'Do not be dismayed by the flames, blazing on Oeta's heights. Hercules,
who conquers all, will conquer the fire you see there: only the human
part, which he owes to his mother, will feel Vulcan's power. What he
derives from me is eternal, beyond the reach of death, and not to be
overcome by any flames. When that part has fulfilled its time on earth,
I shall receive it into the realms of heaven, confident that my action will
be a source of rejoicing to all the gods.' ... Meanwhile Vulcan had
stripped Hercules of whatever fire could ravage, and the form of the hero
was left, quite unrecognisable, retaining none of his likeness to his
mother, but only the signs of his descent from Jove. Just as a serpent
renews its youth, sloughing its old age with its skin, and is left fresh and
shining with its new scales, so when the Tirynthian hero had put off his
mortal shape, the better part of him grew vigorous, and he began to
appear greater than before, a majestic figure of august dignity. Then the
omnipotent father swept him through the hollow clouds in his four-horse
chariot, and set him among the glittering stars.

Ovid *Metamorphoses* IX ll. 248–56, 262–72

16   Like a glad lover the fierce flames he meets,
And tries his first embraces in their sheets.
His shape exact, which the bright flames enfold,
Like the sun's statue stands of burnished gold.
Round the transparent fire about him glows,
As the clear amber on the bee does close.
And as on angels' heads their glories shine,
His burning locks adorn his face divine.
    But when in his immortal mind he felt
His altering form and soldered limbs to melt,
Down on the deck he laid himself and died,
With his dear sword reposing by his side:
And on the flaming plank so rests his head
As one that hugs himself in a warm bed.
The ship burns down and with his relics sinks,

And the sad stream beneath his ashes drinks.
Fortunate boy, if e'er my verse may claim
That matchless grace to propagate thy name,
When Oeta and Alcides [i.e. Hercules] are forgot
Our English youth shall sing the valiant Scot.

> Marvell *The Loyal Scot: Upon Occasion of the*
> *Death of Captain Douglas Burned in One of*
> *his Majesty's Ships at Chatham* ll. 43–62

(c) *Osiris*

(Osiris, the chief Egyptian god, husband of Isis and father of Horus, was murdered by his brother Typhon or Set, dismembered and cast into the Nile. Isis gathered the fragments together. Osiris, who was worshipped as a bull or a crocodile, was identified with Dionysus by the Greeks.)

17   The fact is that the creation and constitution of this world is complex, resulting, as it does, from opposing influences, which, however, are not of equal strength, but the predominance rests with the better. Yet it is impossible for the bad to be completely eradicated, since it is innate, in large amount, in the body and likewise in the soul of the universe, and is always fighting a hard fight against the better. So in the soul intelligence and reason, the ruler and lord of all that is good, is Osiris, and in earth and wind and water and the heavens and stars that which is ordered, established, and healthy, as evidenced by seasons, temperatures, and cycles of revolution, is the efflux of Osiris and his reflected image. But Typhon is that part of the soul which is impressionable, impulsive, irrational and truculent, and of the bodily part the destructible, diseased and disorderly as evidenced by abnormal seasons and temperatures, and by obscurations of the sun and disappearances of the moon, outbursts, as it were, and unruly actions on the part of Typhon ... It is not, therefore, out of keeping that they have a legend that the soul of Osiris is everlasting and imperishable, but that his body Typhon oftentimes dismembers and causes to disappear, and that Isis wander hither and yon in her search for it, and fits it together again; for that which really is and is perceptible and good is superior to destruction and change.

> Plutarch *Isis and Osiris* 371, 373

18   Nor is Osiris seen
In Memphian grove, or green,
   Trampling the unshowered grass with lowings loud:
Nor can he be at rest
Within his sacred chest,
   Nought but profoundest hell can be his shroud,
In vain with timbrelled anthems dark
The sable-stolèd sorcerers bear his worshipped ark.

He feels from Juda's land
The dreaded infant's hand,

The rays of Bethlehem blind his dusky eyn;
Nor all the gods beside,
Longer dare abide,
Not Typhon huge ending in snaky twine:
Our babe to show his Godhead true,
Can in his swaddling bands control the damnèd crew.

Milton 'On the Morning Of Christ's Nativity' ll. 213–28

(Note that though Milton here disparages the pagan gods he nevertheless identifies the child Jesus with the child Hercules, who strangled snakes in his cradle.)

19   Truth indeed came once into the world with her divine Master, and was a perfect shape most glorious to look on: but when he ascended, and his apostles after him were laid asleep, then straight arose a wicked race of deceivers, who as that story goes of the Egyptian Typhon with his conspirators, how they dealt with the good Osiris, took the virgin Truth, hewed her lovely form into a thousand pieces, and scattered them to the four winds. From that time ever since, the sad friends of Truth, such as durst appear, imitating the careful search that Isis made for the mangled body of Osiris, went up and down gathering up limb by limb still as they could find them. We have not yet found them all . . . nor ever shall do, till her Master's second coming; he shall bring together every joint and member, and shall mould them into an immortal feature of loveliness and perfection.

Milton *Areopagitica*

3 Platonism and Neoplatonism

Plato's writings do not expound a coherent philosophical system; his thought changed and developed, with the result that later Platonists attempting to systematise it had to select from contradictory ideas, and often added ideas of their own which Plato would never have accepted. The one central belief common to Plato and his followers (though the terminology may differ) is that of the two worlds. The first, which is intelligible or apprehended by the intellect, is the world of Ideas or Forms, the archetypal patterns of everything existing in the inferior material world. It is the world of Being, stable, eternal, immutable, perfect (1). The second, which is sensible or apprehended by the senses, is not real in itself; its value is in the fact that it is a copy of the real world of Forms. It is the world of Becoming, always subject to change. The human soul comes from the first world and is trapped in the body in the second, from which it seeks to escape (2, 7). The return or ascent of the soul to the world of Forms is the subject of much of Plato's writing, but the way in which the ascent is described varies. In the *Symposium* the two worlds are united by Eros (Love). Love of the beauty of one human being leads to love of physical beauty in general, then to moral beauty, then to intellectual beauty, until finally the Idea of Beauty is reached (1). In the *Republic* the goal is the Idea of Good, and the ascent undertaken by the intellect is far more arduous. Socrates (Plato's teacher and the chief speaker in his dialogues) outlines a long and rigorous scheme for educating the Guardians of the hypothetical republic. The difficulty of the ascent to the world of Ideas and the problem of explaining the relation between the two worlds to untrained minds is illustrated by the allegory of the cave (*Republic* VII). Life in the second, material world is represented by prisoners in a cave, chained so that they cannot move their heads, who spend their time watching shadows cast on a wall by a fire behind them. One of them (representing the philosopher) is forcibly released and made to see his 'reality' for what it is. He is then dragged out of the cave into the sunlight (the first world), where painfully he is able first to discern objects and finally to look straight at the sun itself (the Idea of Good). Having learnt the truth, he returns to the cave to attempt to enlighten his fellow prisoners, who refuse to believe him and want to kill him (Plato is here alluding to the execution of Socrates by the Athenians). This allegory not only illustrates the steps the philosopher must ascend, it also emphasises his social responsibility. The philosopher must descend the ladder from the first to the second world and apply his knowledge for social and political purposes. For life in the second world can only be ordered harmoniously and usefully if its relation to the first is understood (**6**).

There are contradictory tendencies in Plato's accounts of the relationship between the two worlds. One tendency is towards asceticism, intellectual self-discipline and other-worldliness. The soul wants to have nothing to do with the body; death is a longed-for release. The inferiority and insubstantiality of the material world are stressed. This is the version in the *Phaedo* (**7**), Plato's account of the last hours before Socrates' execution. Allied with this asceticism is the belief that the ascent to knowledge of the real world is painful and difficult, as is explained in the *Republic*. The other tendency is towards aesthetic enjoyment of the second world, which is beautiful and good because it is a faithful copy of the real world. This is the version in the *Timaeus*, in which the mythical creator is seen using the world of Ideas as a model (Ch. **6.2**). It is the beauty of the material world that leads the soul to apprehend the Idea of Beauty, and the process is one of rapture or ecstasy (as in the *Symposium*) rather than an arduous climb. Both these tendencies in Platonism are exploited in different ways by later Platonists.

The Platonism revived in the first three centuries AD was religious as much as philosophical; it incorporated magic and elements of late pagan mystery religions, and attempted to shape Plato's thought into a coherent doctrine. Plotinus, the third-century Neoplatonist whose work was as much revered as Plato's in the Renaissance, devised an elaborate hierarchy of being which differs significantly from Plato's accounts of the two worlds. First there is the ultimate principle, the One, which transcends being. Then comes the Divine Mind, whose thoughts are the world of Ideas. Then comes soul, which links the intelligible and the material world; individual souls are part of this greater soul. The individual soul is tripartite (as Plato also believed); one part is concerned with the intelligible and one with the material, while the third is free to turn in either direction. Though the material world is at the foot of the hierarchy it is orderly, beautiful and good. The goal of life is the ascent of the soul to mystical union with the One (**2**), and Plotinus describes the achievement of this state on the basis of his own experience.

Some tenets of Platonism were obviously incompatible with Christianity: for example, that the soul passes through several bodies, and that knowledge is the recollection by the soul of its own previous existence. Further incompatibilities were introduced by the Neoplatonists, some of whom regarded demons and the pagan gods as intermediaries between the intelligible and material worlds. However, of all the ancient philosophies Platonism, because of its doctrine of the two worlds, was most easily assimilated to Christianity. Plotinus' thought is much closer to Christianity than Plato's in one important respect. There is no transcendent principle of unity in Plato, whereas Plotinus' One can easily be identified with the Christian God. Augustine, who passed through a Neoplatonic period (recorded in *Confessions* VII) before his conversion to Christianity, was much influenced by Plotinus, and it is largely through Augustine (and through the late Roman author Boethius and the anonymous Greek Christian Platonist known as Dionysius the Areopagite) that the Platonic tradition reached the Middle Ages. The centre of this diluted Neoplatonism was twelfth-century Chartres. As knowledge of Greek was lost in the West, so the original writings of Plato, Plotinus and other Neoplatonists became inaccessible. There were very few Latin translations of Plato: *Timaeus, Phaedo* and *Meno* were the only texts available in the medieval period. In order for a revival of Platonism in the Renaissance to be possible, therefore, the texts had first to be translated into Latin.

The late fifteenth-century Florentine Neoplatonists, in particular Ficino, were responsible for the dissemination of Platonic and Neoplatonic texts. Ficino translated the complete works of Plato and Plotinus into Latin, wrote commentaries on them, and developed his own system of 'Platonic theology', *Theologica Platonica*. The object of this Platonic theology was to reconcile Platonism and Christianity, but some of Ficino's sources were distinctly unplatonic. The Florentine Neoplatonists attached great importance to a group of writings of late antiquity which they quite wrongly assumed to antedate Plato. (Milton's *Il Penseroso* [ll. 85–96] portrays a Neoplatonist of this kind.) These works of mysticism and magic were attributed to Hermes Trismegistus, Orpheus, Pythagoras and Zoroaster, who were venerated as sages equal in importance to Moses. Plato was supposed to have derived his philosophy from them; thus Greek, Jewish and Christian ideas could be interpreted in terms of one another. It was not until the early seventeenth century that the proper dates of these writings were established. Although Plato frequently resorted to myth to illustrate his more difficult theories, this Renaissance emphasis on magic, mysteries and the occult is quite foreign to true Platonism. Florentine Neoplatonism was essentially syncretic; it drew on contradictory philosophies and beliefs and tried to show their underlying unity. Thus Ficino's follower

Pico della Mirandola wanted to reconcile Plato and Aristotle, the Jewish Cabala and Christianity.

In theological terms Florentine Neoplatonism is important for its emphasis on the freedom of the will. In Ficino's system, which is similar to that of Plotinus, each order in the universal hierarchy (God, angelic mind, soul, body) naturally aspires to that above. Man constantly strives to reach God. However, because of the intermediate position of the soul, man can look upwards or downwards; he is free to reach towards the truth or ignore it. This emphasis on human choice and aspiration differs significantly from the emphasis on divine grace and election in Protestant thought (see Chapter 8).

The most influential aspect of Ficino's thought was his theory of Platonic love. His *De Amore* (on love), a commentary on Plato's *Symposium*, together with Pico's commentary on Benivieni's *Canzone on Divine Love* (**3**), provoked a series of imitative love treatises in sixteenth-century Italy. The argument of one of these, Bembo's *Asolani*, was largely incorporated by Castiglione in Book IV of *The Book of the Courtier* (**4**), a work which helped to spread the social ideals and manners of Renaissance Italy in northern Europe. This theory of love, while following Plato closely in some aspects (the lover begins by loving an individual and finally reaches God), also draws on a quite different tradition, that of medieval courtly love. Courtly love, in which the intangibility of the woman is her chief attraction, can become simply a game in which sexuality is artificially ignored. The association of Ficino's Platonic love with courtly love had the effect of trivialising it; thus the terminology of what was intended as a serious theological system could be used frivolously in love poetry. Platonic love might mean an emotional flirtation denied a proper sexual fulfilment.

The extent of the influence of Italian Neoplatonism on English Renaissance poetry is a disputed matter. Spenser is often claimed as a Platonist, but his emphasis on marriage, fruition and procreation seems fundamentally unplatonic. It is not known how far Spenser was familiar with Platonic literature. Sir Thomas Hoby's translation of *The Book of the Courtier* (1561) was widely read and could have provided enough information, but Spenser may have used Ficino's translation of Plotinus when he wrote *Four Hymns* (**5**). The chief Platonist among the poets is the young Milton. The Pythagorean-Platonic concept of the musical harmony of the world of Ideas which is faintly reflected in the material world (see Chapter 6) is a unifying theme in Milton's early poetry. Milton, who read Plato in the original Greek, wanted to free Christian Neoplatonism from what he saw as its debasement by love poets, but as he moved in the direction of radical Puritanism in his middle years Platonism lost its importance for him, though there are Platonic elements in his later poems. This Christian Platonism is used rather differently by Marvell in his religious poems, which draw wittily on the tradition of Platonic asceticism and ignore Platonic love theory (**10**).

It is in love poetry that the largest number of allusions to Neoplatonism is to be found, but these are often negative and ironic. Critical reference to the Neoplatonic separation of ideal and physical love as untrue to the facts of human experience can be the starting-point for the poet's own definition. This technique is used to great effect by Sidney in *Astrophel and Stella* (**11**) and Donne in *Songs and Sonnets* (**12**). Among cavalier poets the assertion of the rival merits of 'Platonic' and 'antiplatonic' love became an intellectual game and evidently reflected courtly pastime (**13**). It was against this kind of fashionable Platonising that Milton wrote; *Comus* is from one point of view a defence of true against false Neoplatonism (**9**).

Ficino's 'Platonic theology' had few followers in England. However, there was one group of mid-seventeenth-century English Platonic theologians who came too late to have much influence on Renaissance poetry but who are important in the history of thought. The Cambridge Platonists, Whichcote, Smith (**8**), Cudworth and More, reacted against the Calvinist portrayal of divine wrath and human depravity. In their belief in reason, free will, the beauty of religion, and the soul's delight in God, they looked back to the long tradition of Neoplatonism and forward to the rational Latitudinarian theology of the late seventeenth and early eighteenth centuries. The bulk of their work is in the form of sermons and treatises, but Henry More's long poem *Psychozoia* (the life of the soul) is an attempt to expound Plotinus and Ficino through the medium of Spenserian allegory.

THE PLATONIC IDEA OF BEAUTY

1 Socrates recounts what Diotima taught him:
   This beauty is first of all eternal; it neither comes into being nor passes away, neither waxes nor wanes; next, it is not beautiful in part and ugly in part, nor beautiful at one time and ugly at another, nor beautiful in this relation and ugly in that, nor beautiful here and ugly there, as varying according to its beholders; nor again will this beauty appear to him like the beauty of a face or hands or anything else corporeal, or like the beauty of a thought or a science, or like beauty which has its seat in something other than itself, be it a living thing or the earth or the sky or anything else whatever; he will see it as absolute, existing alone with itself, unique, eternal, and all other beautiful things as partaking of it, yet in such a manner that, while they come into being and pass away, it neither

undergoes any increase or diminution nor suffers any change.

Plato *Symposium* 211A–B

THE NEOPLATONIC IDEA OF BEAUTY

2   But how shall we find the way? What method can we devise? How can one see the 'inconceivable beauty' [*Symposium* 218E] which stays within in the holy sanctuary and does not come out where the profane may see it? Let him who can, follow and come within, and leave outside the sight of his eyes and not turn back to the bodily splendours which he saw before. When he sees the beauty in bodies he must not run after them; we must know that they are images, traces, shadows, and hurry away to that which they image ... This would be truer advice. 'Let us fly to our dear country' [*Iliad* II 140]. What then is our way of escape, and how are we to find it? We shall put out to sea, as Odysseus did, from the witch Circe or Calypso ... Our country from which we came is there, our Father is there. How shall we travel to it, where is our way of escape? We cannot get there on foot; for our feet only carry us everywhere in this world, from one country to another ... Shut your eyes, and change to and wake another way of seeing, which everyone has but few use.

Plotinus *Enneads* I vi 8

3   Because man may be understood by the rational soul, either considered apart or in its union to the body; in the first sense, human love is the image of the celestial; in the second, desire of sensible beauty, this being by the soul abstracted from matter, and (as much as its nature will allow) made intellectual. The greater part of men reach no higher than this; others more perfect, remembering that more perfect beauty which the soul (before immersed in the body) beheld, are inflamed with an incredible desire of reviewing it, in pursuit whereof, they separate themselves as much as possible from the body, of which the soul (returning to its first dignity) becomes absolute mistress. This is the image of celestial love, by which man ariseth from one perfection to another, till his soul (wholly united to the intellect) is made an angel. Purged from material dross, and transformed into spiritual flame by his divine power, he mounts up to the intelligible heaven, and happily rests in his Father's bosom.

Pico *A Platonic Discourse* (commentary on
Benivieni's *Canzone on Divine Love*) II xx

4   Bembo speaks:
And therefore burning in this most happy flame, [the soul] ariseth to the noblest part of her which is the understanding, and there no more shadowed with the dark night of earthly matters, seeth the heavenly beauty: but yet doth she not for all that enjoy it altogether perfectly, because she beholdeth it only in her particular understanding, which cannot conceive the passing great universal beauty. Whereupon not

throughly satisfied with this benefit, love giveth unto the soul a greater happiness. For like as through the particular beauty of one body he guideth her to the universal beauty of all bodies: even so in the least degree of perfection through particular understanding he guideth her to the universal understanding. Thus the soul kindled in the most holy fire of true heavenly love, fleeth to couple herself with the nature of angels, and not only clean forsaketh sense, but hath no more need of the discourse of reason, for being changed into an angel, she understandeth all things that may be understood; and without any veil or cloud, she seeth the main sea of the pure heavenly beauty and receiveth it into her, and enjoyeth the sovereign happiness, that cannot be comprehended of the senses.

Castiglione *The Book of the Courtier* IV

5   What time this world's great workmaster did cast
To make all things, such as we now behold,
It seems that he before his eyes had placed
A goodly pattern, to whose perfect mould
He fashioned them as comely as he could;
That now so fair and seemly they appear,
As nought may be amended anywhere.

That wondrous pattern wheresoe'er it be,
Whether in earth laid up in secret store,
Or else in heaven, that no man may it see
With sinful eyes, for fear it to deflower,
Is perfect beauty which all men adore,
Whose face and feature doth so much excel
All mortal sense, that none the same may tell.

Thereof as every earthly thing partakes,
Or more or less by influence divine,
So it more fair accordingly it makes,
And the gross matter of this earthly mine,
Which clotheth it, thereafter doth refine,
Doing away the dross which dims the light
Of that fair beam, which therein is empight.

Spenser 'An Hymn in Honour of Beauty' ll. 29–49

THE ALLEGORY OF THE CAVE

6   The prison dwelling corresponds to the region revealed to us through the sense of sight, and the firelight within it to the power of the sun. The ascent to see the things in the upper world you may take as standing for the upward journey of the soul into the region of the intelligible ... In the world of knowledge, the last thing to be perceived and only with great difficulty is the essential Form of Goodness. Once it is perceived, the

conclusion must follow that, for all things, this is the cause of whatever is right and good; in the visible world it gives birth to light and to the lord of light, while it is itself sovereign in the intelligible world and the parent of intelligence and truth. Without having had a vision of this Form no one can act with wisdom, either in his own life or in matters of state.

Plato *Republic* VII 517

SOUL AND BODY

7   Every seeker after wisdom knows that up to the time when philosophy takes it over his soul is a helpless prisoner, chained hand and foot in the body, compelled to view reality not directly but only through its prison bars, and wallowing in utter ignorance. And philosophy can see that the imprisonment is ingeniously effected by the prisoner's own active desire, which makes him first accessory to his own confinement ... Every pleasure or pain has a sort of rivet with which it fastens the soul to the body and pins it down and makes it corporeal, accepting as true whatever the body certifies. The result of agreeing with the body and finding pleasure in the same things is, I imagine, that it cannot help becoming like it in character and training, so that it can never get clean away to the unseen world, but is always saturated with the body when it sets out, and so soon falls back again into another body, where it takes root and grows. Consequently it is excluded from all fellowship with the pure and uniform and divine.

Plato *Phaedo* 82D–83D

8   The soul is too vigorous and puissant a thing, when it is once restored to the possession of its own being, than to be bounded within the narrow sphere of mortality, or to be straitened within the narrow prison of sensual and corporeal delights; but it will break forth with the greatest vehemency, and ascend upwards towards immortality. And, when it converses more intimately with religion, it can scarce look back upon its own converses, though in a lawful way, with earthly things, without being touched with a holy shamefacedness and modest blushing; and, as Porphyry speaks of Plotinus, 'It seems to be shamed that it should be in the body'. It is true religion only that teaches and enables men to die to this world and to all earthly things, and to rise above that vaporous sphere of sensual and earthly pleasures, which darken the mind, and hinder it from enjoying the brightness of divine light. The proper motion of religion is still upwards to its first original ... Wicked men bury their souls in their bodies; all their objects and designs are bounded within the compass of this earth which they tread upon. The fleshly mind regards nothing but flesh, and never rises above the outward matter, but always creeps up and down, like shadows, upon the surface of the earth; and if it begins, at any time, to make any faint essays upwards, it presently finds itself laden with a weight of sensuality which draws it down again. It was

the opinion of the Academics [*Phaedo* 81C–D] that the souls of wicked men, after their death, could not, of a long season, depart from the graves and sepulchres where their mates were buried; but there wandered up and down in a desolate manner, as not being able to leave those bodies to which they were so much wedded in this life.

John Smith (Cambridge Platonist)
The Excellency and Nobleness of True Religion II

9   The Elder Brother speaks:
So dear to heaven is saintly chastity,
That when a soul is found sincerely so,
A thousand liveried angels lackey her,
Driving far off each thing of sin and guilt,
And in clear dream, and solemn vision
Tell her of things that no gross ear can hear,
Till oft converse with heavenly habitants
Begin to cast a beam on the outward shape,
The unpolluted temple of the mind,
And turns it by degrees to the soul's essence,
Till all be made immortal: but when lust
By unchaste looks, loose gestures, and foul talk,
But most by lewd and lavish act of sin,
Lets in defilement to the inward parts,
The soul grows clotted by contagìon,
Embodies, and imbrutes, till she quite lose
The divine property of her first being.
Such are those thick and gloomy shadows damp
Oft seen in charnel-vaults, and sepulchres
Lingering, and sitting by a new-made grave,
As loth to leave the body that it loved,
And linked itself by carnal sensuality
To a degenerate and degraded state.

Milton *Comus* ll. 452–74 (**8** and **9** draw on
the same passage from the *Phaedo*)

10   Soul: O, who shall from this dungeon raise
A soul, enslaved so many ways,
With bolts of bones, that fettered stands
In feet, and manacled in hands.
Here blinded with an eye; and there
Deaf with the drumming of an ear,
A soul hung up, as 'twere, in chains
Of nerves, and arteries, and veins,
Tortured, besides each other part,
In a vain head, and double heart?

Body: O, who shall me deliver whole,
From bonds of this tyrannic soul,

Which, stretched upright, impales me so,
That mine own precipice I go;
And warms and moves this needless frame
(A fever could but do the same),
And, wanting where its spite to try,
Has made me live to let me die,
A body that could never rest,
Since this ill spirit it possessed?
Marvell 'A Dialogue between the Soul and Body' ll. 1–20

PLATONIC AND ANTIPLATONIC LOVE

11   It is most true that eyes are formed to serve
The inward light, and that the heavenly part
Ought to be king, from whose rules who do swerve,
Rebels to nature, strive for their own smart.
It is most true, what we call Cupid's dart
An image is, which for ourselves we carve,
And, fools, adore in temple of our heart,
Till that good god make church and churchmen starve.
True, that true beauty virtue is indeed,
Whereof this beauty can be but a shade,
Which elements with mortal mixture breed.
True that on earth we are but pilgrims made,
And should in soul up to our country move:
True, and yet true that I must Stella love.
Sidney *Astrophel and Stella* v

12   But O alas, so long, so far
   Our bodies why do we forbear?
They are ours, though they are not we, we are
   The intelligences, they the sphere.

We owe them thanks, because they thus,
   Did us, to us, at first convey,
Yielded their forces, sense, to us,
   Nor are dross to us, but allay.

On man heaven's influence works not so,
   But that it first imprints the air,
So soul into the soul may flow,
   Though it to body first repair.

As our blood labours to beget
   Spirits, as like souls as it can,
Because such fingers need to knit
   That subtle knot, which makes us man:

So must pure lovers' souls descend
   To affections, and to faculties,
Which sense may reach and apprehend,
   Else a great prince in prison lies.

To our bodies turn we then, that so
   Weak men on love revealed may look;
Love's mysteries in souls do grow,
   But yet the body is his book.

Donne 'The Ecstasy' ll. 49–72

13   For shame, thou everlasting wooer,
Still saying grace and ne'er fall to her!
Love that's in contemplation placed,
Is Venus drawn but to the waist.
Unless your flame confess its gender,
And your parley cause surrender,
You are salamanders of a cold desire,
That live untouched amid the hottest fire.

What though she be a dame of stone,
The widow of Pygmalion;
As hard and unrelenting she,
As the new-crusted Niobe;
Or what doth more of statue carry,
A nun of the Platonic quarry?
Love melts the rigour which the rocks have bred,
A flint will break upon a feather-bed.

Cleveland 'The Antiplatonic' ll. 1–16

4 Stoicism

Stoicism (the name derives from the Stoa, the colonnade at Athens where Zeno, the first Stoic philosopher, taught) went through three phases, Early, Middle and Late. Zeno and Chrysippus were the chief writers of the Early Stoa (third to second century BC), Panaetius and Posidonius of the Middle (second to first century BC), and Seneca, Epictetus and Marcus Aurelius of the Late (first to second century AD). It is by historical accident that the Late Stoa is the most important. The writings of the Early and Middle Stoa survive only in fragments, and in the works of historians, critics and popularisers, such as Diogenes Laertius' *Life of Zeno* and Plutarch's essays against the Stoics in the *Moralia*. Our chief source for the Early and Middle Stoa is the philosophical works of Cicero, in particular *Views of Good and Evil, Tusculan Disputations* and *Of Duties*. Stoicism was first introduced to the Romans by Panaetius, in a form adapted to the Roman view of public life. In the mid-first century BC Cicero (himself a follower of the New Academy, or sceptic) undertook to transmit the Greek philosophical tradition to Rome by translating and popularising works of different Greek schools. He had to find or invent Latin equivalents for Greek philosophical terms, and thus created a philosophical vocabulary that is still in use. In *Views of Good and Evil* the Stoic point of view is argued by Cato and attacked by Cicero himself; in *Tusculan Disputations* Cicero's treatment of Stoicism is comprehensive and extremely sympathetic. (For the importance of Cicero in the Renaissance see Chapter 9.) Although we know the works of the Greek Stoics only at second hand, those of the Romans of the Late Stoa survive: the treatises and epistles of Seneca (**4, 5**), politician and playwright, the *Discourses* and *Manual* (**2, 3**) of Epictetus, one-time slave, and the *Meditations* (**1**) of Marcus Aurelius, emperor. Of the three, only Seneca wrote in Latin (it was in Greek that Marcus Aurelius wrote and Epictetus' lectures were taken down); hence Seneca, not the most interesting nor original Stoic author, has been historically the most influential.

The Stoics divided philosophy into three branches, physics, logic and ethics. Although the first two were taken seriously in the Early and Middle Stoa, the writers of the Late Stoa (except Seneca, who produced one scientific work) concentrated on ethics. There was some development and modification of Stoic ethics to fit different political situations, but the principal ideas of the school can be summarised as follows. The object of the study of ethics is that man should learn to live well. Each man has reason implanted in him by God; it is his share of the divine (**1**). The life of virtue is the only road to happiness. Theoretically virtue can be attained by any man who follows nature, which means, since reason is natural and peculiar to man, being ruled by reason. Reason teaches man to distinguish good and evil from things that are indifferent, what is in his power from what is not in his power (**2, 7**). Of things that are indifferent, some are to be preferred as advantages, and some are to be rejected as disadvantages, but ultimately they are of no importance. The man who is ruled by his reason and learns these distinctions is the Stoic sage. He is characterised by his constancy, firmness and self-sufficiency; he alone is free and a king. He has complete tranquillity and peace of mind: whatever his circumstances he can retire into himself. His state is one of 'apathy': he is free from passion. The four passions – fear, lust, delight and distress – are not goods, since they involve reaction to external events and objects. The passionate man is diseased. However, although the wise man is independent of his circumstances, he does not ignore them. He enjoys human relationships, while remembering that friends, wife or children are not his but merely lent to him (**3**). He has a duty to take part in public life, though in a thoroughly corrupt society it is reasonable for him to retire. He need not lead an ascetic life, provided he distinguishes between slavery to and proper enjoyment of prosperity, which is an advantage, not a good. The unequal distribution of prosperity in the world has a purpose. Providence gives riches and health to the vicious man and poverty and suffering to the virtuous man to teach him that fortune and misfortune are neither good nor evil, that the only reward of virtue is the wise man's state of mind. The wise man cannot call himself happy until he has been tested by Providence and can show that he is unaffected by misfortune (**4**). Yet if his sufferings are intolerable, he has the choice of ending his life (**5**). Thus, whether his circumstances are advantageous or disadvantageous, he is detached and free; suicide is the final assertion of freedom.

It is worth noting two points on which Stoicism disagreed with other classical philosophies. Aristotle and his followers the Peripatetic school assumed that material prosperity is necessary to happiness, not merely an advantage, as the Stoics taught. Epicurus believed the object of life to be the pursuit of happiness, achieved through pleasure, whereas the Stoics regarded happiness as the result but not the object of the pursuit of virtue. Epicurus' wise man has no obligation to his fellow men, and always seeks his own happiness in retirement.

In spite of the idealistic rigour of Stoicism (there is no intermediate state between virtue and vice, so the man who is not wise is vicious) it was intended as a practical guide for conduct rather than an abstract system. The apathy of the sage may seem an unattainable ideal, yet the Stoics insisted that he was not merely a convenient fiction. Stoic authors came to concentrate less on the definition of the wise man and more on the stages by which the ordinary man could become wise. The forms of Roman Stoic literature – epistle, consolation, handbook, meditation – reflect this concern with the individual case. Stoic style tends away from logical argument towards epigram and aphorism. Seneca showered practical Stoic advice on his friends and regarded himself as the physician of their souls, yet he was well aware of his own moral failings, and his works are full of self-disparagement. (He amassed a huge private fortune, and as Nero's chief minister he was reluctantly implicated in many of his crimes). Seneca tried to rebuke human weakness in himself and others by holding up examples of moral strength. Hence Stoic literature abounds in exemplary heroes who show their freedom of mind and indifference to circumstances by the bravery of their deaths. The chief Greek hero is Socrates, put to death by the Athenians, the chief Roman hero is Cato, who killed himself after Caesar's defeat of Pompey. Seneca himself, despite his unexemplary life, became a Stoic hero when he killed himself as Nero's command.

After Marcus Aurelius (second century AD) the importance of Stoicism declined; the chief pagan philosophy of the late empire was Neoplatonism. Yet Stoicism had an indirect influence on many early Christian writers, for example Boethius. Seneca assumed a particular importance in the Middle Ages because of the popularity of his supposed correspondence with St Paul (forged in the fourth century); it was even suggested, though not widely believed, that he had been converted to Christianity. However, although extracts from Seneca were included in medieval and early Renaissance school texts, there was no serious revival of Stoicism until the sixteenth and seventeenth centuries. Cicero, the most popular classical author in the Renaissance, was an important source, as was Plutarch, but the texts of Seneca, Epictetus and Marcus Aurelius were also available, both in the original and in Latin and vernacular translations. Important editions of Seneca were those of Erasmus (1515 and 1529) and Justus Lipsius (1604). The Belgian humanist Lipsius attempted a synthesis of Stoicism and Christianity known as Neostoicism, in which the Stoic and the ideal Christian were identified, and the heretical aspects of Stoicism (such as the glorification of suicide and the belief in fate) were suppressed. Lipsius' *Of Constancy* (1584) (**6**) was soon translated into English and widely read in the seventeenth century. However, Neostoicism was more influential in Europe, particularly in France, than in England. An exception is Joseph

Hall: in *Heaven upon Earth* (1606) he attempted to identify Stoic tranquillity with Christian peace, but by making it dependent on divine grace he recognised the essential contradiction between Stoicism and Christianity (**9**).

The development of Christian Neostoicism should be distinguished from interest in secular Stoicism, which seems to have increased in England in the seventeenth century. The poet most influenced by Stoic ethics is Jonson. Jonson preferred Seneca among Stoic authors, copying out passages in *Discoveries*, his commonplace book, and incorporating them in his poems. He was not interested in the conflict between Stoicism and Christianity, but in that between Stoicism and the values of the Renaissance court – honour, fame and magnificence. His Stoic poems assume that there is a small circle of good men who hold themselves aloof from their society and stand firm in the face of changeable fortune (**14**). His part is to define the idea of virtue and to urge his friends to live by it. Images of immobility, rootedness and circular perfection express the Stoic ideals of self-sufficiency and indifference to externals (see Introduction **4**). Jonson remained a courtier and public servant while supporting himself by a Stoic creed. There is a more restricted use of Stoic attitudes and vocabulary in Cavalier poets like Lovelace (**15**), forced into retirement by the Civil War. However, the Stoicism of the Cavaliers is diluted with Epicureanism, and owes more to Horace than to Seneca.

One can suggest several reasons why Stoicism was influential in the sixteenth and seventeenth centuries. Shorn of its physical and logical basis, Stoicism (unlike Neoplatonism) was easily taught and understood, and universal in its appeal. In Europe it was a creed that provided a refuge from religious persecution and from the rival claims of Catholicism and Protestantism: Lipsius, for example, vacillated between the churches, yet his allegiance was elsewhere. Stoicism was one way in which the intellectual at the Renaissance court could overcome his own political impotence: circumstances might be immutable, but they were insignificant compared with the individual's state of mind (**12, 13**). Sixteenth- and seventeenth-century courtiers must have felt a particular attraction to Seneca, tainted by luxury and political corruption, yet kept free and aloof by his Stoic beliefs.

Renaissance objections to Stoicism were made on theological (**9, 10**), psychological and political grounds. Stoicism assumes that the individual can achieve perfect virtue without reference to anything outside himself, but the Christian cannot act unaided by divine grace. The French essayist Montaigne, after a period of sympathy, came to reject the tenets of Stoicism. Montaigne's intellectual development was from Stoicism to scepticism, and from theoretical resistance to pain and death to instinctive enjoyment of life. He came to see the Stoic sage as intellectually arrogant, lacking in humility, and ultimately untrue to human nature (**8**). Stoicism underestimates the human capacity to alter circumstances; it is a creed appropriate to the politically defeated. Hence the fallen angels in *Paradise Lost* I and II bravely voice Stoic slogans, assuming that they can steel themselves against the pains of hell through strength of will, yet forgetting that hell itself is the result of their own degeneracy. Milton's comments on the self-deception of the fallen angels should be compared with the Cavalier poets' pose of self-reliance. Milton's final refutation of the doctrine of the Stoic sage is contained in the portrait of Christ in *Paradise Regained* IV (see Introduction **4**).

THE FUNCTION OF PHILOSOPHY

1   In the life of a man, his time is but a moment, his being an incessant flux, his senses a dim rushlight, his body a prey of worms, his soul an unquiet eddy, his fortune dark, and his fame doubtful. In short, all that is of the body is as coursing waters, all that is of the soul as dreams and vapours; life a warfare, a brief sojourning in an alien land; and after repute, oblivion. Where, then, can man find the power to guide and guard his steps? In one thing and one alone: Philosophy. To be a philosopher is to keep unsullied and unscathed the divine spirit within him, so that it may transcend all pleasure and all pain, take nothing in hand without purpose and nothing falsely or with dissimulation, depend not on another's actions or inactions, accept each and every dispensation as coming from the same Source as itself – and last and chief, wait with a good grace for death, as no more than a simple dissolving of the elements whereof each living thing is composed.

Marcus Aurelius *Meditations* II xvii

FREEDOM AND SLAVERY

2   Some things are under our control, while others are not under our control. Under our control are conception, choice, desire, aversion, and, in a word, everything that is our own doing; not under our control are our body, our property, reputation, office, and, in a word, everything that is not our own doing. Furthermore, the things under our control are by nature free, unhindered, and unimpeded; while the things not under our control are weak, servile, subject to hindrance, and not our own. Remember, therefore, that if what is naturally slavish you think to be free, and what is not your own to be your own, you will be hampered, will grieve, will be in turmoil, and will blame both gods and men; while if you think only what is your own to be your own, and what is not your own

to be, as it really is, not your own, then no one will ever be able to exert compulsion upon you, no one will hinder you, you will blame no one, will find fault with no one, will do absolutely nothing against your will, you will have no personal enemy, no one will harm you, for neither is there any harm that can touch you.

Epictetus *Manual* i

ADVANTAGES ARE ONLY LENT

3   Never say about anything, 'I have lost it', but only 'I have given it back.' Is your child dead? It has been given back. Is your wife dead? She has been given back. 'I have had my farm taken away.' Very well, this too has been given back. 'Yet it was a rascal who took it away.' But what concern is it of yours by whose instrumentality the Giver called for its return? So long as he gives it you, take care of it as of a thing that is not your own, as travellers treat their inn.

Epictetus *Manual* xi

THE WISE MAN IN ADVERSITY

4   The invulnerable thing is not that which is not struck, but that which is not hurt; by this mark I will show you the wise man ... So you must know that the wise man, if no injury hurts him, will be of a higher type than if none is offered to him, and the brave man, I should say, is he whom war cannot subdue, whom the onset of a hostile force cannot terrify, not he who battens at ease among the idle populace. Consequently I will assert this – that the wise man is not subject to any injury. It does not matter, therefore, how many darts are hurled against him, since none can pierce him. As the hardness of certain stones is impervious to steel, and adamant cannot be cut or hewed or ground, but in turn blunts whatever comes into contact with it; as certain substances cannot be consumed by fire, but, though encompassed by flame, retain their hardness and their shape; as certain cliffs, projecting into the deep, break the force of the sea, and, though lashed for countless ages, show no traces of its wrath, just so the spirit of the wise man is impregnable.

Seneca *On the Firmness of the Wise Man* iii 3–5
(Compare Jonson 'An Ode to James, Earl of Desmond')

5   Why do [good men] suffer certain hardships? It is that they may teach others to endure them; they were born to be a pattern. Think, then, of God as saying: 'What possible reason have you to complain of me, you who have chosen righteousness? ... To you I have given the true and enduring goods ... "Yet," you say, "many sorrows, things dreadful and hard to bear, do befall us." Yes, because I could not withdraw you from their path, I have armed your minds to withstand them all; endure with fortitude. In this you may outstrip God; he is exempt from enduring evil,

while you are superior to it. Scorn poverty; no one lives as poor as he was born. Scorn pain; it will either be relieved or relieve you. Scorn death, which either ends you or transfers you. Scorn Fortune; I have given her no weapon with which she may strike your soul. Above all, I have taken pains that nothing should keep you here against your will; the way out lies open. If you do not choose to fight, you may run away. Therefore of all things that I have deemed necessary for you, I have made nothing easier than dying.'

Seneca *On Providence* vi 3–7

6   These grievous afflictions sent of God do commonly either exercise the good, chastise offenders or punish the wicked; and all this for our good ... We see daily the best sort of men to be subject to calamities either privately or else to be partakers thereof with the wicked: we mark and marvel thereat, because we neither sufficiently conceive the cause, nor consider the consequence thereof. The cause is God's love towards us, and not hatred. The end or consequence, not our hurt, but our benefit. For this our exercising furthereth us more ways than one: it confirmeth or strengtheneth us; it trieth or proveth us; it maketh us mirrors of patience unto others.

Lipsius *Two Books of Constancy* II viii

CHRISTIAN CRITICISM OF STOICISM

7   The meaning of the Stoic assertion that passions do not touch a wise man is probably that passions in no way cloud with error that wisdom in virtue of which he is wise, nor can they undermine and overthrow it. However, they do happen to his soul, but that is because of circumstances which the Stoics call 'advantageous' or 'disadvantageous', being unwilling to describe them as 'good' or 'evil' ... The Stoic insistence that such things are not to be called 'good', but 'advantageous', should be regarded as a quibble about words, not a question of the realities they signify. What does it matter whether they are more properly called 'goods', or 'advantages', seeing that Stoic and Peripatetic alike turn pale with dread at the prospect of their loss?

Augustine *City of God* IX iv

8   'Oh, what a vile and abject thing is man (saith [Seneca]) unless he raise himself above humanity!' Observe here a notable speech and a profitable desire; but likewise absurd. For to make the handful greater than the hand, and the embraced greater than the arm, and to hope to straddle more than our legs' length, is impossible and monstrous: nor that man should mount over and above himself and humanity; for he cannot see but with his own eyes, nor take hold but with his own arms. He shall raise himself up, if it please God extraordinarily to lend him his helping hand. He may elevate himself by forsaking and renouncing his own means, and suffering himself to be elevated and raised by mere heavenly means. It

is for our Christian faith, not for his Stoic virtue, to pretend or aspire to this divine metamorphosis, or miraculous transmutation.

Montaigne *An Apology of Raymond Sebond* conclusion

9 The mind of man is too weak to bear out itself hereby against all onsets ... The wisest and most resolute moralist that ever was [Socrates], looked pale when he should taste of his hemlock; and by his timorousness made sport to those that envied his speculations. The best of the heathen emperors [Antoninus Pius], that was honoured with the title of piety, justly magnified that courage of Christians which made them insult over their tormentors, and by their fearlessness of earthquakes and deaths argued the truth of their religion. It must be, it can be, none but a divine power that can uphold the mind against the rage of many afflictions; and yet the greatest crosses are not the greatest enemies to inward peace. Let us therefore look up above ourselves, and from the rules of an higher art supply the defects of natural wisdom; giving such infallible directions for tranquillity, that whosoever shall follow cannot but live sweetly and with continual delight; applauding himself at home when all the world besides him shall be miserable.

Joseph Hall *Heaven upon Earth* iii

(NB Hall misrepresents Plato's account in *Phaedo* 117B; Socrates did not look pale. The letter of Antoninus is now regarded as a forgery.)

10 There are singular pieces in the philosophy of Zeno, and doctrine of the Stoics, which I perceive, delivered in a pulpit, pass for current divinity: yet herein are they in extremes, that can allow a man to be his own assassin, and so highly extol the end and suicide of Cato; this is indeed not to fear death, but yet to be afraid of life. It is a brave act of valour to contemn death, but where life is more terrible than death, it is then the truest valour to dare to live, and herein religion hath taught us a noble example; for all the valiant acts of Curtius, Scaevola, or Codrus, do not parallel or match that one of Job.

Browne *Religio Medici* I

STOICISM IN POETRY

11 The man of life upright,
  Whose guiltless heart is free
From all dishonest deeds,
  Or thought of vanity,

The man whose silent days
  In harmless joys are spent,
Whom hopes cannot delude
  Nor sorrow discontent,

That man needs neither towers
  Nor armour for defence,

Nor secret vaults to fly
   From thunder's violence.

He only can behold
   With unaffrighted eyes
The horrors of the deep,
   And terrors of the skies.

Thus, scorning all the cares
   That fate, or fortune brings,
He makes the heaven his book,
   His wisdom heavenly things,

Good thoughts his only friends,
   His wealth a well-spent age,
The earth his sober inn
   And quiet pilgrimage.

                       Thomas Campion

12   Since all the good we have rests in the mind,
   By whose proportions only we redeem
   Our thoughts from out confusion, and do find
The measure of our selves, and of our powers.
   And that all happiness remains confined
   Within the kingdom of this breast of ours.
Without whose bounds, all that we look on, lies
   In others' jurisdictions, others' powers,
   Out of the circuit of our liberties.

All glory, honour, fame, applause, renown,
   Are not belonging to our royalties,
   But to others' wills, wherein they are only grown
And that unless we find us all within,
   We never can without us be our own:
   Nor call it right our life, that we live in:
But a possession held for others' use,
   That seem to have most interest therein.

      Daniel 'To the Lady Lucy, Countess of Bedford' ll. 50–66

13   How happy is he born and taught,
That serveth not another's will;
Whose armour is his honest thought,
And simple truth his utmost skill.

Whose passions not his masters are,
Whose soul is still prepared for death:
Untied unto the world by care
Of public fame, or private breath.

Who envies none that chance doth raise,

Nor vice hath ever understood;
How deepest wounds are given by praise,
Nor rules of state, but rules of good.

Who hath his life from rumours freed,
Whose conscience is his strong retreat;
Whose state can neither flatterers feed,
Nor ruin make oppressors great.

Who God doth late and early pray,
More of his grace than gifts to lend:
And entertains the harmless day
With a religious book, or friend.

This man is freed from servile bands,
Of hope to rise, or fear to fall:
Lord of himself, though not of lands,
And having nothing, yet hath all.
Sir Henry Wotton 'The Character of a Happy Life'

14   Thou hast begun well, Roe, which stand well too,
And I know nothing more thou hast to do.
He that is round within himself, and straight,
Need seek no other strength, no other height;
Fortune upon him breaks herself, if ill,
And what would hurt his virtue makes it still.
That thou at once, then, nobly mayest defend
With thine own course the judgement of thy friend,
Be always to thy gathered self the same:
And study conscience, more than thou would'st fame.
Though both be good, the latter yet is worst,
And ever is ill got without the first.
Jonson 'To Sir Thomas Roe' *Epigrams* 98

15   Thou best of men and friends! we will create
     A genuine summer in each other's breast,
And spite of this cold time and frozen fate,
     Thaw us a warm seat to our rest.
. . . . . .
Thus richer than untempted kings are we,
     That asking nothing, nothing need:
Though lord of all what seas embrace, yet he
     That wants himself is poor indeed.
Lovelace 'The Grasshopper' ll. 21–4, 37–40

5 Views of History

Renaissance views of history (in the sense both of the course of events and the recording of those events) were formed by three traditions of historiography, classical, Christian and British. Although the assumptions of classical and Christian historians about the meaning and shape of history in the first sense, and about its function in the second, were largely contradictory, Renaissance historians and poets drew on both.

There are important differences in the methods and aims of Greek and Roman historiography, yet we can define broadly the classical attitude to history. Classical history is concerned with political life, as lived in the Greek city states and the Roman republic and empire, and classical historians take as their subject the conflict between great political powers, for example, Greece and Persia (Herodotus), Athens and Sparta (Thucydides), Rome and Carthage (Livy), Rome and Greece (Polybius), or the struggle for power within a particular state, for example, Athens (Thucydides), republican Rome (Sallust), imperial Rome (Tacitus). Within this framework their narratives tend to concentrate on the ambitions and careers of politicians and generals, and on the analysis of character and motive. There is thus a strong biographical emphasis, some histories (such as Plutarch's *Lives*) taking the form of biography. The object of these narratives is moral; the assumed reader of classical history is a citizen, who will profit from the mistakes and victories of the past and apply the lessons learned to his own political life (**3, 4**). The reading of history serves as practical training. This view of the function of history (recorded narrative) arises from the classical interpretation of history (the course of events): human nature is constant, events are cyclical, men and empires rise and fall, Fortune presides over the inevitable change in human affairs. The patterns of the past will repeat themselves in the future (**1**); men can learn to accommodate themselves to the cycle of events and steel themselves against Fortune.

Some distinctions need to be borne in mind. There were two separate approaches to the writing of history in antiquity. One saw history as a science based on the accumulation of empirical evidence, the other as an art form, associating it with epic, tragedy, oratory and myth. 'Scientific' historians like Thucydides and Polybius dissociated themselves from poets and tragedians; both experienced politicians, they thought such experience was necessary for the historian. At the other extreme, some Roman historians drew heavily on myth in their account of Rome's fulfilment of its destiny as mistress of the world: Livy's idea of Rome is close to that of Virgil in the *Aeneid*. In Roman history the cyclical view of events conflicts with a linear view: on the one hand Roman historians lament the degeneration of Rome from the heroic and mythical early republic (**4**); on the other they see the world domination of Rome as the culmination of the historical process (**2**). In this respect the Roman view of history differs from the Greek but shares aspects of the Christian view.

With Christian history we find a radical alteration of perspective. Classical history is narrated from the point of view of man as citizen of a secular state, Christian history from the point of view of God. The course of events is not directed by capricious Fortune, but by beneficent Providence. The pattern is linear: God's promises are fulfilled. Events will not recur endlessly; history has a beginning, the Creation, a central point, the Incarnation, and an end, the Last Judgement (**9**). Time will give place to eternity. It is the task of the Christian historian to bring man's perspective, that of time, into harmony with God's, that of eternity. Hence, as R. G. Collingwood puts it, 'any history written on Christian principles will be of necessity universal, providential, apocalyptic, and periodized'.

Like the Romans, the Jews had a sense of national destiny, but a destiny ordained by God. The Christian view of history, drawing heavily on the prophetic books of the Old Testament, particularly Daniel (**7**), made this national destiny universal. The Book of Revelation (or Apocalypse), the other chief source for the Christian view of history, incorporated and transformed the Jewish apocalyptic tradition. Revelation predicts the thousand-year reign of Christ and the saints on earth after the destruction of Babylon and the beast, and the binding of Satan (**10**). Literal belief in this prediction (known as millenarianism) was widespread among the Christians of the first two centuries, but with the allegorical interpretation of Revelation it became a heresy. However, Christian history remained apocalyptic in that, unlike classical history, it was less concerned with the past than with the future, less with men's actions than with their final goal.

Although the patterns of Christian history were biblical in origin, it was not until the fourth century, when the Roman empire became officially Christian, that a tradition of Christian historiography was properly established. Eusebius, the author of the first *Ecclesiastical History*, described the sufferings of the early Church and its victory under Constantine, and in his *Chronology* (made available to the Latin West in Jerome's translation, and drawn on by the seventh-century encyclopedist Isidore) provided synchronised tables of classical, Jewish and Christian history that remained in use until the sixteenth century. In *The City of God* Augustine narrated the history of the world from the Creation to the Last Judgement. In arguing the superiority of Christian to classical religion, philosophy and culture Augustine attacked both the cyclical theory of history (**11**) and the pagan belief in Rome's special destiny. He took over three traditional Christian schemes for dividing history into periods and for interpreting its meaning: the Four World Monarchies, the Six Ages (**13**), and the Three Eras. He also created a new scheme, that of the Two Cities (**12**). The Scheme of the Four Monarchies derives from Daniel's interpretation of Nebuchadnezzar's dream and his own vision (2:31–45; 7:17–27) (**7**). The Four Monarchies were traditionally identified as Assyria, Persia, Greece and Rome; the fall of one marks the rise of the next, until the last one, Rome, is finally overcome by Christ's kingdom (the Fifth Monarchy). The related but more worldly idea of *translatio imperii* (translation of empire) was extremely influential in the Middle Ages, when the Roman empire was 'translated' first to the Franks under Charlemagne and subsequently to the Germans as the Holy Roman Empire, and in a rather different form in the Renaissance, when Spain, France and England all saw themselves as heirs to Rome.

The scheme of the Six Ages is based on the divisions of Old Testament history; each age was supposed to last for a thousand years, though Augustine repudiated this rigidity (**13**). The Ages are: (1) Adam to Noah (2) Noah to Abraham (3) Abraham to David (4) David to the Babylonian Captivity (5) the Babylonian Captivity to the Incarnation (6) the Incarnation to the Last Judgement. The Seventh Age is eternity. This scheme tended to be absorbed into the simpler one of the Three Eras (Augustine, *On The Trinity* IV iv): *ante legem* (the state of nature, before the giving of the Law to Moses), *sub lege* (under the Law, the old dispensation of Moses), *sub gratia* (under grace, the new dispensation of Christ).

Augustine's own scheme of the Two Cities was the most striking (**12**). Two cities coexist in history, Babylon and Jerusalem, the earthly and the heavenly; every man is a member of one of them. Historically, Babylon takes a different form in different ages; in Augustine's time, it was Rome. The citizen of Babylon is a secular political being; the citizen of Jerusalem is only a pilgrim (*peregrinus* or resident alien) in Babylon, waiting for his true home. The temporal Babylon will finally give place to the eternal Jerusalem. Through this scheme of the Two Cities Augustine repudiated what he considered the narrow concern of classical historians with political events. The sack of Rome in 410, a disaster for the pagans, was, Augustine tried to show, relatively insignificant when seen from the true perspective.

This Christian view of history with its accompanying schemes of periodisation was dominant until the fourteenth century. With the humanist rediscovery of classical historiography there was a return to classical views of history (see Chapter 9). For the humanists, beginning with Petrarch, the fall of Rome was not to be explained away as part of the divine plan; it was a political and cultural disaster, and the ensuing period of a thousand years was the dark age from which the humanists believed themselves to be emerging into the light. Humanist historians abandoned the schemes of universal Christian history and concentrated on military and political narratives. The Florentine Machiavelli in *The Prince* and *Discourses on Livy* revived Polybius' theory of political cycles and the role of Fortune; the French Jean Bodin in *Method for the Easy Comprehension of History* attacked Christian schemes like that of the Four Monarchies. The humanist concern with the political obligations of the man of letters entailed a return to the pragmatic and moral interpretation of the function of history: history both teaches men the art of political survival and, by rewarding men with good and bad fame according to their deserts, provides an incitement to virtue. The classical works which embodied these views were widely read in the Renaissance; between the 1530s and the 1630s the major Greek and Roman historians were translated into English (notable examples being Philemon Holland's Livy, Sir Thomas North's Plutarch, Sir Henry Savile's Tacitus (**17**), and Thomas Hobbes's Thucydides). Tacitus, an author scarcely known in late antiquity or the Middle Ages, achieved a new popularity in the later sixteenth and early seventeenth centuries.

The humanist revival of classical history did not, however, imply an eclipse of the Christian view of history; on the contrary, the Reformation gave it fresh impetus (see Chapter 7). The break with the Church of Rome involved a new interpretation of the Book of Revelation and a revival of millenarianism. Whereas for the early Christians Babylon represented pagan Rome and Antichrist persecuting emperors such as Nero and Domitian, for the Protestants Babylon represented Catholic Rome, and Antichrist the Pope. The most influential work of Protestant historiography in England in the sixteenth century, John Foxe's *Acts and Monuments* (usually known as Foxe's Book of Martyrs), recasts Augustine's scheme of the Two Cities as the Two Churches (**14**). The providential view of history, with events from Creation to Last Judgement guided by God, was still widely held. Of the many universal histories written during the period the most popular was Ralegh's *History of the World*. Ralegh's frontispiece shows the all-seeing eye of Providence surveying the globe, which is supported by *Magistra Vitae* (the Instructress of Life, Cicero's phrase for history), who in turn tramples on *Mors* and *Oblivio* (Death and Oblivion) (**18**). In the Preface

Ralegh gives a prudential reason for not writing modern political history: 'Whosoever in writing a modern history, shall follow truth too near the heels, it may haply strike out his teeth.' Yet he also seems pessimistic about the moralistic claim of humanist historians that men can learn from history.

Renaissance historians drew on a third extremely popular historical tradition, now regarded largely as fiction: British history, or the Matter of Britain. The chief figure in the disseminating of this tradition is the twelfth-century monk Geoffrey of Monmouth, whose *History of Britain* narrates how the Trojan Brutus conquered Albion, renamed it Britain, and founded the city of New Troy. Britain achieved its greatest glory under Arthur, whose army swept across Europe and finally defeated the Romans in Gaul. Arthur is known to modern readers largely through medieval romance, but the chronicle tradition is more relevant to the Renaissance. We find two divergent treatments of the Matter of Britain in the sixteenth century: it is questioned as history while it flourishes as propaganda and myth. The Italian humanist historian Polydore Vergil, whose *English History* was dedicated to Henry VIII, denied the authenticity of the Trojan and Arthurian stories. Because of the uproar this criticism occasioned, the antiquarian William Camden was more cautious in his questioning of the material in *Britannia*. Yet by the time Milton wrote his *History of Britain* in the 1640s antiquarian research into Anglo-Saxon England had demolished the Matter of Britain as history (Milton consequently found himself unable to use Arthur as the subject of an epic). However, the Tudors consciously manipulated the material as myth. One useful British legend was the prophecy of Arthur's second coming: he was *rex quondam rexque futurus* (the once and future king). The Welsh (i.e. British) Henry VII drew on this legend to support his claim to the English throne, even naming his elder son Arthur. We can see here a deliberate imitation of Virgil's use of the legend of the Trojan Aeneas to support the political position of Augustus. Just as empire had passed from Troy to Rome, so now it passed to New Troy, London. It is important to realise that a number of possible and contradictory meanings for Rome was available in Renaissance historical thought. There was the Rome of Virgil and Augustus, whose power, so the imperialist propagandists of Spain, France and England contended, had passed to their own monarchs; there was the Rome of Augustine's Two Cities, representing ultimately insignificant earthly government; there was the Rome seen by the Protestants, presided over by Antichrist, whose defeat would, in millenarian thought, herald the Fifth Monarchy of Christ.

In determining the use made of the various historiographical traditions in poetry, we should distinguish between historical poems which give a narrative account of specific historical events, such as the *Mirror for Magistrates*, Daniel's *The Civil Wars*, or Drayton's *The Barons' Wars*, and poems which explore and define certain views of history, such as *The Faerie Queene* and *Paradise Lost*. Spenser's sense of the shape and meaning of history is the most complex. In making the hinge of his story Arthur's search for Gloriana and presumably his eventual union with her, Spenser was alluding to the idea of the return of Arthur in the form of Elizabeth. The idea is reinforced by the superimposed settings of Britain and Faeryland. Spenser sets out the British and Elvish genealogies in detail in Books II x, III iii, and III ix. By his use of Tudor Arthurian propaganda with its Virgilian emphasis on prophecy and fulfilment Spenser achieves a deliberate fusion of past and present, history and myth. Yet the perspective is not simply that of the idealised Arthurian past against which the present is measured. Spenser uses the scheme of the Two Cities, but with what we might call a Roman orientation. His cities are the heavenly Jerusalem and the earthly city representing Elizabeth's London, which appears in two guises: Cleopolis, the city of glory, Gloriana's capital, and the British Troynovant. In I x Red Cross Knight is shown the heavenly city, but taught that his present obligations are to the earthly one (**15**). The perspective of eternity is thus briefly introduced and then withdrawn, a reminder of what lies beyond the temporal action of the poem. This perspective is again introduced in the Mutability Cantos, when Nature defeats Mutability with two arguments: first, change means not permanent alteration but repetition and continuity; second, change will one day have an end and time will be overtaken by eternity (**16**).

Milton's use of Christian history is much more confident and assertive than Spenser's; he rejects the imperial Roman and the cyclical theories which play a large part in *The Faerie Queene*. Michael's prophecy to Adam (*Paradise Lost* XI and XII) constitutes a universal history, leading to the Last Judgement, 'the race of time,/Till time stand fixed'. Though human life is arduous, it is the certain knowledge of God's eventual fulfilment of his promises that enables man to endure with patience and to make the right choices. However, it is worth noting that Milton's sense of man's ability to foresee the stages of God's plan altered considerably. In the early 1640s he was strongly attracted to millenarianism, and appeared to regard the Long Parliament as precipitating the Second Coming; but the failure of the Puritan cause destroyed this view. In *Paradise Regained* the emphasis shifts to the inscrutability of God's purposes (**20**).

Some poets explored the problem of history in a much more detached and experimental manner. Marvell in his poems on Cromwell appears to be testing views of history and their relevance to immediate situations. In 'An Horatian Ode' Cromwell's rise is explained in terms that Polybius would have understood, while in *The First Anniversary* cyclical and millenarian views of history, with their appropriate terminology, are set against each other (**19**). Marvell is comparing two traditions, as Spenser does in the Mutability Cantos, but the effect is very different: Marvell is paradoxically using the Christian perspective of history for immediate political ends.

CLASSICAL VIEWS OF HISTORY

1   It may well be that my history will seem less easy to read because of the absence in it of a romantic element. It will be enough for me, however, if these words of mine are judged useful by those who want to understand clearly the events which happened in the past and which (human nature being what it is) will, at some time or other and in much the same ways, be repeated in the future. My work is not a piece of writing designed to meet the taste of an immediate public, but was done to last for ever.

Thucydides *The Peloponnesian War* I i

2   Fortune having guided almost all the affairs of the world in one direction and having forced them to incline towards one and the same end, a historian should bring before his readers under one synoptical view the operations by which she has accomplished her general purpose ... I therefore thought it quite necessary not to leave unnoticed or allow to pass into oblivion this the finest and most beneficent of the performances of Fortune. For though she is ever producing something new and ever playing a part in the lives of men, she has not in a single instance ever accomplished such a work, ever achieved such a triumph, as in our own times [i.e. the rise of Rome].

Polybius *The Histories* I iv

3   There are two ways by which all men can reform themselves, the one through their own mischances, the other through those of others, and of these the former is the more impressive, but the latter the less hurtful. Therefore we should never choose the first method if we can help it, as it corrects by means of great pain and peril, but ever pursue the other, since by it we can discern what is best without suffering hurt. Reflecting on this we should regard as the best discipline for actual life the experience that accrues from serious history; for this alone makes us, without inflicting any harm on us, the most competent judges of what is best at every time and in every circumstance.

Polybius I xxxv

4   I invite the reader's attention to the much more serious consideration of the kind of lives our ancestors lived, of who were the men, and what the means both in politics and war by which Rome's power was first acquired

and subsequently expanded; I would then have him trace the process of our moral decline, to watch, first, the sinking of the foundations of morality as the old teaching was allowed to lapse, then the rapidly increasing disintegration, then the final collapse of the whole edifice, and the dark dawning of our modern day when we can neither endure our vices nor face the remedies needed to cure them. The study of history is the best medicine for a sick mind; for in history you have a record of the infinite variety of human experience plainly set out for all to see; and in that record you can find for yourself and your country both examples and warnings; fine things to take as models, base things, rotten through and through, to avoid.

Livy *The History of Rome* I i

5   It seems to me a historian's foremost duty to ensure that merit is recorded, and to confront evil deeds and words with the fear of posterity's denunciations.

Tacitus *Annals* III lxv

BIBLICAL VIEWS OF HISTORY

6   Lord, thou hast been our dwelling place in all generations.
Before the mountains were brought forth, or ever thou hadst formed the earth and the world, even from everlasting to everlasting, thou art God.
. . . . . .
For a thousand years in thy sight are but as yesterday when it is past, and as a watch in the night.

Psalm 90:1–2, 4

7   The interpretation of Daniel's vision:
These great beasts, which are four, are four kings, which shall arise out of the earth.
But the saints of the most High shall take the kingdom, and possess the kingdom for ever, even for ever and ever.
. . . . . .
... The fourth beast shall be the fourth kingdom upon earth, which shall be diverse from all kingdoms, and shall devour the whole earth, and shall tread it down, and break it in pieces.
And the ten horns out of this kingdom are ten kings that shall arise: and another shall rise after them; and he shall be diverse from the first, and he shall subdue three kings.
And he shall speak great words against the most High, and shall wear out the saints of the most High, and think to change times and laws: and they shall be given into his hand until a time and times and the dividing of time.
But the judgement shall sit, and they shall take away his dominion, to consume and to destroy it unto the end.

And the kingdom and dominion, and the greatness of the kingdom under the whole heaven, shall be given to the people of the saints of the most High, whose kingdom is an everlasting kingdom, and all dominions shall serve and obey him.

Daniel 7:17–18, 23–7

8   When they therefore were come together, they asked of him, saying, Lord, wilt thou at this time restore again the kingdom to Israel?

And he said unto them, It is not for you to know the times or the seasons, which the Father hath put in his own power.

Acts 1: 6–7 (compare **13, 20**)

9   ... There shall come in the last days scoffers, walking after their own lusts,

And saying, Where is the promise of his coming? for since the fathers fell asleep, all things continue as they were from the beginning of the creation.

For this they willingly are ignorant of, that by the word of God the heavens were of old, and the earth standing out of the water and in the water:

Whereby the world that then was, being overflowed with water, perished:

But the heavens and the earth, which are now, by the same word are kept in store, reserved unto fire against the day of judgement and perdition of ungodly men.

But, beloved, be not ignorant of this one thing, that one day is with the Lord as a thousand years, and a thousand years as one day. [compare **6**]

. . . . . .

But the day of the Lord will come as a thief in the night; in the which the heavens shall pass away with a great noise, and the elements shall melt with fervent heat, the earth also and the works that are therein shall be burned up.

. . . . . .

Nevertheless we, according to his promise, look for new heavens and a new earth, wherein dwelleth righteousness.

II Peter 3: 3–8, 10, 13

10   And I saw an angel come down from heaven, having the key of the bottomless pit and a great chain in his hand.

And he laid hold on the dragon, that old serpent, which is the Devil, and Satan, and bound him a thousand years,

And cast him into the bottomless pit, and shut him up, and set a seal upon him, that he should deceive the nations no more, till the thousand years should be fulfilled: and after that he must be loosed a little season.

And I saw thrones, and they sat upon them, and judgement was given unto them: and I saw the souls of them that were beheaded for the witness of Jesus, and for the word of God, and which had not worshipped the beast, neither his image, neither had received his mark upon their foreheads, or in their hands; and they lived and reigned with Christ a thousand years.

Revelation 20:1–4

AUGUSTINE'S VIEW OF HISTORY

11 [Advocates of the cyclical view of history] asserted that by those cycles all things in the universe have been continually renewed and repeated, in the same form, and thus there will be hereafter an unceasing sequence of ages, passing away and coming again in revolution. These cycles may take place in one continuing world, or it may be that at certain periods the world disappears and reappears, showing the same features, which appear as new, but which in fact have been in the past and will return in the future. And they are utterly unable to rescue the immortal soul from this merry-go-round, even when it has attained wisdom; it must proceed on an unremitting alternation between false bliss and genuine misery. For how can there be true bliss, without any certainty of its eternal continuance, when the soul in its ignorance does not know of the misery to come, or else unhappily fears its coming in the midst of its blessedness? But if the soul goes from misery to happiness, nevermore to return, then there is some new state of affairs in time, which will never have an end in time. If so, why cannot the same be true of the world? And of man, created in the world? And so we may escape from these false circuitous courses . . .

Augustine *The City of God* XII xiv

12 We see then that the two cities were created by two kinds of love: the earthly city was created by self-love reaching the point of contempt for God, the Heavenly City by the love of God carried as far as contempt of self. In fact, the earthly city glories in itself, the Heavenly City glories in the Lord. The former looks for glory from men, the latter finds its highest glory in God, the witness of a good conscience. The earthly lifts up its head in its own glory, the Heavenly City says to its God: 'My glory, and the lifter up of mine head' [Psalm 3:3]. In the former, the lust for domination lords it over its princes as over the nations it subjugates; in the other both those put in authority and those subject to them serve one another in love, the rulers by their counsel, the subjects by obedience. The one city loves its own strength shown in its powerful leaders; the other says to its God, 'I will love thee, O Lord, my strength' [Psalm 18: 1].

. . . Scripture tells us that Cain founded a city, whereas Abel, as a pilgrim, did not found one. For the City of the saints is up above, although it produces citizens here below, and in their persons the City is on pilgrimage until the time of its kingdom comes. At that time it will assemble all those citizens as they rise again in their bodies; and then they will be given the promised kingdom, where with their Prince, the king of ages, they will reign, world without end.

City of God XIV xxviii, XV i

13   Now if the epochs of history are reckoned as 'days', following the apparent temporal scheme of Scripture, this Sabbath period will emerge more clearly as the seventh of those epochs. The first 'day' is the first period, from Adam to the Flood; the second from the Flood to Abraham. Those correspond not by equality in the passage of time, but in respect of the number of generations, for there are found to be ten generations in each of those periods. From that time, in the scheme of the evangelist Matthew, there are three epochs, which take us down to the coming of Christ; one from Abraham to David, a second from David to the Exile in Babylon, and the third extending to the coming of Christ in the flesh. Thus we have a total of five periods. We are now in the sixth epoch, but that cannot be measured by the number of generations, because it is said, 'It is not for you to know the times or the seasons, which the Father hath put in his own power' [Acts 1: 7; see [8]. After this present age God will rest, as it were, on the seventh day, and he will cause us, who are the seventh day, to find our rest in him.

City of God XXII xxx

PROTESTANT HISTORY

14   For first to see the simple flock of Christ, especially the unlearned sort, so miserably abused, and all for ignorance of history, not knowing the course of times, and true descent of the Church, it pitied me, that part of diligence so long to have been unsupplied in this my country Church of England ... Which therefore I have here taken in hand, that as other storywriters heretofore have employed their travail to magnify the Church of Rome: so in this history might appear to all Christian readers the image of both churches, as well of the one as of the other: especially of the poor oppressed and persecuted Church of Christ. Which persecuted Church though it hath been of long season trodden underfoot by enemies, neglected in the world, nor regarded in histories, and almost scarce visible or known to worldly eyes, yet hath it been the true Church only of God.

Foxe *Acts and Monuments* 'A Protestation to the whole Church of England'

VIEWS OF HISTORY IN RENAISSANCE POETRY

15   The hermit Contemplation shows Red Cross Knight the new Jerusalem and foretells his earthly and heavenly glory as St George:
'Fair knight,' quoth he, 'Hierusalem that is,
The new Hierusalem, that God has built
For those to dwell in that are chosen his,

His chosen people, purged from sinful guilt
With precious blood, which cruelly was spilt
On cursèd tree, of that unspotted lamb,
That for the sins of all the world was kilt:
Now are they saints all in that City sam, [i.e. together]
More dear unto their God than younglings to their dam.'

'Till now,' said then the knight, 'I weenèd well,
That great Cleopolis, where I have been,
In which that fairest Faery Queene doth dwell
The fairest city was that might be seen;
And that bright tower, all built of crystal clean,
Panthea, seemed the brightest thing that was;
But now by proof all otherwise I ween,
For this great City that does far surpass,
And this bright angels' tower quite dims that tower of glass.'

'Most true,' then said the holy agèd man;
'Yet is Cleopolis, for earthly frame,
The fairest piece that eye beholden can;
And well beseems all knights of noble name,
That covet in the immortal book of fame
To be eternisèd, that same to haunt,
And doen their service to that sovereign Dame,
That glory does to them for guerdon grant;
For she is heavenly born, and heaven may justly vaunt.'

Spenser The Faerie Queene 1 x stanzas 57–9

16 Nature has over-ruled Mutability's arguments:
When I bethink me on that speech whilere
Of Mutability, and well it way!
Me seems, that though she all unworthy were
Of the heavens' rule; yet, very sooth to say,
In all things else she bears the greatest sway:
Which makes me loathe this state of life so tickle,
And love of things so vain to cast away;
Whose flowering pride, so fading and so fickle,
Short Time shall soon cut down with his consuming sickle.

Then gin I think on that which Nature said,
Of that same time when no more change shall be,
But steadfast rest of all things, firmly stayed
Upon the pillars of Eternity,
That is contrair to Mutability;
For all that moveth doth in change delight:
But thenceforth all shall rest eternally
With Him that is the God of Sabaoth hight:
O! that great Sabaoth God, grant me that Sabaoth's sight.

The Faerie Queene VII viii stanzas 1–2 (see Ch. 6.16)

17   Although to write be lesser than to do,
      It is the next deed, and a great one too.
      We need a man that knows the several graces
      Of history, and how to apt their places;
      Where brevity, where splendour, and where height,
      Where sweetness is required, and where weight;
      We need a man, can speak of the intents,
      The counsels, actions, orders, and events
      Of state, and censure them: we need his pen
      Can write the things, the causes, and the men.
      But most we need his faith (and all have you)
      That dares nor write things false, nor hide things true.

                        Jonson 'To Sir Henry Savile' (the translator
                              of Tacitus) *Epigrams* 95 ll. 25–36

18   From death and dark oblivion (near the same)
      The mistress of man's life, grave history,
      Raising the world to good, or evil fame,
      Doth vindicate it to eternity.

      High Providence would so: that nor the good
      Might be defrauded, nor the great secured,
      But both might know their ways are understood
      And the reward and punishment assured.

      This makes, that lighted by the beamy hand
      Of truth, which searcheth the most hidden springs,
      And guided by experience, whose straight wand
      Doth mete, whose line doth sound the depth of things;

      She cheerfully supporteth what she rears:
      Assisted by no strengths, but are her own.
      Some note of which each varied pillar bears,
      By which, as proper titles, she is known,

      Time's witness, herald of antiquity,
      The light of truth, and life of memory.

                        Jonson 'The Mind of the Front' [ispiece]
                            (to Ralegh's *History of the World*.
                         The last two lines are a translation
                         from Cicero *On the Orator* II ix 36)

19   Marvell tentatively casts Cromwell in a millenarian role:
      Hence oft I think if in some happy hour
      High grace should meet in one with highest power,
      And then a seasonable people still
      Should bend to his, as he to heaven's will,
      What we might hope, what wonderful effect
      From such a wished conjuncture might reflect.
      Sure, the mysterious work, where none withstand,

Would forthwith finish under such a hand:
Foreshortened time its useless course would stay,
And soon precipitate the latest day.
But a thick cloud about that morning lies,
And intercepts the beams of mortal eyes,
That 'tis the most which we determine can,
If these the times, then this must be the man.

> Marvell *The First Anniversary of the Government* ll. 131–44

20 The Son rejects Satan's millenarian temptation:

If kingdom move thee not, let move thee zeal,
And duty; zeal and duty are not slow;
. . . . . .
So shalt thou best fulfil, best verify
The prophets old, who sung thy endless reign,
The happier reign the sooner it begins,
Reign then; what canst thou better do the while?
    To whom our Saviour answer thus returned.
All things are best fulfilled in their due time,
And time there is for all things, Truth hath said:
If of my reign prophetic writ hath told,
That it shall never end, so when begin
The Father in his purpose hath decreed,
He in whose hand all times and seasons roll.

> Milton *Paradise Regained* III ll. 171–2, 177–87 (compare **8**)

6 Cosmology

The Greek cosmos (κόσμος, Latin *mundus*), meaning both order and ornament, was first used by the Pythagoreans as a term for the universe, conceived as harmoniously shaped and bounded, in opposition to shapeless and boundless chaos (1). The traditional Greek cosmology, emphasising the order, finiteness and constancy of the cosmos, dominated Western thought for almost 2,000 years, until in the hundred years from about 1550 to 1650 it was overthrown by the new cosmology in what is known as the Copernican revolution. The traditional cosmology provided a coherent account of the constitution of all existing things and the relationship between them, from the great cosmos or macrocosm, the universe, to the small cosmos or microcosm, man. Although certain modifications had to be made to the tradition to accommodate it to Christian belief, it remained extraordinarily consistent, deriving as it did from a few crucial texts. The most important of these were Plato's *Timaeus* (an account of the creation of the world and the relationship between macro- and microcosm), and Aristotle's *On the Heavens, Physics, Metaphysics, On Generation and Corruption* and *On the Soul* (works which modified the Platonic account significantly, and which provided what were to become the accepted definitions of concepts such as motion, function, growth and decay, stability and change). Other classical writers contributed to aspects of the tradition: Ptolemy to astronomy, Hippocrates and Galen to medicine, Strabo to geography, Pliny to natural history. This traditional cosmology was transmitted to the early Middle Ages through the works of encyclopedists and commentators, such as Chalcidius' commentary on the *Timaeus*, Macrobius' *Commentary on the Dream of Scipio* (the vision at the end of the *Republic* of Cicero, modelled on the myth of Er at the end of the *Republic* of Plato), and Boethius' *Consolation of Philosophy*. Although Aristotle's writings on logic were translated by Boethius, his scientific writings were not generally accessible until the twelfth and thirteenth centuries, when the bulk of the Aristotelian corpus was translated into Latin, some of it from Arabic versions of the Greek. From the thirteenth century Aristotle, christianised by Aquinas, was the recognised authority on philosophy (which included what we should now call science). In the sixteenth and seventeenth centuries the English universities still based the teaching of science largely on Aristotle, while popular encyclopedias such as *Batman upon Bartholomew* and de la Primaudaye's *The French Academy* helped to disseminate the tradition more widely.

The christianised Aristotelian–Ptolemaic cosmology rests on a fundamental opposition between the earthly, which is characterised by generation and corruption, flux, mutability and inconstancy, and the heavenly, which is constant, orderly and eternal (**4, 6**). (Aristotle's view that the cosmos had always existed was incompatible with the Genesis account of creation and had to be rejected, whereas the Platonic myth (**2**) could be incorporated. However, there was always a certain amount of tension between the Greek tradition of a pre-existent chaos out of which cosmos arose (**3**), and the Christian belief that God created the world out of nothing, *ex nihilo*.) The whole cosmos is a perfect, finite sphere, enclosing within itself a number of concentric transparent spheres, each with its particular motion. At the centre of the cosmos is the stationary earth; at the centre of the earth (as in Dante's *Inferno*) is sometimes placed the Christian hell. The constituent materials of the terrestrial sphere and its inhabitants are the four elements: earth, which is cold and dry; water, cold and wet; air, hot and wet; and fire, hot and dry. (The theory of the four elements was derived by Plato and Aristotle from Empedocles, who taught that they are given shape by two conflicting forces, Love and Strife, which alternately combine and separate them (**8**).) The elements themselves are arranged in concentric spheres: the earth at the centre, enclosed in turn by the spheres of water, air and fire. The next sphere is that of the moon, which is especially important as the boundary between the earthly, the sublunary, and the heavenly, the trans- or superlunary. The characteristic motion of the imperfect sublunary elements is rectilinear: up, in the case of fire and air, down, in the case of water and earth. Everything in the region above the moon is formed of a different, perfect fifth element, the quintessence or aether (**4**). The characteristic motion of these spheres is circular. There is no space or void in the cosmos; each sphere, carrying a heavenly body embedded in it, moves separately, impelled partly by the motion of the sphere outside it. The number of spheres might vary with refinements of the cosmological scheme, but the cosmology received in the Renaissance contained ten. First are the seven planets, in the order Moon, Mercury, Venus, Sun, Mars, Jupiter, Saturn; then the sphere of the fixed stars, or firmament; then the Crystalline sphere (a late addition); and finally the Primum Mobile, the outermost moving sphere which initiates the motion of all the rest. Beyond the Primum Mobile is the abode of God, the Empyrean Heaven, whose existence is of a different nature from that of the cosmos and incomprehensible to man. The Aristotelian Unmoved Mover, who moves the cosmos because he is an object of love (**5**), becomes the Christian God, who moves the cosmos through his active love of his Creation.

As the heavenly spheres revolve, the friction causes each to give out a different note, the resulting harmony or scale composing the music of the spheres. This Pythagorean theory, taken up by Plato in *Republic* X (**11**), was repudiated by Aristotle in *On the Heavens* II ix (**12**), but it was popularised by Macrobius (*Commentary* II iii) and became fused with Aristotle's theory of an unmoved mover or intelligence for each sphere (*Metaphysics* XII viii). Plato supposed that eight sirens sang the heavenly notes; these later were identified with the nine Muses, and ultimately with the nine orders of angels (Seraphim, Cherubim, Thrones, Dominations, Powers, Virtues, Princedoms, Archangels and Angels). Thus the angelic choirs came to be associated both with the Pythagorean–Platonic celestial harmony and with the Aristotelian intelligences. The correspondence between heavenly and earthly music was explained by Boethius in *The Principles of Music* I ii (**13**). The music of the spheres or cosmic music (*musica mundana*) is inaudible to human ears, but the harmony can be approximated by the harmonious human life (*musica humana*) and by instrumental music (*musica instrumentis constituta*).

This correspondence between different kinds of music, and hence different levels of the cosmos, illustrates an extremely important aspect of the traditional cosmology. The separation between the earthly and the heavenly could be seen pessimistically, as showing the irremediable imperfection of the sublunary world (although Aristotle himself was far more interested in the changing processes of terrestrial life than in the constancy of the heavens). Alternatively, and more optimistically, the relationship between macro- and microcosm and the interdependence of the various planes of existence could be stressed. The dualistic cosmos, therefore, was also seen as a hierarchy, a series of gradations from the lowest to the highest forms of existence, from stones, plants, animals, men, angels, up to God (**14**). This hierarchy was known as the *scala naturae*, the ladder of nature, or the chain of being – sometimes symbolised by Jacob's ladder (Genesis 28: 12) or the golden chain with which Homer's Zeus threatened to hang earth from Olympus (*Iliad* VIII ll. 18–27).

The central position in the scale of nature is held by man, the microcosm (**22–6**). His bodily structure mirrors the terrestrial sphere. The four humours (classified by Hippocrates in *The Nature of Man* IV), melancholy (cold and dry), phlegm (cold and wet), blood (hot and wet) and choler (hot and dry), parallel the four elements and the four seasons. The fact that he is compounded of body and soul shows that he is an amphibious creature, linked to both earthly and heavenly spheres (**24**).

Man's tripartite soul (the account was adapted from Aristotle *On the Soul* II) itself embodies the scale of nature: the vegetative, shared by plants, animals and man, capable of growth and reproduction; the sensitive, shared by animals and man, capable of sensation; and the rational, shared by man and angels, capable of thought and choice (**22**). (Aristotle's term psyche ($\psi\upsilon\chi\acute{\eta}$) means life rather than soul, and does not imply a separate existence for the soul apart from the body, but it was readily adapted to the Platonic–Christian scheme.)

One way in which the belief in the interaction of the levels of existence found expression was the 'science' of astrology. Astrology, the study of the influence of the heavenly bodies on the earthly sphere, may now seem very different from astronomy, but the distinction was blurred until the end of the Renaissance period. The astronomer who engaged in pure observation or computation was also a practising astrologer who cast horoscopes and predicted future events; this activity was known as judicial astrology. The planets, identified with the pagan gods, were believed to influence a wide range not only of forms of life, from the characteristics of stones and plants to the humours of men, but also of events, from changes in the climate to the rise and fall of nations. Astrology in its first, more limited aspect was universally accepted, but where it implied moral and historical determinism and was seen to conflict with man's free will and God's providence it was condemned by theologians. (The problem is explored by Ralegh, *History of the World* I i 11.)

The traditional cosmology was thus not only intellectually and aesthetically satisfying, it had religious and moral significance. Man's position at the centre of the universe was paradoxical: imperfect and earthbound, he was unhappily aware of the difference between the earthly and heavenly spheres of existence, yet he also knew that the cosmos had been created for him, and that through a proper exercise of the celestial faculties with which he was endowed he could aspire to the heavens. This religious and moral significance supported the long belief in the traditional cosmology. Yet this cosmology failed because it did not fit the observed facts: by the end of the seventeenth century it no longer survived as science, but only as poetic myth.

From the beginning Greek cosmology had been concerned with the problem of 'saving the appearances', that is of reconciling theories about the structure of the cosmos with observations of the heavenly bodies. Plato and Aristotle insisted that these movements were circular, yet it was difficult to show that this was true of the apparently irregular planets. Ptolemy devised an extremely elaborate system of eccentrics and epicycles to account for planetary motion, and although this was accepted as functioning mathematically it was clearly an absurd and implausible way of saving the appearances. Some other cosmology than Aristotle's was needed if a truer picture of the cosmos was to be given, yet the problem was that a change in the moral and religious perspectives of the traditional cosmology would be entailed.

Alternatives existed in the early Greek cosmologies rejected by Aristotle and in rival ones developed after him. Thus, among pre-Aristotelian philosophers, it was held by the Pythagoreans that fire is at the centre of the universe; by Anaxagoras that the heavenly bodies are formed of the same matter as earth; by the atomists, Democritus and Leucippus, that the universe is boundless, has no centre, and contains a plurality of worlds. (The views of the atomists were incorporated after Aristotle in the Epicurean philosophy, and propagated by the Roman poet Lucretius in *The Nature of the Universe* I–II. The text of Lucretius, unknown in the Middle Ages, was rediscovered in 1417; it profoundly influenced Bruno, who, drawing both on Lucretius and on the fifteenth-century Neoplatonist Nicholas of Cusa, was the first Renaissance philosopher to propose the theory of an infinite universe (**28**).) Among post-Aristotelians Aristarchus held that the sun is at the centre of the universe with the planets, including the earth, revolving around it and rotating on their own axes. Such views, held only by a minority, were generally regarded in antiquity and later as impious and absurd, yet many of them were incorporated into the new Copernican cosmology.

The Copernican revolution was largely the work of four astronomers: initiated by Copernicus, it was developed by Tycho Brahe, Kepler and Galileo. Copernicus realised that the difficulties of explaining planetary motion encountered in the Aristotelian–Ptolemaic system could be resolved if it were accepted that the earth rotated diurnally on its axis and annually (together with the other planets) around the sun (**27**). However, although Copernicus much enlarged distances within his heliocentric cosmos, he retained an essentially Aristotelian system, with a finite outer sphere and concentric inner spheres carrying the heavenly bodies. Copernicus was cautious of disseminating his views and finally published them fully in the year of his death, 1543, in *On the Revolutions of the Celestial Spheres*. The implications of the Copernican system were worked out within the next seventy years. Tycho Brahe, the first astronomer to make adequately detailed and precise observations, devised a system of his own with the sun revolving round the earth but the other planets revolving round the sun. Tycho's importance lies in the conclusions he drew from his observations of a new star and of the motion of comets (hitherto regarded as a sublunary phenomenon): the supposedly constant Aristotelian heavens were, like the earth, subject to change and capable of non-circular motion. In addition, Tycho denied the existence of the concentric spheres: instead, the heavenly bodies revolved in a void. Further evidence for Tycho's breakdown of the distinction between the earthly and the heavenly was provided by Galileo. In his influential *Starry Messenger* (1610) Galileo recorded how he observed the heavens through the newly invented telescope and discovered that the surface of the moon, far from being perfectly spherical, shows the same irregularities as the earth, that the universe contains stars invisible to the naked eye, that such stars make up the Milky Way, and that Jupiter has four moons revolving round it. Kepler, using Tycho's observations, finally demonstrated that the motion of the planets is not circular, as the traditional cosmology demanded, but elliptical; he assumed that it was magnetic attraction that kept the planets in their orbits. Yet Kepler's cosmos was in many ways conservative; in two works, the *Cosmographic Mystery* (1596) and the *Harmony of the World* (1619), he argued, as had Plato in the *Timaeus*, that the structure of the cosmos is based on geometrical and musical proportion, and he rejected the theories of cosmic infinity and a plurality of worlds.

The Copernican cosmology provoked varied responses. The Catholic Church was hostile: the heliocentric theory, which seemed to conflict with Scripture (**30–32**), was condemned in 1616, and Galileo, after the publication of his *Dialogue Concerning the Two Chief World Systems* in 1632 (**29**), was forced to recant and kept under arrest (Milton visited him in 1638). Many divines, Protestant as well as Catholic, thought that the new cosmology, by moving the earth from the centre and breaking down the distinction between the earthly and the heavenly, undermined the Christian view of man's dual nature and his special position in the creation. Yet in England the response was often more positive and ultimately more fruitful, in terms of both science and theology. Scientists like Robert Recorde, Thomas Digges, John Dee and William Gilbert were early espousers of aspects of Copernicanism. One reason for the success of the Copernican cosmology in overthrowing the Aristotelian was the hostility towards Aristotelianism coupled with the revival of Pythagoreanism and Platonism which was generated by the humanists: Copernicus regarded his system as Pythagorean. Another kind of anti-Aristotelianism was represented by the Baconian emphasis on experiment and the role of science in controlling nature for the benefit of man. Bacon, not himself a scientist but a philosopher of science, set out in *The New Organon* (1620) his utilitarian programme and described in *The New Atlantis* (1627) his ideal scientific community, which ultimately was realised by the founding of the Royal Society in 1662. In theological terms, the overthrow of the Aristotelian finite cosmos came to be seen by the end of the seventeenth century not as undermining God's order and man's moral nature but rather as magnifying God's power as the creator of an infinite, unknowable cosmos and concentrating man's attention on self-knowledge. The Cambridge Platonist Henry More enthusiastically propounded the theory of infinite space in which God is immanent.

The traditional cosmology with its system of correspondences profoundly influenced the subject matter, the theory and the structure of Renaissance poetry. Although the Renaissance produced no major poem like Dante's *Divine Comedy* with its meticulously ordered Aristotelian cosmology, an enormous number of poets expounded aspects of the traditional system: the macro- and microcosm (**23, 25, 26**), the superlunary and sublunary, the music of the spheres (**20, 21**), the aether and the elements (**17, 18**), and the dual nature of man. Sometimes the object is didactic and encyclopedic, as in the very popular *Divine Weeks and Works* of Du Bartas, translated from the French by Joshuah Sylvester (**23, 33**), which roundly condemns Copernican interference with the received cosmology. More often there is a significant connection between the poem itself and the cosmological ideas it embodies. Thus the work of art is itself a microcosm, like the greater cosmos a unified, ordered, finite whole. (See also Chapters 11 and 13.) The involved and apparently disorderly structure of a poem like *The Faerie Queene*, which the modern reader has difficulty in unravelling, itself illustrates the cosmic principle of *concordia discors* or *discordia concors*, concord through discord, and unity through variety (**7, 8, 15**). (The most influential classical poem to work out this idea was Ovid's *Metamorphoses*, particularly Books I and XV (**9, 10**).) Just as in God's cosmos there exist correspondences and analogies between macro- and microcosm, between the several planes of existence, so in the poet's cosmos these correspondences and analogies are evoked by means of metaphor and conceit. A conceit which compares two apparently dissimilar objects from separate planes (like the soul and the dew in Marvell's 'On a Drop of Dew') is illustrating the fundamental unity of the cosmos. This is the characteristic technique of 'metaphysical' poetry (the theory underlying it has been described as the 'poetic of correspondence').

Spenser's cosmos is the traditional one: the goddess Mutability, viewing apparent disorder from a false earthly perspective, is defeated in her attempt to establish the dominance of change in the regions below and above the moon (**16**). The poets who responded most eagerly to the new cosmology were Donne and Milton. Donne's reading of the 'new philosophy' of Kepler and Galileo (which is evident in his satire on the Jesuits, *Ignatius his Conclave*) led him in the *Anniversaries* to scepticism about the possibility of any real scientific knowledge, and hence to reliance on faith (**35, 36**). Yet Donne repeatedly drew for his conceits on both old and new cosmologies (**25**), often in a spirit of intellectual play. Milton's treatment of cosmology in *Paradise Lost* shows scientific curiosity, poetic audacity and Christian humility, which do not altogether cohere. His system is predominantly Aristotelian–Ptolemaic with Copernican and idiosyncratic components. It has four localities: above, the Empyrean; hanging suspended from it, the created cosmos or world, with the earth at the centre; beneath it, Hell; and surrounding the whole, Chaos. Throughout the poem Milton's system of correspondences and parallelisms is based on the old cosmology, yet he uses Satan's voyage through Chaos to earth (Book II) to explore aspects of the new, such as the plurality of worlds. In the dialogue on astronomy (Book VIII) Adam is taught by Raphael that disputes about cosmological systems are unimportant, that knowledge of nature is of value only in so far as it leads man to God, and that self-knowledge should be his aim (**37**). This advice has seemed to some to be belied by Milton's own enthusiastic voyages through the cosmos as narrator of *Paradise Lost*.

THE TERM 'COSMOS'

1   We are told on good authority ... that heaven and earth and their respective inhabitants are held together by the bonds of society and love and order and discipline and righteousness, and that is why the universe is called an ordered whole or cosmos and not a state of disorder and licence.

Plato *Gorgias* 508

THE CREATION OF THE COSMOS

2   This was the plan of the eternal god when he gave to the god about to come into existence a smooth and unbroken surface, equidistant in every direction from the centre, and made it a physical body whole and complete, whose components were also complete physical bodies. And he put soul in the centre and diffused it through the whole and enclosed the body in it. So he established a single spherical universe in circular motion, alone but because of its excellence needing no company other than itself, and satisfied to be its own acquaintance and friend. His creation, then, for all these reasons, was a blessed god.

Plato *Timaeus* 34

3   Before there was any earth or sea, before the canopy of heaven stretched overhead, Nature presented the same aspect the world over, that to which men have given the name of Chaos. This was a shapeless unco-ordinated mass, nothing but a weight of lifeless matter, whose ill-assorted elements

were indiscriminately heaped together in one place ... Nothing had any
lasting shape, but everything got in the way of everything else; for, within
that one body, cold warred with hot, moist with dry, soft with hard, and
light with heavy. This strife was finally resolved by a god, a natural force
of a higher kind, who separated the earth from heaven, and the waters
from the earth, and set the clear air apart from the cloudy atmosphere.
When he had freed these elements, sorting them out from the heap where
they had lain, indistinguishable from one another, he bound them fast,
each in its separate place, forming a harmonious union.

Ovid *Metamorphoses* I ll. 5–9, 17–25

THE FIFTH ELEMENT

4   The primary body of all is eternal, suffers neither growth nor diminution,
but is ageless, unalterable and impassive ... Throughout all past time,
according to the records handed down from generation to generation, we
find no trace of change either in the whole of the outermost heaven or in
any one of its proper parts. It seems too that the name of this first body
has been passed down to the present time by the ancients ... Thus they,
believing that the primary body was something different from earth and
fire and air and water, gave the name *aither* to the uppermost region,
choosing its title from the fact that it 'runs always' [ἀεὶ θεῖν] and
eternally.

Aristotle *On the Heavens* I iii

THE UNMOVED MOVER

5   There is something which is eternally moved with an unceasing motion,
and that circular motion ... Then there is also something which moves
it. And since that which is moved while it moves is intermediate, there
is something which moves without being moved; something eternal
which is both substance and actuality ... It causes motion as being an
object of love, whereas all other things cause motion because they are
themselves in motion ... Such, then, is the first principle upon which
depend the sensible universe and the world of nature. And its life is like
the best which we temporarily enjoy [i.e. thought].

Aristotle *Metaphysics* XII vii

THE SPHERES

6   Africanus shows the cosmos to Scipio:
These are the nine circles, or rather spheres, by which the whole is joined.
One of them, the outermost, is that of heaven; it contains all the rest, and
is itself the supreme God, holding and embracing within itself all the

other spheres; in it are fixed the eternal revolving courses of the stars.
Beneath it are seven other spheres which revolve in the opposite direction
to that of heaven. One of these globes is that light which on earth is called
Saturn's. Next comes the star called Jupiter's, which bring fortune and
health to mankind. Beneath it is that star, red and terrible to the dwellings
of man, which you assign to Mars. Below it and almost midway of the
distance is the Sun, the lord, chief, and ruler of the other lights, the mind
and guiding principle of the universe, of such magnitude that he reveals
and fills all things with his light. He is accompanied by his companions,
as it were – Venus and Mercury in their orbits, and in the lowest sphere
revolves the Moon, set on fire by the rays of the Sun. But below the Moon
there is nothing except what is mortal and doomed to decay, save only
the souls given to the human race by the bounty of the gods, while above
the Moon all things are eternal. For the ninth and central sphere, which
is the earth, is immovable and the lowest of all, and toward it all
ponderable bodies are drawn by their own tendency downward.

Cicero 'The Dream of Scipio' *Republic* VI xvii
(note that there is no crystalline sphere in this system,
and that the spheres are numbered from the outside)

HARMONY FROM DISCORD AND UNITY IN VARIETY

7   Things taken together are whole and not whole, something which is being
brought together and brought apart, which is in tune and out of tune; out
of all things there comes a unity, and out of a unity all things.

Heraclitus Fragment 10

8   And these things never cease from continual shifting, at one time all
coming together, through Love, into one, at another each borne apart
from the others through Strife. So, in so far as they have learnt to grow
into one from many, and again, when the one is sundered, are once more
many, thus far they come into being and they have no lasting life; but in
so far as they never cease from continual interchange of places, thus far
are they ever changeless in the cycle.

Empedocles Fragment 17

9   Although fire and water are always opposites, none the less moist heat is
the source of everything, and this discordant harmony [*discors con-cordia*] is suited to creation.

Ovid *Metamorphoses* I ll. 432–3

10   Pythagoras is speaking:
Nothing is constant in the whole world. Everything is in a state of flux,
and comes into being as a transient appearance. Time itself flows on with
constant motion, just like a river: for no more than a river can the fleeting
hour stand still. As wave is driven on by wave, and, itself pursued,
pursues the one before, so the moments of time at once flee and follow,

and are ever new. What was before is left behind, that which was not comes to be, and every minute gives place to another ... Time, the devourer, and the jealous years that pass, destroy all things and, nibbling them away, consume them gradually in a lingering death. Even the things which we call elements do not remain constant ... Nor does anything retain its own appearance permanently. Ever-inventive nature continually produces one shape from another. Nothing in the entire universe ever perishes, believe me, but things vary, and adopt a new form. The phrase 'being born' is used for beginning to be something different from what one was before, while 'dying' means ceasing to be the same. Though this thing may pass into that, and that into this, yet the sum of things remains unchanged.

Ovid *Metamorphoses* XV ll. 177–85, 234–7, 252–8

THE MUSIC OF THE SPHERES

11   The Spindle [by which the circles of the planets revolved] turned on the knees of Necessity. Upon each of its circles stood a Siren, who was carried round with its movement, uttering a single sound on one note, so that all the eight made up the concords of a single scale. Round about, at equal distances, were seated, each on a throne, the three daughters of Necessity, the Fates, robed in white with garlands on their heads, Lachesis, Clotho, and Atropos, chanting to the Sirens' music, Lachesis of things past, Clotho of the present, and Atropos of things to come.

Plato *Republic* X 617

12   It seems to some thinkers that bodies so great must inevitably produce a sound by their movement: even bodies on the earth do so ... and as for the sun and the moon, and the stars, so many in number and enormous in size, all moving at a tremendous speed, it is incredible that they should fail to produce a noise of surpassing loudness ... To meet the difficulty that none of us is aware of this sound, they account for it by saying that the sound is with us right from birth and has thus no contrasting silence to show it up ... Now this theory, I repeat, shows great feeling for fitness and beauty, but nevertheless it cannot be true ... When so many bodies are in motion, if the noise which travels here is in proportion to the size of the moving body, it must be many times greater then thunder when it reaches us, and of insupportable force and violence. No, there is a good reason why we neither hear anything ourselves nor see violence done to inanimate objects, namely that the movement is noiseless.

Aristotle *On the Heavens* II ix

13   There are three types of music. The first type is the music of the universe (*musica mundana*), the second type, that of the human being (*musica humana*), and the third type is that which is created by certain instruments (*musica instrumentis constituta*) ... Now the first type, that is the music of the universe, is best observed in those things which one

perceives in heaven itself, or in the structure of the elements, or in the diversity of the seasons ... Now one comes to understand the music of the human being by examining [one's] own being. For what unites the incorporeal existence of the reason with the body except a certain harmony ... and, as it were, a careful tuning of low and high pitches in such a way that they produce one consonance?

Boethius *The Principles of Music* I ii

RENAISSANCE VIEWS OF COSMIC ORDER

14   Behold the four elements whereof the body of man is compact, how they be set in their places called spheres, higher or lower according to the sovereignty of their natures, that is to say, the fire as the most pure element, having in it nothing that is corruptible, in his place is highest and above other elements. The air, which next to the fire is most pure in substance, is in the second sphere or place. The water, which is somewhat consolidate, and approacheth to corruption, is next unto the earth. The earth, which is of substance gross and ponderous, is set of all elements most lowest. Behold also the order that God hath put generally in all his creatures, beginning at the most inferior or base, and ascending upward ... Every kind of trees, herbs, birds, beasts, and fishes, beside their diversity of forms, have (as who saith) a peculiar disposition appropered unto them by God their creator: so that in everything is order, and without order may be nothing stable or permanent; and it may not be called order, except it do contain in it degrees, high and base, according to the merit or estimation of the thing that is ordered.

Elyot *The Governor* I i

15   Scudamour describes the figure of Concord in the Temple of Venus:
On either side of her two young men stood,
Both strongly armed, as fearing one another;
Yet were they brethren both of half the blood,
Begotten by two fathers of one mother,
Though of contrary natures each to other:
The one of them hight Love, the other Hate.
Hate was the elder, Love the younger brother;
Yet was the younger stronger in his state
Than th' elder, and him mastered still in all debate.

Nathless that Dame so well them tempered both,
That she them forcèd hand to join in hand,
Albe that Hatred was thereto full loth,
And turned his face away, as he did stand,
Unwilling to behold that lovely band.
Yet she was of such grace and virtuous might,
That her commandment he could not withstand,
But bit his lip for felonous despite,
And gnashed his iron tusks at that displeasing sight.

Concord she clepèd was in common rede,
Mother of blessed Peace and Friendship true;
They both her twins, both born of heavenly seed,
And she herself likewise divinely grew;
The which right well her works divine did show:
For strength and wealth and happiness she lends
And strife and war and anger does subdue:
Of little much, of foes she maketh friends,
And to afflicted minds sweet rest and quiet sends.

By her the heaven is in his course contained,
And all the world in state unmovèd stands,
As their Almighty maker first ordained,
And bound them with inviolable bands;
Else would the waters overflow the lands,
And fire devour the air, and hell [i.e. cover] them quite,
But that she holds them with her blessed hands.
                    Spenser *The Faerie Queene* IV x stanzas 32–5

16   Mutability summarises her argument:
Then, since within this wide great Universe
Nothing doth firm and permanent appear,
But all things tossed and turned by transverse,
What then should let [i.e. prevent], but I aloft should rear
My trophy, and from all the triumph bear?
Now judge then (O thou greatest goddess true)
According as thyself doest see and hear,
And unto me addoom that is my due;
That is, the rule of all, all being ruled by you.

Nature's reply:
I well consider all that ye have said,
And find that all things steadfastness do hate
And changèd be: yet, being rightly weighed,
They are not changèd from their first estate;
But by their change their being do dilate,
And turning to themselves at length again,
Do work their own perfection so by fate:
Then over them change doth not rule and reign,
But they reign over change, and do their states maintain.
          Faerie Queene VII vii stanzas 56, 58 (compare **10**; see also Ch. **5.16**)

17   First stepped the Light, and spread his cheerful rays
Through all the Chaos; darkness headlong fell,
Frighted with sudden beams, and new-born days;
And plunged her ugly head in deepest hell:
      Not that he meant to help his feeble sight
      To frame the rest, he made the day of night:
All else but darkness; he the true, the only Light.

Fire, Water, Earth, and Air (that fiercely strove)
His sovereign hand in strong alliance tied,
Binding their deadly hate in constant love:
So that great Wisdom tempered all their pride,
   (Commanding strife and love should never cease)
   That by their peaceful fight, and fighting peace,
The world might die to live, and lessen to increase.
Phineas Fletcher The Purple Island I i stanzas 40–1
(compare 3 and 8)

18   Uriel describes the creation:
   I saw when at his word the formless mass,
   This world's material mould, came to a heap:
   Confusion heard his voice, and wild uproar
   Stood ruled, stood vast infinitude confined;
   Till at his second bidding darkness fled,
   Light shone, and order from disorder sprung:
   Swift to their several quarters hasted then
   The cumbrous elements, earth, flood, air, fire,
   And this ethereal quintessence of heaven
   Flew upwards, spirited with various forms,
   That rolled orbicular, and turned to stars
   Numberless, as thou seest, and how they move;
   Each had his place appointed, each his course,
   The rest in circuit walls this universe.
Milton Paradise Lost III ll. 708–21 (compare 3)

COSMIC MUSIC IN RENAISSANCE LITERATURE

19   There is a music wherever there is a harmony, order or proportion; and thus far we may maintain the music of the spheres; for those well-ordered motions, and regular paces, though they give no sound unto the ear, yet to the understanding they strike a note most full of harmony. Whatsoever is harmonically composed, delights in harmony; which makes me much distrust the symmetry of those heads which declaim against all church music. For myself, not only from my obedience but my particular genius, I do embrace it; for even that vulgar and tavern music, which makes one man merry, another mad, strikes in me a deep fit of devotion, and a profound contemplation of the First Composer, there is something in it of divinity more than the ear discovers. It is an hieroglyphical and shadowed lesson of the whole world, and creatures of God, such a melody to the ear, as the whole world well understood, would afford the understanding. In brief, it is a sensible fit of that harmony, which intellectually sounds in the ears of God.
Browne Religio Medici II

20   The Genius of the Wood speaks:

But else in deep of night when drowsiness
Hath locked up mortal sense, then listen I
To the celestial sirens' harmony.
That sit upon the nine enfolded spheres,
And sing to those that hold the vital shears,
And turn the adamantine spindle round,
On which the fate of gods and men is wound.
Such sweet compulsion doth in music lie,
To lull the daughters of Necessity,
And keep unsteady nature to her law,
And the low world in measured motion draw
After the heavenly tune, which none can hear
Of human mould with gross unpurgèd ear.

Milton *Arcades* ll. 61–73 (compare **11**, and see also
Prolusion II *On the Harmony of the Spheres* and 'At a solemn music')

21   Such was God's poem, this world's new essay,
So wild and rude in its first draught it lay;
The ungoverned parts no correspondence knew,
An artless war from thwarting motions grew;
Till they to number and fixed rules were brought
By the eternal Mind's poetic thought.
Water and air he for the tenor chose,
Earth made the bass, the treble flame arose,
To the active Moon a quick brisk stroke he gave,
To Saturn's string a touch more soft and grave.
The motions straight, and round, and swift, and slow,
And short, and long, were mixed and woven so,
Did in such artful figures smoothly fall,
As made this decent measured dance of all.
And this is music . . .

Cowley *Davideis* I

RENAISSANCE VIEWS OF THE NATURE OF MAN

22   Truly, just as God is God not only because He understands all things, but
because in Himself He assembles and unites the total perfection of the true
substance of things, so also man (although differently, as we shall show,
else he would not be the image of God, but God) collects and joins to the
completeness of his substance all the natures of the world. We cannot say
this of any other creature, angelic, heavenly, or sensible. The difference
between God and man is that God contains all things in Himself as their
origin, and man contains all things in himself as their centre. Hence in God
all things are of better stamp than in themselves, whereas in man inferior
things are of nobler mark and the superior are degenerate.

Pico della Mirandola *Heptaplus* V vi (see also opening of
On the Dignity of Man)

23 There's under sun (as Delphos God did show)
No better knowledge than our self to know:
There is no theme more plentiful to scan,
Than is the glorious goodly frame of man:
For, in man's self is fire, air, earth and sea;
Man's (in a word) the world's epitome
Or little map . . .

Du Bartas *Divine Weeks and Works*
'The Sixth Day of the First Week'

24 That we are the breath and similitude of God, it is indisputable, and upon
record of Holy Scripture; but to call ourselves a microcosm, or little
world, I thought it only a pleasant trope of rhetoric, till my near
judgement and second thoughts told me there was a real truth therein: for
first we are a rude mass, and in the rank of creatures, which only are, and
have a dull kind of being not yet privileged with life, or preferred to sense
or reason; next we live the life of plants, the life of animals, the life of
men, and at last the life of spirits, running on in one mysterious nature
those five kinds of existences, which comprehend the creatures, not only
of the world, but of the universe; thus is man that great and true
Amphibium, whose nature is disposed to live not only like other creatures
in divers elements, but in divided and distinguished worlds; for though
there be but one to sense, there are two to reason; the one visible, the
other invisible.

Browne *Religio Medici* I (see also Ralegh
History of the World I ii 5)

25 I am a little world made cunningly
Of elements, and an angelic sprite,
But black sin hath betrayed to endless night
My world's both parts, and, oh, both parts must die.
You which beyond that heaven which was most high
Have found new spheres, and of new lands can write,
Pour new seas in mine eyes, that so I might
Drown my world with my weeping earnestly . . .

Donne *Holy Sonnet* v ll. 1–8

26   Man is all symmetry,
Full of proportions, one limb to another,
   And all to all the world besides:
  Each part may call the farthest, brother:
For head with foot hath private amity,
   And both with moons and tides.

      Nothing hath got so far,
But man hath caught and kept it, as his prey.
   His eyes dismount the highest star:
   He is in little all the sphere.

Herbs gladly cure our flesh; because that they
    Find their acquaintance there.

Herbert 'Man' ll. 13–24

THE NEW COSMOLOGY

27   We therefore assert that the centre of the Earth, carrying the Moon's path, passes in a great circuit among the other planets in an annual revolution round the Sun; that near the Sun is the centre of the universe; and that whereas the Sun is at rest, any apparent motion of the Sun can be better explained by motion of the Earth. Yet so great is the universe that though the distance of the Earth from the Sun is not insignificant compared with the size of any other planetary path, in accordance with the ratios of their sizes, it is insignificant compared with the distances of the sphere of the fixed stars. I think it easier to believe this than to confuse the issue by assuming a vast number of spheres, which those who keep Earth at the centre must do ... In the middle of all sits Sun enthroned. In this most beautiful temple could we place this luminary in any better position from which he can illuminate the whole at once? He is rightly called the lamp, the mind, the ruler of the universe; Hermes Trismegistus names him the visible God, Sophocles' Electra calls him the all-seeing. So the Sun sits as upon a royal throne ruling his children the planets which circle round him.

Copernicus *On the Revolutions of the Celestial Spheres* I x

28   Democritus and Epicurus, who maintained that everything throughout infinity suffereth renewal and restoration, understood these matters more truly than those who would at all costs maintain belief in the immutability of the universe ... Make then your forecasts, my lords Astrologers, with your slavish physicians, by means of those astrolabes with which you seek to discern the fantastic nine moving spheres ... We know that the Supreme Ruler cannot have a seat so narrow, so miserable a throne ... On the contrary we recognise a noble image, a marvellous conception, a supreme figure, an exalted shadow, an infinite representation of the represented infinity, a spectacle worthy of the supremacy of Him who transcendeth understanding, comprehension, or grasp. Thus is the excellence of God magnified and the greatness of his kingdom made manifest; he is glorified not in one, but in countless suns, not in a single earth, a single world, but in a thousand thousand, I say in an infinity of worlds.

Bruno *On the Infinite Universe and Worlds* 'Introductory Epistle'

29   The Copernican Salviati addresses the Aristotelian Simplicio:
    I declare that we do have in our age new events and observations such that if Aristotle were now alive, I have no doubt he would change his opinion. This is easily inferred from his own manner of philosophising, for when he writes of considering the heavens inalterable, etc., because

no new thing is seen to be generated there or any old one dissolved, he seems implicitly to let us understand that if he had seen any such event he would have reversed his opinion and properly preferred the sensible experience to natural reason ... Excellent astronomers have observed many comets generated and dissipated in places above the lunar orbit, besides the two new stars of 1572 and 1604, which were indisputably beyond all the planets. And on the face of the sun itself, with the aid of the telescope, they have seen produced and dissolved dense and dark matter, appearing much like clouds upon the earth ... Now, if Aristotle had seen these things, what do you think he would have said and done, Simplicio?

> Galileo *Dialogue Concerning the Two Chief World Systems* 'The First Day' (compare **4**)

BIBLICAL TEXTS CITED AGAINST THE NEW COSMOLOGY

30 ... [Joshua] said in the sight of Israel, Sun, stand thou still upon Gibeon; and thou, Moon, in the valley of Ajalon.

And the sun stood still, and the moon stayed, until the people had avenged themselves upon their enemies ... So the sun stood still in the midst of heaven, and hasted not to go down about a whole day.

> Joshua 10:12–13

31 The Lord reigneth, he is clothed with majesty; the Lord is clothed with strength, wherewith he hath girded himself: the world also is established, that it cannot be moved.

> Psalm 93:1

32 One generation passeth away, and another generation cometh: but the earth abideth for ever.

The sun also ariseth, and the sun goeth down, and hasteth to his place where he arose.

> Ecclesiastes 1:4–5

KNOWLEDGE OF GOD THROUGH THE CREATION

33 The world's a school, where (in a general story)
God always reads dumb lectures of his glory:
A pair of stairs, whereby our mounting soul
Ascends by steps above the archèd pole:
A sumptuous hall, where God (on every side)
His wealthy shop of wonders opens wide:
A bridge, whereby we may pass o'er (at ease),
Of sacred secrets the broad boundless seas.
......

> The world's a book in folio, printed all
> With God's great works in letters capital:
> Each creature is a page; and each effect
> A fair character, void of all defect.
> But, as young truants, toying in the schools,
> Instead of learning, learn to play the fools:
> We gaze but on the babies [i.e. pictures] and the cover,
> The gawdy flowers, and edges gilded over;
> And never farther for our lesson look
> Within the volume of this various book;
> Where learned nature rudest ones instructs,
> That, by his wisdom, God the world conducts.
> . . . . . .
> But he that wears the spectacles of faith,
> Sees through the spheres, above the highest height:
> He comprehends the Arch-mover of all motions,
> And reads (though running) all these needful notions.
>   Du Bartas *Divine Weeks and Works* 'The First Day of the First Week'

34   The world was made to be inhabited by beasts, but studied and contemplated by man: 'tis the debt of our reason we owe unto God, and the homage we pay for not being beasts; without this the world is still as though it had not been, or as it was before the sixth day when as yet there was not a creature that could conceive, or say there was a world. The wisdom of God receives small honour from those vulgar heads, that rudely stare about, and with a gross rusticity admire his works; those highly magnify him whose judicious inquiry into his acts, and deliberate research into his creatures, return the duty of a devout and learned admiration.

Browne *Religio Medici* I

SCIENTIFIC SCEPTICISM AND MORAL KNOWLEDGE

35   We think the heavens enjoy their spherical,
Their round proportion embracing all.
But yet their various and perplexèd course,
Observed in divers ages, doth enforce
Men to find out so many eccentric parts,
Such divers down-right lines, such overthwarts,
As disproportion that pure form. It tears
The firmament in eight and forty shares,
And in these constellations then arise
New stars, and old do vanish from our eyes.
                    Donne *The First Anniversary* ll. 251–60

36   Have not all souls thought
For many ages, that our body is wrought

Of air, and fire, and other elements?
And now they think of new ingredients,
And one soul thinks one, and another way
Another thinks, and 'tis an even lay.
. . . . . .
What hope have we to know our selves, when we
Know not the least things, which for our use be?
. . . . . .
Thou look'st through spectacles; small things seem great
Below; but up unto the watch-tower get,
And see all things despoiled of fallacies:
Thou shalt not peep through lattices of eyes,
Nor hear through labyrinths of ears, nor learn
By circuit, or collection to discern.
In heaven thou straight knowest all, concerning it,
And what concerns is not, shalt straight forget.

> Donne *The Second Anniversary* ll. 263–8, 279–80, 293–300

37 Raphael to Adam:
To ask or search I blame thee not, for heaven
Is as the book of God before thee set,
Wherein to read his wondrous works, and learn
His seasons, hours, or days, or months, or years:
This to attain, whether heaven move or earth,
Imports not, if thou reckon right, the rest
From man or angel the great architect
Did wisely to conceal, and not divulge
His secrets to be scanned by them who ought
Rather admire; or if they list to try
Conjecture, he his fabric of the heavens
Hath left to their disputes, perhaps to move
His laughter at their quaint opinions wide
Hereafter, when they come to model heaven
And calculate the stars, how they will wield
The mighty frame, how build, unbuild, contrive
To save appearances, how gird the sphere
With centric and eccentric scribbled o'er,
Cycle and epicycle, orb in orb:
. . . . . .
Solicit not thy thoughts with matters hid,
Leave them to God above, him serve and fear;
. . . . . .heaven is for thee too high
To know what passes there; be lowly wise:
Think only what concerns thee and thy being;
Dream not of other worlds . . .

> Milton *Paradise Lost* VIII ll. 66–84, 167–8, 172–5

7 Reformation and Counter-Reformation

The English Reformation was an anomalous aspect of a European movement. For convenience we can distinguish three main areas with which Protestant reformers of whatever nationality or persuasion were concerned: organisation (the source and distribution of authority in the church), worship and discipline (preaching, the administration of the sacraments, prayers, ceremonies, the furnishing of churches), and doctrine. There was much more dispute between Catholics and Protestants and among Protestants themselves about the first two, although the last was most important. The reformation of the English church was not a sudden and final event, but a slow and uneven process lasting over a hundred years. From the 1530s, when Henry VIII broke with Rome, to the 1660s, when with the Restoration of Charles II Anglicanism was re-established, the church underwent various metamorphoses. Anglicanism, praised by its supporters as the *via media*, the path of moderation between the extremes of Catholic Rome and Calvinist Geneva (**13**, **14**, **21**), was regarded by its Puritan critics as an ineffectual compromise, an incompletely reformed system (**18**). Twice in the period Anglicanism was defeated: in the 1550s, when the church for the duration of Mary's reign reacknowledged the authority of Rome, and in the 1640s and 1650s, when in the period of the Puritan revolution the distinctive features of the Anglican church were abolished. Yet ultimately it was the Anglican compromise, however unsatisfactory, that survived.

The chief architects of the continental Reformation towards whom the English reformers looked with various degrees of approbation were Martin Luther in Saxony and Ulrich Zwingli and Jean Calvin in Switzerland. In some respects the continental reformers were not original, but drew on and developed existing criticisms of the Church of Rome. The fourteenth-century English reformer John Wycliffe and his Bohemian follower John Huss anticipated many of Luther's teachings. The hostility of many states towards the temporal political power of the papacy had long been expressed. There was widespread condemnation of notorious abuses in the medieval church: the unchastity of the supposedly celibate clergy, the luxury and extravagance of the monasteries whose inmates were vowed to lives of poverty, pluralism (the holding of several benefices) and absenteeism among the clergy, the dubious financial dealings of the papacy, such as the sale of offices (simony) and indulgences (which promised remission of time to be spent in purgatory). Indeed Luther's attack on the sale of indulgences in 1517 first brought him notoriety. More important than these specific criticisms, however, were the weapons provided by humanism (see Chapter 9) against the traditional authority of the church. Humanist insistence on the recovery of the past and the return to original texts directed attention away from the work of medieval theologians and back to the Bible and the early Fathers (especially Jerome and Augustine); it also revealed how far removed the medieval church was in its practices from the primitive church of the first centuries and the Christianity of the gospels and epistles. Further, humanist philological methods revealed serious weaknesses in the claims of the church. Thus the Italian humanist Lorenzo Valla demonstrated that the so-called Donation of Constantine giving temporal power to the papacy was a forgery, and Erasmus in his edition of the New Testament of 1516 pointed out errors in Jerome's Latin translation, the Vulgate, which had been used by the church for centuries. However, though humanism can be seen to have done a good deal to prepare the ground for the Protestant Reformation, there were fundamental differences between the two movements. Erasmus and Luther disagreed violently over the question of the dignity or depravity of human nature (see Chapter 8), and Erasmus remained uncomfortably within the Church of Rome (his writings were, however, to be condemned by Rome after his death). Above all it was Luther's theology, added to longstanding political, social and moral criticisms of Rome, and armed with humanist literary and historical techniques, that made Protestantism a revolutionary force.

There was much disagreement in the sixteenth century between continental Lutheran and Reformed (Calvinist) churches over secondary questions of church government and worship, paralleled by that in England in the late sixteenth and early seventeenth centuries between Anglicans and Puritans. But such disagreement is insignificant compared with what the Protestant churches held in common, which can be summarised as follows. The source of authority for Christians is the Bible (**2–4**), and the central doctrine taught in the Bible is that of justification by faith alone (see Chapter 8). On these tenets the remaining articles of Protestantism depend. The Bible must be available in the vernacular for each individual to read (**6–9**); worship must be conducted in the vernacular so that the individual can take part. Neither the pope nor the traditions of the church have any divine claims to authority. The seven Catholic sacraments (Baptism, Confirmation, the Eucharist, Penance, Extreme Unction, Ordination and Matrimony) are reduced to two (Baptism and the Eucharist). The Eucharist (the Lord's Supper or Communion) is not a sacrifice as in the Catholic mass, but a visible sign of invisible grace (**10**); the Real Presence of Christ's body and blood in the bread and wine is denied (there was however much disagreement among reformers about the exact meaning of the Lord's Supper). Since the Christian is saved by faith alone, not by good works, a number of Catholic beliefs, practices and institutions are irrelevant and unchristian: the intercession of saints, masses for the souls of the dead, purgatory, penance, indulgences, monastic vows of poverty, chastity and obedience, self-mortification (**11**). The role of the priesthood is diminished: Protestant Christianity is a priesthood of all believers, each of whom can interpret the Bible for himself (**1**). The Protestant minister is above all a teacher and exhorter; he is not set apart as an intermediary between God and man like the Catholic priest. His function as preacher is stressed more than his function as administrator of the sacraments. Hence the coming of reform to a European city or state meant immediate, visible changes in the life of the church: monasteries were dissolved, monks, nuns and priests were free to marry, churches were stripped of many images, the pulpit became the focal point, clerical dress was simplified, liturgies were altered, the congregation participated actively through the singing of hymns (in Lutheran churches) and metrical psalms (in Reformed and Anglican churches).

In England the Reformation was the fusion of three separate forces: native Lollardy (the Wycliffite movement), continental Protestantism, and the constitutional conflict between Henry VIII and the church, resulting from the pope's refusal to allow Henry to divorce Katherine of Aragon and marry Anne Boleyn. In the 1530s Henry broke with Rome, made himself the Supreme Head of the church, divorced Katherine, dissolved the monasteries and appropriated their wealth. However, Henry remained hostile to Protestant theology (he gained his title of *Fidei Defensor*, defender of the faith, from the pope for writing against Luther). Lutheranism spread rapidly in Henry's reign among Lollards and especially at Cambridge, but it was not until the reign of Edward VI that the Church of England, under the direction of Archbishop Thomas Cranmer, took recognisable shape. Cranmer was responsible for creating a new liturgy in the Book of Common Prayer (**15**), which was first issued in 1549 and revised in 1552. This revised edition was reissued in 1559 as part of the Elizabethan Settlement of the church; Puritan hostility brought about its abolition in 1645, but it was reissued in what has been its most lasting form in 1662. Cranmer was also responsible for the formulation of Anglican doctrine. His Forty-Two Articles of 1553 formed the basis of the Thirty-Nine Articles adopted in final form in 1571 (**3, 10, 16**; Ch. **8.16, 19, 31**). In addition Cranmer was the principal author of the first Book of

Homilies (or sermons to be read in churches) of 1547; a second book (largely by John Jewel) was issued in 1571. The Homilies (no longer in use, unlike the Thirty-Nine Articles and the Book of Common Prayer) provide clear expositions of sixteenth-century Anglican theological, political, social and moral teaching (**4**, **7**, **11**; Ch. **8.13**). These works, together with the English translations of the Bible, form the literary basis of the Anglican church.

The version of the Bible used by the Catholic church was the Vulgate, St Jerome's fourth-century Latin translation. The uneducated could not understand it, and the church controlled its interpretation. The primary aim of the reformers was to translate the Bible into the vernacular. Two Wycliffite versions had a limited circulation in manuscript in the fifteenth century, but a layman required a bishop's licence to read them. The invention of printing and the development of humanist linguistic scholarship were decisive factors in the spread of knowledge of the Bible in the sixteenth century. The Spanish Cardinal Ximenes' edition, known as the Complutensian Polyglot (1522), printed the original Hebrew and Greek alongside the Vulgate. Erasmus' several editions of the Greek New Testament with his own Latin translation contained important prefatory material on the study of Scripture. The preface to the first edition of 1516, the 'Paraclesis' or exhortation, urged that the words of Christ should be on the lips of all Christians from childhood (**6**). Luther translated both New and Old Testaments into German (1522 and 1534), not from the Vulgate, but from Erasmus' Greek edition and the Hebrew, and wrote commentaries on specific books (Romans, Galatians, Hebrews, and Genesis, Psalms, Isaiah, Habbakuk and Jonah). Luther's own preference (for St John, I Peter, Romans, Galatians and Ephesians) and dislike (for the Epistle of James) strongly influenced Protestant interpretation of the New Testament. The work of both Erasmus and Luther was drawn on by William Tyndale, the most important individual in the corporate creation of the English Bible. Tyndale received no support for his projected translation in England, and so worked on the continent. The first edition of his New Testament, published in 1525, reached England in 1526; because of its Lutheran phraseology and ideas (some of the prefaces were translations of Luther's commentaries (Ch. **8.15**, **26**)) Tyndale's translation was attacked, notably by Sir Thomas More in his *Dialogue Concerning Heresies*. More wished the church to safeguard interpretation and was prepared to envisage only a limited circulation of a vernacular Bible. Tyndale also published part of the Old Testament from the Hebrew, and left further parts translated but unpublished at his death (he was executed for heresy in 1536).

The subsequent history of English Bible translation is a complicated matter, but Tyndale's version remained at the heart of it. After Henry VIII's break with Rome the English church asked for an official translation. The first complete version was that of Miles Coverdale, published initially on the continent and then in England in 1537, drawing on Luther, Tyndale and the Vulgate. Coverdale's translation of the psalms was included by Cranmer in the Book of Common Prayer, and has consequently remained more familiar through use than the psalms in the Authorised Version. The Great Bible, the first official Bible to be supplied to all parish churches by an injunction of 1538, was Coverdale's revision of Matthew's Bible of 1537, itself a revision of Tyndale and Coverdale's earlier version. The Great Bible was revised and reissued under Elizabeth in 1568 as the Bishops' Bible. Although it was the official version read in churches, the Bishops' Bible was never popular. Its rival was the Geneva Bible (**8**), largely by William Whittingham, issued in 1557 and 1560 by the community of Marian exiles (Protestants who had fled to the continent to escape persecution under Mary, and who returned following the accession of Elizabeth in 1558). The Geneva Bible, based on French as well as earlier English translations, was supplied with extensive Calvinist annotation. It was the first English Bible to be divided into numbered verses, and this practice was followed by the Authorised Version. The Geneva Bible (although officially frowned upon) remained popular well after the publication of the latter. A Catholic translation from the Vulgate was issued by the English College at Rheims and Douai in 1582 and 1609–10, to counteract the doctrinal tendentiousness of the English Protestant versions, and was quite widely known in England among Protestants as well as Catholics. Because of the uneasy coexistence of the Bishops' and Geneva Bibles, James I was petitioned by the Puritans at the beginning of his reign for a new official translation. The Authorised Version or King James Bible (**9**), published in 1611 without doctrinal annotation, was the work of fifty theological and linguistic experts, whose task was to revise the Bishops' Bible in comparison with the Geneva and in the light of the earlier versions of Tyndale and Coverdale. The Douai–Rheims Bible was also used. The Authorised Version was thus not a new Bible: rather it was the considered culmination of ninety years of biblical scholarship, translation and evangelism. Much of Tyndale's original rendering remained. Thus stylistically the Authorised Version was an anachronism; in comparison with ornate and witty late Elizabethan and early Jacobean prose, its vocabulary and sentence structure were archaic and simple. This style itself came to exercise an influence on seventeenth-century prose.

Doctrinally the Church of England was unequivocally Protestant; in terms of worship and government its position was more ambiguous. In its liturgy and vestments the church retained Catholic features, and, more important, it continued to be governed by bishops (the system known as episcopacy or prelacy). This compromise was deplored by the Puritan members (also known as the godly or the precise), who wished to purify the church of these vestiges of popery (**18**). The Puritans, many of whom had adopted Calvinist ideas of church government in Germany or Switzerland during the Marian exile, argued that the Bible must be the only authority not only for doctrine but for every aspect of church life. Thus practices not sanctioned by the Bible (which included most of the Anglican liturgy and ceremonies) should be abolished, as should episcopacy; instead, the church should be governed by elected elders or presbyters (hence presbyterianism). The Puritans attached great importance to extempore preaching and prayer (though some set forms were allowed), and attempted in the 1580s to replace the prescribed Book of Common Prayer by Walter Travers' *Book of Discipline*, so as to bring the Church of England into line with the continental Reformed churches. The classic defence of the Anglican system against Puritan attacks was made by Richard Hooker in *The Laws of Ecclesiastical Polity* (Books I–IV 1593, V 1597, VI–VIII posthumously) (**5, 12**). Hooker broadened the basis of Protestant thought by drawing on classical and medieval philosophies of natural law and reason (see Chapter 8). On the question of worship and discipline, Hooker used the Lutheran concept of 'things indifferent' against Calvinist rigidity. Human traditions and ceremonies, though not necessary for salvation, should not be destroyed if they have been found effective. Hooker conceded that episcopacy was not positively demanded by Scripture, but it was convenient.

Under Elizabeth the Puritan wing of the church was contained; under the Stuarts the disagreement between Anglicans and Puritans grew. The disagreement concerned both doctrine and discipline. Some Anglicans became attracted to Arminianism, the anti-Calvinist teaching of the Dutch theologian Arminius (see Chapter 8), particularly after the Dutch Synod of Dort of 1618–19 condemned Arminianism and reaffirmed Calvinism. Under Archbishop Laud the Church of England seemed to Puritans to be moving back to Rome (**19**). Laud placed great stress on ceremony (**17**) and the 'beauty of holiness' (Psalm 96:9), valued the administration of the sacraments above preaching, and argued that episcopacy was not simply convenient but scriptural and of divine right. This seemed like sacerdotalism, a return to the sacrificial view of priesthood. Laud's strict censorship of his Puritan critics and enforcement of his views of church discipline hastened the Civil War.

In the 1640s the Long Parliament abolished episcopacy, and the Westminster Assembly (set up to reform the church) issued the

Westminster Confession of Faith as a substitute for the Thirty-Nine Articles and the Directory of Public Worship as a substitute for the Book of Common Prayer. But a presbyterian system of church government was never achieved. This was because of the increasing fragmentation of Puritanism during the years of Anglican control. A tendency to fragmentation was implicit in the Protestant emphasis on the sole authority of Scripture combined with the individual's right to interpret Scripture for himself. The Presbyterians were able to impose their discipline neither on the Independents, who wanted not a national church but a loose association of self-governing churches, nor on the many sects who expected toleration for a wide range of beliefs and practices. However, many Puritans had emigrated to America to escape Laud's persecution, and in New England, as in Scotland earlier, theocracies based on Calvin's Geneva were established.

The Protestant and especially Puritan view of the Church of Rome remained stereotyped in its prejudices. To the moderate Anglican the pope was the Bishop of Rome, to the Puritan he was Antichrist (**19**). This hostility was fed by Catholic political blunders (the burning of 300 Protestants in Mary's reign, the papal bull excommunicating Elizabeth and releasing her subjects from their allegiance, the abortive invasion by the Spanish Armada, the Gunpowder Plot to blow up James and the Houses of Parliament), and it was perpetuated by John Foxe's *Acts and Monuments* (or Book of Martyrs) (Ch. **5.14**), which was officially placed in churches with the Bible. For many Protestants the Inquisition and the Index (prohibiting heretical books) characterised the Counter-Reformation. But the Counter-Reformation was much more than a movement to combat Protestantism; it was also an alternative Catholic Reformation concerned with correcting abuses in the church, improving the education and efficiency of the priesthood, clarifying doctrine and defining the conditions of the Christian life. Some of the required reform was achieved by the Council of Trent, which met at intervals from 1545 to 1563 to establish the church's position on doctrine and discipline. The Council confirmed the Vulgate as the official Bible, affirmed the church's sole right to interpret it, and assigned as much authority to the traditions of the church as to Scripture. Traditional teaching on the seven sacraments, transubstantiation, the sacrifice of the mass, justification and merit were clarified and Protestant positions condemned. Clerical celibacy, confession, indulgences and the use of relics and images were retained. Seminaries for the education of priests were to be established in each diocese. Perhaps the most significant new institution of the Counter-Reformation was the Society of Jesus, or Jesuits, founded in Rome by the Spaniard St Ignatius Loyola in 1540, which rapidly became the church's chief instrument for education, propaganda and missionary activity, both in Europe and overseas. Jesuit priests from the English college at Douai were sent to England as missionaries in the 1580s, to support the recusants (Catholics who did not attend Church of England services) and convert the Protestants. Many were executed for treason, including the poet Robert Southwell. Two influential literary works of the Counter-Reformation were the *Spiritual Exercises* of St Ignatius (published 1548) and the *Introduction to the Devout Life* of St François de Sales (1609). Such spiritual handbooks stressed self-examination, asceticism, active commitment to good works, obedience, subordination of the will, and meditation on the life and passion of Christ (**23**). They were widely read in England by Anglicans as well as Catholics, and influenced the structure and subject matter of devotional poetry (**24**).

It is impossible to appreciate fully the work of the religious poets of the sixteenth and seventeenth centuries without paying some attention to the conflicting versions of Christian doctrine and discipline that shaped their lives. A poet's religious affiliations or disaffections, his conversion to or withdrawal from a particular church or movement, are not merely reflected in the doctrinal core of his work but condition his vocabulary, the structure of his arguments, his patterning of Christian experience. Many poets (Southwell, Donne, Giles Fletcher, Herbert, Crashaw) were in holy orders; many changed their allegiances (Alabaster from Anglicanism to Catholicism and back, Donne from Catholicism to Anglicanism, Milton from Anglicanism to Presbyterianism to Separatism, Crashaw from Anglicianism to Catholicism). Spenser's triumphant marriage of Red Cross Knight to Una (*Faerie Queene* I xii) can only be understood in the light of the success of the Elizabethan settlement, Greville's paradoxes in *Caelica* in the light of the Puritan separation of the realms of nature and grace, Herbert's stress on the Eucharist in *The Temple* in the light of Laudian sacramentalism, Milton's sense of history in *Paradise Lost* and *Paradise Regained* in the light of the collapse of the Puritan revolution, Crashaw's adulation of St Teresa in *Carmen Deo Nostro* in the light of Counter-Reformation devotion (**25, 26**).

Bible translation and the liturgical innovations of the Protestant churches were themselves productive of certain kinds of poetry. Whereas Lutheran congregations sang hymns (many by Luther himself), Reformed and Anglican congregations sang only metrical versions of the psalms. Three official versions were very widely used: in England, that of Sternhold and Hopkins (first complete edition 1562); in Massachusetts, the Bay Psalm Book (1640); in Scotland, the second Scottish Psalter (1650). Yet many individuals made paraphrases of the psalms for their own use, among them Wyatt, Surrey, Sidney and his sister the Countess of Pembroke (the most technically innovative version), Sandys, Carew and Milton. The Bible is present in poetry in many other ways: some of

Herbert's poems are modelled on the parables (see Introduction 2), and some of Vaughan's are meditations on specific verses of the New Testament. The writing of metrical psalms and devotional poetry can be seen both as kind of spiritual exercise, and as an extension of liturgy.

THE PRIESTHOOD OF ALL BELIEVERS

1   All Christians are truly of the spiritual estate ... We are all consecrated priests through baptism ... A priest in Christendom is nothing else but an officeholder ... If we are all priests ... and all have one faith, one gospel, one sacrament, why should we not also have the power to test and judge what is right or wrong in matters of faith?

Luther *To the Christian Nobility of the German Nation*

THE SUFFICIENCY OF SCRIPTURE

2   Unless I am convicted by the testimony of Scripture or plain reason (for I believe neither in Pope nor councils alone, since it is agreed that they have often erred and contradicted themselves), I am bound by the Scriptures I have quoted, and my conscience is captive to the Word of God.

Luther 'Answer before the Emperor and the Diet of Worms' 1521

3   Holy Scripture containeth all things necessary to salvation: so that whatsoever is not read therein, nor may be proved thereby, is not to be required of any man, that it should be believed as an article of faith, or be thought requisite or necessary to salvation.

The Thirty-Nine Articles VI 'Of the Sufficiency of the Holy Scriptures for Salvation'

4   Therefore forsaking the corrupt judgement of fleshly men, which care not but for their carcass; let us reverently hear and read Holy Scriptures, which is the food of the soul. Let us diligently search for the well of life in the books of the New and Old Testament, and not run to the stinking puddles of men's traditions, devised by men's imagination, for our justification and salvation.

The Book of Homilies I 'A Fruitful Exhortation to the Reading of Holy Scripture'

5   Two opinions therefore there are concerning sufficiency of Holy Scripture, each extremely opposite unto the other, and both repugnant unto truth. The schools of Rome teach Scripture to be so unsufficient, as if, except traditions were added, it did not contain all revealed and supernatural truth, which absolutely is necessary for the children of men in this life to know that they may in the next be saved. Others justly condemning this opinion grow likewise unto a dangerous extremity, as if Scripture did not only

contain all things in that kind necessary, but all things simply, and in such sort that to do anything according to any other law were not only unnecessary but even opposite unto salvation, unlawful and simple . . . We must . . . take great heed, lest in attributing unto Scripture more than it can have, the incredibility of that do cause even those things which indeed it hath most abundantly to be less reverently esteemed.

Hooker *Of the Laws of Ecclesiastical Polity* II viii

THE TRANSLATION AND STUDY OF THE BIBLE

6 Truly it is one degree to good living, yea the first (I had almost said the chief) to have a little sight in the Scripture, though it be but a gross knowledge, and not yet consummate. (Be it in case that some would laugh at it, yea and that some should err and be deceived) I would to God, the ploughman would sing a text of the Scripture at his ploughbeam. And that the weaver at his loom, with this would drive away the tediousness of time. I would the wayfaring man with this pastime, would expel the weariness of his journey. And to be short, I would that all the communication of the Christian should be of the Scripture . . . If any man being inspired with the Holy Ghost do preach, and teach these and such other things, if any man exhort, entice, and bolden his neighbour unto these things, he is a very and true divine, though he be a weaver, yea though he dig and delve.

'An exhortation to the diligent study of Scripture, made by Erasmus Roterodamus' (Erasmus' 'Paraclete', trans. W. Roy, Tyndale's amanuensis)

7 And concerning the hardness of Scripture; he that is so weak that he is not able to brook strong meat, yet he may suck the sweet and tender milk, and defer the rest until he wax stronger, and come to more knowledge [Heb. 5:12–14]. For God receiveth the learned and unlearned, and casteth away none, but is indifferent unto all. And the Scripture is full, as well of low valleys, plain ways, and easy for every man to use and to walk in; as also of high hills and mountains, which few men can climb unto . . . If we read once, twice, or thrice, and understand not, let us not cease so, but still continue reading, praying, asking of other, and so by still knocking, at the last the door shall be opened; as St Augustine saith, Although many things in the Scripture be spoken in obscure mysteries, yet there is nothing spoken under dark mysteries in one place, but the self-same thing in other places is spoken more familiarly and plainly, to the capacity both of learned and unlearned. And those things in the Scripture that be plain to understand, and necessary for salvation, every man's duty is to learn them, to print them in memory, and effectually to exercise them. And as for the dark mysteries, to be contented to be ignorant in them, until such time as it shall please God to open those things unto him.

The Book of Homilies I (see p. 143)

8   We are especially bound (dear brethren) to give [God] thanks without ceasing for his great grace and unspeakable mercies, in that it hath pleased him to call us unto this marvellous light of his gospel, and mercifully to regard us after so horrible backsliding and falling away from Christ to Antichrist [i.e. in the reign of Mary], from light to darkness, from the living God to dumb and dead idols, and that after so cruel murder of God's saints, as alas, hath been among us, we are not altogether cast off . . . but received again to grace with most evident signs and tokens of God's especial love and favour. To the intent therefore that we may not be unmindful of these great mercies . . . it behoveth us so to walk in his fear and love, that all the days of our life we may procure the glory of his holy name. Now forasmuch as this thing chiefly is attained by the knowledge and practising of the word of God (which is the light to our paths, the key of the kingdom of heaven, our comfort in affliction, our shield and sword against Satan, the school of all wisdom, the glass wherein we behold God's face, the testimony of his favour, and the only food and nourishment of our souls) we thought that we could bestow our labours and study in nothing which could be more acceptable to God and comfortable to his church than in the translating of the Holy Scriptures into our native tongue.

Preface to the Geneva Bible

9   Translation it is that openeth the window, to let in the light; that breaketh the shell, that we may eat the kernel; that putteth aside the curtain that we may look into the most holy place; that removeth the cover of the well, that we may come by the water, even as Jacob rolled away the stone from the mouth of the well, by which means the flocks of Laban were watered.

Preface to the Authorised Version

THE LORD'S SUPPER

10   The Supper of the Lord is not only a sign of love that Christians ought to have among themselves one to another; but rather it is a sacrament of our redemption by Christ's death: insomuch that to such as rightly, worthily, and with faith, receive the same, the bread which we break is a partaking of the body of Christ; and likewise the cup of blessing is a partaking of the blood of Christ.

Transubstantiation (or the change of the substance of bread and wine) in the Supper of the Lord, cannot be proved by holy Writ; but it is repugnant to the plain words of Scripture, overthroweth the nature of a sacrament, and hath given occasion to many superstitions.

The body of Christ is given, taken, and eaten, in the Supper, only after an heavenly and spiritual manner. And the mean whereby the body of Christ is received and eaten in the Supper is faith.

The Thirty-Nine Articles XXVIII 'Of the Lord's Supper'

THE PROTESTANT VIEW OF ROME

11   Let us rehearse some other kinds of papistical superstitions and abuses,
as of beads, of lady psalters, and rosaries ... of purgatory, of masses
satisfactory, of stations and jubilees, of feigned relics, of hallowed beads,
bells, bread, water, palms, candles, fire, and such other; of superstitious
fastings, of fraternities or brotherhoods, of pardons, with such like
merchandise, which were so esteemed and abused to the great prejudice
of God's glory and commandments, that they were made most high and
most holy things, whereby to attain to the everlasting life, or remission
of sin: yea also vain inventions, unfruitful ceremonies, and ungodly laws,
decrees, and councils of Rome, were in such wise advanced, that nothing
was thought comparable in authority, wisdom, learning, and godliness
unto them ... Thus was the people through ignorance so blinded with the
godly show and appearance of those things, that they thought the keeping
of them to be a more holiness, a more perfect service and honouring of
God, and more pleasing to God, than the keeping of God's commandments.

The Book of Homilies V 'Of Good Works'

THE CHURCH OF ENGLAND

12   The Church of England being to alter her received laws concerning such
orders, rites, and ceremonies, as had been in former times an hindrance
unto piety and religious service of God, was to enter into consideration
first, that the change of laws, especially concerning matter of religion,
must be warily proceeded in. Laws, as all other things human, are many
times full of imperfection; and that which is supposed behoveful unto
men, proveth oftentimes most pernicious. The wisdom which is learned
by tract of time, findeth the laws that have been in former ages
established, needful in later to be abrogated. Besides, that which
sometime is expedient doth not always so continue: and the number of
needless laws unabolished doth weaken the force of them that are
necessary. But true withal it is, that alteration though it be from worse to
better hath in it inconveniences, and those weighty ...

Hooker *Of the Laws of Ecclesiastical Polity* IV xiv

13   There is no church whose every part so squares unto my conscience,
whose articles, constitutions and customs seem so consonant unto reason,
and as it were framed to my particular devotion, as this whereof I hold
my belief, the Church of England, to whose faith I am a sworn subject,
and therefore in a double obligation, subscribe unto her articles, and
endeavour to observe her constitutions: whatsoever is beyond, as points
indifferent, I observe according to the rules of my private reason, or the
humour and fashion of my devotion, neither believing this, because
Luther affirmed it, or disproving that, because Calvin hath disavouched
it. I condemn not all things in the Council of Trent, nor approve all in the

Synod of Dort. In brief, where the Scripture is silent, the church is my text; where that speaks, 'tis but my comment: where there is a joint silence of both, I borrow not the rules of my religion from Rome or Geneva, but the dictates of my own reason.

Browne *Religio Medici* I

14   To the churches of the Roman communion we can say that ours is reformed; to the Reformed churches we can say that ours is orderly and decent; for we were freed from the impositions and lasting errors of a tyrannical spirit, and yet from the extravagancies of a popular spirit too. Our reformation was done without tumult, and yet we saw it necessary to reform. We were zealous to cast away the old errors, but our zeal was balanced with the consideration and the results of authority: not like women or children when they are affrighted with fire in their clothes; we shaked off the coal indeed, but not our garments, lest we should have exposed our churches to that nakedness, which the excellent men of our sister-churches complained to be among themselves.

Taylor *An Apology for Authorised and Set Forms of Liturgy*
Preface (compare the image in **21**)

ANGLICAN CEREMONY

15   Some [ceremonies] are put away, because the great excess and multitude of them hath so increased in these latter days, that the burden of them was intolerable ... This our excessive multitude of ceremonies was so great, and many of them so dark, that they did more confound and darken, than declare and set forth Christ's benefits unto us. And beside this, Christ's gospel is not a ceremonial law (as much of Moses' law was), but it is a religion to serve God, not in bondage of the figure or shadow, but in the freedom of the spirit; being content only with those ceremonies which do serve to a decent order and godly discipline, and such as be apt to stir up the dull mind of man to the remembrance of his duty to God, by some notable and special signification, whereby he might be edified.

The Book of Common Prayer 'Of Ceremonies,
why some be abolished, and some retained'

16   It is not necessary that traditions and ceremonies be in all places one, or utterly like; for at all times they have been divers, and may be changed according to the diversities of countries, times, and men's manners, so that nothing be ordained against God's Word. Whosoever through his private judgement, willingly and purposely, doth openly break the traditions and ceremonies of the church, which be not repugnant to the Word of God, and be ordained and approved by common authority, ought to be rebuked openly (that others may fear to do the like), as he that offendeth against the common order of the church, and hurteth the authority of the magistrate, and woundeth the consciences of the weak brethren.

The Thirty-Nine Articles XXXIV
'Of the Traditions of the Church'

17   For my own part, I take myself bound to worship with body as well as in soul, whenever I come where God is worshipped. And were this kingdom such as would allow no holy table standing in its proper place (and such places some there are), yet I would worship God when I came into his house. And were the times such as would beat down churches, and all the 'curious carved work thereof, with axes and hammers', as in Psalm 74: 6 (and such times have been), yet would I worship in what place soever I came to pray, though there were not so much as a stone laid for Bethel. But this is the misery, it is superstition nowadays for any man to come with more reverence into a church, than a tinker and his bitch come into an ale-house.

Laud: Speech at the Censure of Bastwick,
Burton and Prynne 1637

PURITAN CRITICISM OF THE CHURCH OF ENGLAND

8   I thought it my duty even for the kind affection which I bear to that church in which I have been born and brought up and therefore love most dearly for good causes . . . to desire and beseech this church earnestly and carefully to think of this so great a benefit, whereby it may be established forever, and most earnestly to exhort and admonish it to abolish that popish tyranny which yet remaineth in the government thereof, and to restore again the most holy policy of ruling the church which our Saviour Christ hath left unto us, and to fear lest that the Lord will punish us and will be revenged of us if we continue still to despise his discipline . . . When [the supporters of episcopacy] understand the good cause that we have to reprieve the one and require the other, they may join together with us in earnest prayers unto God and humble suit unto her Majesty that, this popish tyranny being at the last utterly abolished and clean taken away, in place thereof a better and more holy government of the church according to God's word may be established.

Travers *A Full and Plain Declaration of Ecclesiastical Discipline*
(trans. from Latin by Thomas Cartwright 1574; basis of later
Book of Discipline)

19   Now I appeal to all wise men, what an excessive waste of treasury hath been within these few years in this land not in the expedient, but in the idolatrous erection of temples beautified exquisitely to outvie the papists, the costly and dear-bought scandals and snares of images, pictures, rich copes, gorgeous altar-cloths . . . What can we suppose this will come to? . . . The sour leaven of human traditions mixed in one putrified mass with

the poisonous dregs of hypocrisy in the hearts of prelates that lie basking
in the sunny warmth of wealth and promotion, is the serpent's egg that
will hatch an Antichrist wheresoever, and engender the same monster as
big or little as the lump is which breeds him. If the splendour of gold and
silver begin to lord it once again in the Church of England, we shall see
Antichrist shortly wallow here, though his chief kennel be at Rome.

Milton *Of Reformation* II

POEMS ON THE RIVAL CHURCHES

20   Show me, dear Christ, thy spouse, so bright and clear.
What, is it she, which on the other shore
Goes richly painted? or which robbed and tore
Laments and mourns in Germany and here?
Sleeps she a thousand, then peeps up one year?
Is she self truth and errs? now new, now outwore?
Doth she, and did she, and shall she evermore
On one, on seven, or on no hill appear?
Dwells she with us, or like adventuring knights
First travail we to seek and then make love?
Betray, kind husband, thy spouse to our sights,
And let mine amorous soul court thy mild dove,
Who is most true, and pleasing to thee, then
When she is embraced and open to most men.

Donne *Holy Sonnet* xviii

21   I joy, dear Mother, when I view
Thy perfect lineaments, and hue
            Both sweet and bright.

Beauty in thee takes up her place,
And dates her letters from thy face,
            When she doth write.

A fine aspect in fit array,
Neither too mean, nor yet too gay,
            Shows who is best.

Outlandish looks may not compare:
For all they either painted are,
            Or else undressed.

She on the hills, which wantonly
Allureth all in hope to be
            By her preferred,

Hath kissed so long her painted shrines,
That even her face by kissing shines,
            For her reward.

She in the valley is so shy
Of dressing, that her hair doth lie
    About her ears:

While she avoids her neighbour's pride,
She wholly goes on the other side,
    And nothing wears.

But dearest Mother (what those miss)
The mean thy praise and glory is,
    And long may be.

Blessed be God, whose love it was
To double-moat thee with his grace,
    And none but thee.
Herbert 'The British Church'

22   Avenge O Lord thy slaughtered saints, whose bones
      Lie scattered on the Alpine mountains cold,
      Even them who kept thy truth so pure of old
      When all our fathers worshiped stocks and stones,
    Forget not: in thy book record their groans
      Who were thy sheep and in their ancient fold
      Slain by the bloody Piedmontese that rolled
      Mother with infant down the rocks. Their moans
    The vales redoubled to the hills, and they
      To heaven. Their martyred blood and ashes sow
      O'er all the Italian fields where still doth sway
    The triple tyrant: that from these may grow
      A hundredfold, who having learnt thy way
      Early may fly the Babylonian woe.
Milton 'On the late Massacre in Piedmont' (of the Protestant
Vaudois by the Catholic Duke of Savoy in 1655)

COUNTER-REFORMATION DEVOTION

23   Colloquy. Imagining Christ our Lord present before me on the cross, to make a colloquy with him, asking him how it is that being the creator, he has come to make himself man, and from eternal life has come to temporal death, and in this manner to die for my sins. Again, reflecting on myself, to ask what have I done for Christ, what am I doing for Christ, what ought I to do for Christ. Then beholding him in such a condition, and thus hanging upon the cross, to make the reflections which may present themselves.
St Ignatius Loyola *Spiritual Exercises* First Week; First Exercise

24   Fat soil, full spring, sweet olive, grape of bliss,
    That yields, that streams, that pours, that dost distil,

Untilled, undrawn, unstamped, untouched of press,
Dear fruit, clear brooks, fair oil, sweet wine at will:
Thus Christ unforced prevents [i.e. anticipates] in shedding blood
The whips, the thorns, the nails, the spear, and rood.

He pelican's, he phoenix' fate doth prove,
Whom flames consume, whom streams enforce to die,
How burneth blood, how bleedeth burning love?
Can one in flame and stream both bathe and fry?
How could he join a phoenix' fiery pains
In fainting pelican's still bleeding veins?

Elias once to prove God's sovereign power
By prayer procured a fire of wondrous force
That blood and wood and water did devour,
Yea stones and dust, beyond all nature's course:
Such fire is love that fed with gory blood
Doth burn no less than in the dryest wood.

O sacred fire come show thy force on me
That sacrifice to Christ I may return,
If withered wood for fuel fittest be,
If stones and dust, if flesh and blood will burn,
I withered am and stony to all good,
A sack of dust, a mass of flesh and blood.

> Southwell 'Christ's bloody Sweat' (the poem refers to the Agony
> in the Garden, Luke 22: 44; compare 'The Burning Babe', and
> Donne 'Good Friday, 1613, Riding Westward')

25   It pleased the Lord that I should see this angel in the following way. He
was not tall, but short, and very beautiful, his face so aflame that he
appeared to be one of the highest types of angel who seem to be all afire
... In his hands I saw a long golden spear and at the end of the iron tip
I seemed to see a point of fire. With this he seemed to pierce my heart
several times so that it penetrated to my entrails. When he drew it out,
I thought he was drawing them out with it and he left me completely afire
with a great love for God. The pain was so sharp that it made me utter
several moans; and so excessive was the sweetness caused me by this
intense pain that one can never wish to lose it, nor will one's soul be
content with anything less than God. It is not bodily pain, but spiritual,
though the body has a share in it – indeed, a great share.

> St Teresa of Avila *The Life of Teresa of Jesus* xxix

26   O heart! the equal poise of love's both parts
Big alike with wound and darts.
Live in these conquering leaves; live all the same;
And walk through all tongues one triumphant flame.
Live here, great heart; and love and die and kill;
And bleed and wound; and yield and conquer still

. . . . . .
O sweet incendiary! show here thy art,
Upon this carcass of a hard, cold heart,
Let all thy scattered shafts of light, that play
Among the leaves of thy large books of day,
Combined against this breast at once break in
And take away from me my self and sin,
This gracious robbery shall thy bounty be;
And my best fortunes such fair spoils of me.
O thou undaunted daughter of desires!
By all thy dower of lights and fires;
By all the eagle in thee, all the dove;
By all thy lives and deaths of love;
By thy large draughts of intellectual day,
And by thy thirsts of love more large than they;
By all thy brim-filled bowls of fierce desire
By the last morning's draught of liquid fire;
By the full kingdom of that final kiss
That seized thy parting soul, and sealed thee his;
By all the heavens thou hast in him
(Fair sister of the seraphim!)
By all of him we have in thee;
Leave nothing of my self in me.
Let me so read thy life, that I
Unto all life of mine may die.

> Crashaw 'The Flaming Heart upon the Book and
> Picture of the Seraphical Saint Teresa' ll. 75–108

8 Protestant Theology

Protestant theology represents not so much a new departure as an emphasis on and a reinterpretation of certain ideas that were always present in Christian thought but not always stressed. Luther and Calvin evolved their theology largely from two sources, the writings of St Paul and St Augustine. In doing so they turned away from the rational theology of medieval Catholicism, especially as represented in the thirteenth century by St Thomas Aquinas, who had tried to reconcile Aristotelian philosophy and theology, reason and faith, man and God, in a harmonious, hierarchically ordered system. Instead they emphasised, as Augustine and some fourteenth-century Augustinians had done, the basic paradoxes of Christianity, the limitations of human reason, the great gap between man's sin and God's grace. Important sources were Paul's Epistles, especially Romans and Galatians, Augustine's *City of God*, his later writings against the Pelagians (see below), for example *On the Spirit and the Letter* and *On Grace and Free Will*, and the *Enchiridion* (handbook) in which he summarised his teaching. Luther and Calvin propagated and popularised their reinterpretation of Paul and Augustine in a large number of works written in Latin for ecclesiastical readers and in German and French for laymen; of these the most important are Luther's *The Freedom of a Christian* (1520), *On the Bondage of the Will* (1525), his many commentaries on the books of the Bible, especially the Preface to Romans (1522); and Calvin's *Institutes of the Christian Religion* (several editions both Latin and French, 1536–60). Lutheran and Calvinist ideas were diffused in England both directly through translation, for example, Tyndale's versions of Luther's commentaries (**15, 26**), and, indirectly but more widely, through incorporation in other men's books. England produced no comparable original theologian, yet the vast religious literature of all kinds and purposes – sermons, controversial writings, catechisms, handbooks of devotion and practical piety, theological textbooks – made every reading Protestant familiar with the ideas and terminology of the continental reformers.

The Protestant view of the relationship between man and God is based on a series of antitheses defined in St Paul's Epistles: between law and gospel, flesh and spirit, works and faith, nature and grace, bondage and freedom, the first and the second Adam. It can be set out in a simplified form as follows. God created the first man, Adam, in his own image, a being in whom reason and will were perfectly integrated, who was free to exercise his reason and will as he chose, and capable of perfect obedience to God. God knew that Adam would exercise his choice wrongly, that he would fail the test of obedience, yet he allowed him full responsibility. Adam's original sin, his disobedience to God represented by eating the fruit of the Tree of Knowledge, has had calamitous consequences for the human race. Fallen man's nature has become utterly depraved and corrupt. He is a mass of sin. He retains some vestiges of his original reason, but whereas Adam could freely and of his own efforts follow the dictates of his reason, the reason and will of fallen man are so vitiated that he can of his own efforts only choose to sin. Because of his sin man is condemned by God to a double death, the mortality of the body and the eternal damnation of the soul. Unaided, man is incapable of righteousness; he is in bondage to the law which demands righteousness but which he cannot fulfil. Hence he is justly condemned by God, since the corruption of his nature which makes righteousness impossible is the responsibility of the first man who freely disobeyed God (**1–4**).

God's justice, which punishes man for the sin of disobedience, is matched by his mercy, which forgives man. Yet his justice demands satisfaction. This is achieved through the mediation of God's greatest gift to man, his Son, the second Adam, whose perfect obedience cancels the disobedience of the first Adam, and who gives himself as a sacrifice, thereby taking on himself man's sin and redeeming him from damnation. The disobedience of the first Adam brought man death; the obedience of the second Adam brings man eternal life. Just as Christ takes on man's sin, though he is himself sinless, so he imputes to man his righteousness, though fallen man is himself incapable of righteousness. God accepts Christ's imputed righteousness or merits as man's, and thus grants man salvation (**5–9**). This process of redemption, whereby man is released from sin and death and the impossible demands of the law, is the promise of the gospel.

Man's salvation is thus achieved not by his own efforts but by God's grace. He is justified (i.e. accepted by God as righteous through Christ although in himself he is unrighteous) by faith alone, *sola fide* (**10–13**). (This is the crucial doctrine of Protestantism; Luther's conversion depended on his understanding of the phrase 'The just shall live by faith', Romans 1:17 (**12**).) Faith does not mean simply intellectual assent to the Christian creed, but trust that God will fulfil his promises. The man who is justified by faith is chosen by God for salvation: he is one of the elect. His faith is a gift of God. He is now adopted by God and regenerate, freed from his corrupt nature; through this change in his nature he has assurance that he is one of the elect. He is granted perseverance by God so that he can continue in a state of grace. The sacraments of baptism and the Lord's supper are signs of God's promise of salvation to him. The justified man through God's grace cannot help producing good works and living a sanctified life, and hence he has evidence that he is of the elect. However, good works are the result not the cause of justification. Works contribute nothing to justification; works without faith do not justify, but faith without works is an impossibility (**15**).

This state in which a man lives by faith, assured of the fulfilment of God's promises and of his own election and ultimate salvation, free from the burden of the law, is that of Christian liberty. The law, the covenant of works of the Old Testament which demanded that man should be justified by his observance of the moral and ceremonial and civil code, but which his corrupt nature prevented him from fulfilling, has been abrogated by the gospel, the covenant of grace of the New Testament which promises that man shall be justified by faith in the redeeming sacrifice of Christ (**22–27**). Christian liberty does not mean that man is free from observance of the moral or civil law, though he is free from Jewish ceremonial law; it means that his justification does not depend on his observance of the law, though he will observe it in so far as he can, not coerced into obedience through fear of God's wrath, but obeying freely through love. The justified man is not morally perfect; only Christ as man was capable of moral perfection. Sanctification in this life is incomplete. The justified man, though liable to occasional sin, does not thereby fall from a state of grace. (Antinomianism, the doctrine that defines Christian liberty as meaning man's freedom from any obligation to observe the moral law, was characteristic of some extreme Protestant sects but was repudiated by orthodox Protestantism.)

Who are the elect, and why does God choose them? These were among the most difficult questions put by Protestant theologians. Only a few (known variously as the elect, the remnant, the saints, the godly) are to be saved. Augustine, following Paul (**17–18**), elaborated the doctrine of predestination that was to be given a sterner emphasis by Calvin. The whole of mankind, because of sin, merits damnation; God predestinates a few to salvation, not because of their merit but out of his free grace (*City of God* XIV xxvi, *Enchiridion* xxv). Man does not deserve grace; it is freely given by God. Although God has foreknowledge of man's acts, his predestination of the few is not governed by this foreknowledge. All men are responsible for their sins (**28**), though it is only God's free gift of grace to the predestined that makes their good works possible. Calvin carried the doctrine further, and supposed a system of double predestination (*Institutes of the Christian*

Religion III xxi–xxiv). Not only has God from all eternity predestinated the few to salvation, he has also reprobated the many to damnation (**20**). This decree admittedly seems horrible to man; it is incomprehensible, yet it is also just. The decree is final. The elect cannot resist God's grace, nor can the reprobate avoid damnation. However, Calvin denied that this took away human responsibility or made God the author of evil. God can bring good out of evil, and use the reprobate as instruments of his good, but they are fully responsible for their sin.

The problem of reconciling God's grace with man's free will was the basis of some important controversies. Those who stressed the magnitude of God's grace, his free gifts to man, and man's nothingness, tended to limit man's freedom of choice; those who stressed man's freedom to work out his own salvation in co-operation with grace tended to diminish the part played by grace and to limit God's power. It was on this issue that the humanist Erasmus, after a period of sympathy with the cause of reform, finally condemned Luther. In *On the Freedom of the Will* (1524) Erasmus argues that man may co-operate with or turn away from grace (**29**); Luther in his reply, *On the Bondage of the Will* (1525), argues that man is only free to choose sin: the faith which justifies is a gift of grace (**30**). A similar controversy with more far-reaching consequences was that between Arminians and Calvinists in the early seventeenth century. Arminius argued that God wills the salvation of all, that Christ died for all, not just for the elect, that grace is freely offered to all, but that man may resist or co-operate with grace as he chooses. These views were put forward after Arminius' death in the Five Articles of the Remonstrants (1610) and condemned by the Synod of Dort (see Chapter 7).

These controversies, which turn on the question of how far human nature has been corrupted by the fall, themselves echo one of the most important controversies in the history of the formation of Christian theology: that between Augustine and Pelagius in the early fifth century. Pelagius denied that man inherits original sin and that his nature is corrupt, and deplored Augustine's stress on the weakness and helplessness of man's will. Man is capable of freely choosing good or evil, of moving towards or away from God, of perfecting himself morally. Here there are some connections between Pelagianism and a classical philosophy such as Stoicism (see Chapter 4) which envisages man as a free, self-sufficient being capable of living a life governed by reason. In response to Pelagius Augustine elaborated his teaching on original sin, prevenient grace (which 'comes before' or precedes repentance and makes it possible), predestination, and the perseverance of the elect.

Strict Protestantism argues that man's reason is corrupt and cannot save him; it is antithetical to faith, which is God's gift (**36**). However, many Protestants, especially those with humanist sympathies, were reluctant to allow that reason had been so weakened or that man was totally depraved as a result of the fall. Instead of the depravity of man they upheld the dignity of man, and while granting that man's reason had been impaired by the fall they insisted that it could guide his conduct and lead him to knowledge of God. Here they drew both on the classical concept of right reason (*recta ratio*) as expounded by Cicero (*Republic* III xxii) and on Paul's acknowledgement (Romans 2:14) that the gentiles or pagans without the benefit of revelation are capable of acting morally, because knowledge of the law is written in their hearts (**37**). Right reason, which can also be designated conscience, is as much a gift of God as faith. Its functioning is explained by Hooker in *Of the Laws of Ecclesiastical Polity* I v–x (**32, 38**). Man is endowed with a natural faculty of reason which prescribes to the will what it should choose as good. By the light of reason man is able to discern what is good without the help of revelation; the good is what men have generally and perpetually agreed to be so. This is the law of nature. However, since man's nature is corrupt he cannot fulfil the law of nature (although he can discern it) without supernatural help, the revelation of the gospel. Thus for Hooker reason and faith, law and gospel are complementary, not antithetical. Hooker's tradition of rational theology was continued in the seventeenth century by men such as Hales, Chillingworth and the Cambridge Platonists (More, Cudworth, Whichcote and Smith); it was this tradition that by the end of the seventeenth century came to dominate the Church of England as Latitudinarianism and largely superseded Lutheran and Calvinist theology.

This attempt to fuse classical ethics with Christian faith is characteristic of Christian humanism (see Chapter 9). Milton fully explored the complexities and contradictions inherent in such a fusion, though he was unable to resolve them satisfactorily. He produced an idiosyncratic work of systematic theology for his own use, *Christian Doctrine*, before embarking on *Paradise Lost*. Milton rejects Calvinist double predestination and adopts instead the Arminian doctrine of salvation offered to all (**21, 33**). However, his rationalist approach to theology leaves him open to criticism of a kind that Luther and Calvin avoid through their fideism (their reliance on faith for knowledge of God and their denigration of reason). Where Calvin admits the mysteriousness of God's decrees, Milton sets out to explain them, and here most readers have found the chief weakness of *Paradise Lost*. Milton's emphasis on reason may damage his portrait of God, yet it leads also to his particular definition of Christian liberty, which is the core of the poem. Liberty lies in obeying the dictates of right reason; to obey nature is the same as to obey God (**39–41**). The man who understands and completes this

process is of the elect; the choice is his as much as God's. Yet against
this rational statement of man's capacity to choose good Milton sets an
Augustinian sense of history as a record of man's sinfulness, of
voluntary servitude.

It is important to realise that although there might have been general
agreement among Protestants as to the meaning of terms such as faith,
works, reason and law, in practice these could be very differently
emphasised. A doctrine baldly stated is very different from a doctrine
lived or a doctrine explored in poetry. Belief in an elect or in
predestination is not in itself pessimistic, though it may appear so in its
outlines: to Luther it was a joyful liberation from the appalling burden
of a religion of works and merit (**12**). The same doctrine provokes
different responses in different poets: for Greville, the contrast between
God's grace and man's insignificance leads almost to despair and
disgust at his own condition; for Donne and Herbert, it leads to faith in
redemption and a certainty that God's wrath is subsumed in his mercy.

ORIGINAL SIN

1   God created man aright, for God is the author of natures, though he is
     certainly not responsible for their defects. But man was willingly
     perverted and justly condemned, and so begot perverted and condemned
     offspring. For we were all in that one man, seeing that we all *were* that
     one man who fell into sin through the woman who was made from him
     before the first sin. We did not yet possess forms individually created and
     assigned to us for us to live in them as individuals; but there already
     existed the seminal nature from which we were to be begotten. And of
     course, when this was vitiated through sin, and bound with death's fetters
     in its just condemnation, man could not be born of man in any other
     condition. Hence from the misuse of free will there started a chain of
     disasters: mankind is led from that original perversion, a kind of
     corruption at the root, right up to the disaster of the second death, which
     has no end. Only those who are set free through God's grace escape from
     this calamitous sequence.

                                            Augustine *City of God* XIII xiv

2   We must, therefore, distinctly note these two things. First, we are so
     vitiated and perverted in every part of our nature that by this great
     corruption we stand justly condemned and convicted before God, to
     whom nothing is acceptable but righteousness, innocence, and purity . . .
     Then comes the second consideration: that this perversity never ceases in
     us, but continually bears new fruits . . . just as a burning furnace gives
     forth flames and sparks, or water ceaselessly bubbles up from a spring . . .
     Those who have said that original sin is 'concupiscence' [i.e. Augustine]
     have used an appropriate word, if only it be added – something that most

will by no means concede – that whatever is in man, from the understanding to the will, from the soul even to the flesh, has been defiled and crammed with this concupiscence. Or, to put it more briefly, the whole man is of himself nothing but concupiscence.

Calvin *Institutes of the Christian Religion* II i 8

3   My God, my God, what am I put to when I am put to consider and put off the root, the fuel, the occasion of my sickness? What Hippocrates, what Galen, could show me that in my body? It lies deeper than so, it lies in my soul; and deeper than so, for we may well consider the body before the soul came, before inanimation, to be without sin; and the soul, before it comes to the body, before that infection, to be without sin: sin is the root and the fuel of all sickness, and yet that which destroys body and soul is in neither, but in both together. It is the union of the body and soul, and, O my God, could I prevent that, or can I dissolve that? The root and the fuel of my sickness is my sin, my actual sin; but even that sin hath another root, another fuel, original sin; and can I divest that? Wilt thou bid me to separate the leaven that a lump of dough hath received, or the salt, that the water hath contracted, from the sea? Dost thou look, that I should so look to the fuel or embers of sin, that I never take fire? The whole world is a pile of faggots, upon which we are laid, and (as though there were no other) we are the bellows.

Donne *Devotions* Expostulation xxii

4   Wrapped up, O Lord, in man's degeneration;
The glories of thy truth, thy joys eternal,
Reflect upon my soul dark desolation,
And ugly prospects o'er the sprites infernal.
    Lord, I have sinned, and mine iniquity.
    Deserves this hell; yet Lord deliver me.

Thy power and mercy never comprehended,
Rest lively-imaged in my conscience wounded;
Mercy to grace, and power to fear extended,
Both infinite, and I in both confounded;
    Lord, I have sinned, and mine iniquity,
    Deserves this hell, yet Lord deliver me.

If from this depth of sin, this hellish grave,
And fatal absence from my Saviour's glory,
I could implore his mercy, who can save,
And for my sins, not pains of sins, be sorry:
    Lord, from this horror of iniquity,
    And hellish grave, thou would'st deliver me.

Greville *Caelica* xcviii

REDEMPTION THROUGH THE MEDIATION OF CHRIST, THE SECOND ADAM

5   For as by one man's disobedience many were made sinners, so by the obedience of one shall many be made righteous.

Moreover the law entered, that the offence might abound. But where sin abounded, grace did much more abound:

That as sin hath reigned unto death, even so might grace reign through righteousness unto eternal life by Jesus Christ our Lord.

Romans 5:19–21

6   For since by man came death, by man came also the resurrection of the dead.

For as in Adam all die, even so in Christ shall all be made alive.

1 Corinthians 15:21–2

7   When Adam was made – being made an upright man – there was no need for a mediator. Once sin, however, had widely separated the human race from God, it was necessary for a mediator, who alone was born, lived, and was put to death without sin, to reconcile us to God, and provide even for our bodies a resurrection to life eternal – and all this in order that man's pride might be exposed and healed through God's humility. Thus it might be shown man how far he had departed from God, when by the incarnate God he is recalled to God; that man in his contumacy might be furnished an example of obedience by the God-Man; that the fount of grace might be opened up; that even the resurrection of the body – itself promised to the redeemed – might be previewed in the resurrection of the Redeemer himself; that the devil might be vanquished by that very nature he was rejoicing over having deceived – all this, however, without giving man ground for glory in himself, lest pride spring up anew.

Augustine Enchiridion xxviii

8   A tree was first the instrument of strife,
Where Eve to sin her soul did prostitute,
A tree is now the instrument of life,
Though ill that trunk, and this fair body suit:
Ah, cursèd tree, and yet O blessèd fruit!
    That death to him, this life to us doth give:
    Strange is the cure, when things past cure revive,
And the physician dies, to make his patient live.
   . . . . . .
A man was first the author of our fall,
A man is now the author of our rise,
A garden was the place we perished all,
A garden is the place he pays our price,
And the old serpent with a new device,
    Hath found a way himself for to beguile,

So he, that all men tangled in his wile,
Is now by one man caught, beguiled with his own guile.
                Giles Fletcher *Christ's Triumph over Death* stanzas 13, 15
                        (compare Herbert 'The Sacrifice', 'The Agony',
                                and Donne 'Hymn to God my God')

9   God the Father addresses God the Son:
                Well thou know'st how dear,
To me are all my works, nor man the least
Though last created, that for him I spare
Thee from my bosom and right hand, to save,
By losing thee awhile, the whole race lost.
Thou therefore whom thou only canst redeem,
Their nature also to thy nature join;
And be thy self man among men on earth,
Made flesh, when time shall be, of virgin seed,
By wondrous birth: be thou in Adam's room
The head of all mankind, though Adam's son.
As in him perish all men, so in thee
As from a second root shall be restored,
As many as are restored, without thee none.
His crime makes guilty all his sons, thy merit
Imputed shall absolve them who renounce
Their own both righteous and unrighteous deeds,
And live in thee transplanted, and from thee
Receive new life. So man, as is most just,
Shall satisfy for man, be judged and die,
And dying rise, and rising with him raise
His brethren, ransomed with his own dear life.
                                Milton *Paradise Lost* III ll. 276–97

JUSTIFICATION BY FAITH

10   Now we know that what things soever the law saith, it saith to them who are under the law: that every mouth may be stopped, and all the world may become guilty before God.

Therefore by the deeds of the law there shall no flesh be justified in his sight: for by the law is the knowledge of sin.

But now the righteousness of God without the law is manifested, being witnessed by the law and the prophets;

Even the righteousness of God which is by faith of Jesus Christ unto all and upon all them that believe ...

For all have sinned, and come short of the glory of God;

Being justified freely by his grace through the redemption that is in Christ Jesus.

. . . . . .

Therefore we conclude that a man is justified by faith without the deeds of the law.

Romans 3:19–24, 28

11   For as many as are of the works of the law are under the curse: for it is written, Cursed is every one that continueth not in all things which are written in the book of the law to do them.

But that no man is justified by the law in the sight of God, it is evident: for, The just shall live by faith.

And the law is not of faith: but, The man that doeth them shall live in them.

Christ hath redeemed us from the curse of the law, being made a curse for us: for it is written, Cursed is every one that hangeth on a tree.

Galatians 3:10–13

12   My case was this: however irreproachable my life as a monk, I felt myself in the presence of God to be a sinner with a most unquiet conscience, nor could I believe him to be appeased by the satisfaction I could offer. I did not love – nay, I hated this just God who punishes sinners, and if not with silent blasphemy, at least with huge murmuring I was indignant against God, as if it were really not enough that miserable sinners, eternally ruined by original sin, should be crushed with every kind of calamity through the law of the Ten Commandments, but that God through the gospel must add sorrow to sorrow, and even though the gospel bring his righteousness and wrath to bear on us. And so I raged with a savage and confounded conscience; yet I knocked importunely at Paul in this place [Romans 1: 17], with a parched and burning desire to know what he could mean. At last, as I meditated day and night, God showed mercy and I turned my attention to the connection of the words, namely – 'For therein is the righteousness of God revealed from faith to faith: as it is written, The just shall live by faith' – and there I began to understand that the righteousness of God is the righteousness in which a just man lives by the gift of God, in other words by faith, and that what Paul means is this: the righteousness of God, revealed in the gospel, is passive, in other words that by which the merciful God justifies us through faith, as it is written. 'The just shall live by faith.' At this I felt myself straightway born afresh and to have entered through the open gates into paradise itself.

Luther 'Autobiographical Fragment'

13   But this saying, that we be justified by faith only, freely, and without works, is spoken for to take away clearly all merit of our works, as being unable to deserve our justification at God's hands, and thereby most plainly to express the weakness of man, and the goodness of God; the great infirmity of ourselves, and the might and power of God; the imperfectness of our own works, and the most abundant grace of our saviour Christ; and therefore wholly to ascribe the merit and deserving of our justification unto Christ only, and his most precious blood-shedding. This faith the Holy Scripture teacheth us; this is the strong rock

and foundation of Christian religion; this doctrine all old and ancient authors of Christ's church do approve; this doctrine advanceth and setteth forth the true glory of Christ, and beateth down the vain-glory of man; this whosoever denieth, is not to be accounted for a Christian man, nor for a setter-forth of Christ's glory; but for an adversary to Christ and his gospel, and for a setter-forth of men's vain-glory.

The Book of Homilies III 'Of the Salvation of Mankind'

GOOD WORKS

14   Pure religion and undefiled before God and the Father is this, To visit the fatherless and widows in their affliction, and to keep himself unspotted from the world.

James 1:27

15   Faith is a lively thing, mighty in working, valiant, and strong, ever doing, ever fruitful; so that it is impossible that he who is endued therewith should not work always good works without ceasing. He asketh not whether good works are to be done or not, but hath done them already, ere mention be made of them; and is always doing, for such is his nature; for quick faith in his heart, and lively moving of the Spirit, drive him and stir him thereunto. Whosoever doth not good works, is an unbelieving person, and faithless, and looketh round about him, groping after faith and good works, and wotteth not what faith or good works mean, though he babble never so many things of faith and good works. Faith is, then, a lively and a steadfast trust in the favour of God, wherewith we commit ourselves altogether unto God ... And such trust, wrought by the Holy Ghost through faith, maketh a man glad, lusty, cheerful, and true-hearted unto God and unto all creatures: whereof, willingly and without compulsion, he is glad and ready to do good to every man, to do service to every man, to suffer all things, that God may be loved and praised, which hath given him such grace; so that it is impossible to separate good works from faith, even as it is impossible to separate heat and burning from fire.

Tyndale *Prologue upon the Epistle of St Paul to the Romans*
(trans. from Luther's *Preface to the Epistle to the Romans*)

16   Works done before the grace of Christ, and the inspiration of his Spirit, are not pleasant to God, forasmuch as they sprang not of faith in Jesus Christ, neither do they make men meet to receive grace ... yea rather, for that they are not done as God hath willed and commanded them to be done, we doubt not but they have the nature of sin.

The Thirty-Nine Articles XIII 'Of Works before Justification'

PREDESTINATION

17   And we know that all things work together for good to them that love God, to them who are the called according to his purpose.

For whom he did foreknow, he also did predestinate to be conformed to the image of his Son, that he might be the firstborn among many brethren.

Moreover whom he did predestinate, them he also called: and whom he called, them he also justified: and whom he justified, them he also glorified.

What shall we then say to these things? If God be for us, who can be against us?

Romans 8:28–31

18   As it is written, Jacob have I loved, but Esau have I hated.

What shall we say then? Is there unrighteousness with God? God forbid.

For he saith to Moses, I will have mercy on whom I will have mercy, and I will have compassion on whom I will have compassion.

So then it is not of him that willeth, nor of him that runneth, but of God that showeth mercy.

. . . . . .

Thou wilt say then unto me, Why doth he yet find fault? For who hath resisted his will?

Nay but, O man, who art thou that repliest against God? Shall the thing formed say to him that formed it, Why hast thou made me thus?

Hath not the potter power over the clay, of the same lump to make one vessel unto honour, and another unto dishonour?

Romans 9:13–16, 19–21

19   Predestination to life is the everlasting purpose of God, whereby (before the foundations of the world were laid) he hath constantly decreed by his counsel secret to us, to deliver from curse and damnation those whom he hath chosen in Christ out of mankind, and to bring them by Christ to everlasting salvation, as vessels made to honour. Wherefore, they which be endued with so excellent a benefit of God be called according to God's purpose by his Spirit working in due season: they through grace obey the calling: they be justified freely: they be made sons of God by adoption: they be made like the image of his only-begotten son Jesus Christ: they walk religiously in good works, and at length, by God's mercy, they attain to everlasting felicity.

The Thirty-Nine Articles XVII 'Of Predestination and Election'

20   As Scripture, then, clearly shows, we say that God once established by his eternal and unchangeable plan those whom he long before determined once for all to receive into salvation, and those whom, on the other hand, he would devote to destruction. We assert that, with respect to the elect, this plan was founded upon his freely given mercy, without regard to human worth; but by his just and irreprehensible but incomprehensible judgement he has barred the door of life to those whom he has given over to damnation. Now among the elect we regard the call as a testimony of election. Then we hold justification another sign of its manifestation, until they come into the glory in which the fulfilment of that election lies. But as the Lord seals his elect by call and justification, so by shutting off the reprobate from knowledge of his name or from the sanctification of his Spirit, he, as it were, reveals by these marks what sort of judgement awaits them.

Calvin *Institutes of the Christian Religion* III xxi 7

21   It is quite clear, then, that God has predestined from eternity all who would believe and persist in their belief. It follows, therefore, that there is no reprobation except for those who do not believe or do not persist, and that this is rather a matter of consequence than of an express decree by God. Thus there is no reprobation from eternity of particular men. For God has predestined to salvation all who use their free will, on one condition, which applies to all. None are predestined to destruction except through their own fault.

Milton *Christian Doctrine* I iv

THE BONDAGE OF THE LAW AND THE LIBERTY OF THE GOSPEL

22   For as many as are led by the Spirit of God, they are the sons of God.

For ye have not received the spirit of bondage again to fear; but ye have received the Spirit of adoption, whereby we cry, Abba, Father.

Romans 8:14–15

23   But before faith came, we were kept under the law, shut up unto the faith which should afterwards be revealed.

Wherefore the law was our schoolmaster to bring us unto Christ, that we might be justified by faith.

But after that faith is come, we are no longer under a schoolmaster.

For ye are all the children of God by faith in Christ Jesus.

For as many of you as have been baptised into Christ have put on Christ.

There is neither Jew nor Greek, there is neither bond nor free, there is neither male nor female; for ye are all one in Christ Jesus.

And if ye be Christ's, then are ye Abraham's seed, and heirs according to the promise.

Galatians 3:23–9

24   And you, being dead in your sins and the uncircumcision of your flesh, hath he quickened together with him, having forgiven you all trespasses;

Blotting out the handwriting of ordinances that was against us, which was contrary to us, and took it out of the way, nailing it to his cross.

Colossians 2:13–14

25   A Christian is a perfectly free lord of all, subject to none. A Christian is
a perfectly dutiful servant of all, subject to all ... A Christian has all that
he needs in faith and needs no works to justify him; and if he has no need
of works, he has no need of the law; and if he has no need of the law,
surely he is free from the law ... Faith alone is the righteousness of a
Christian and the fulfilling of all the commandments, for he who fulfils
the First Commandment has no difficulty in fulfilling all the rest.

Luther *The Freedom of a Christian*

26   The Old Testament is a book, wherein is written the law of God, and
the deeds of them which fulfil them, and of them also which fulfil them
not.

The New Testament is a book, wherein are contained the promises of
God; and the deeds of them which believe them, or believe them not.

Evangelion (that we call the gospel) is a Greek word; and signifieth
good, merry, glad and joyful tidings, that maketh a man's heart glad, and
maketh him sing, dance, and leap for joy: as when David had killed
Goliah the giant, came glad tidings unto the Jews, that their fearful and
cruel enemy was slain, and they delivered out of all danger: for gladness
whereof, they sung, danced, and were joyful. In like manner is the
Evangelion of God (which we call gospel, and the New Testament) joyful
tidings; and, as some say, a good hearing published by the apostles
throughout all the world, of Christ the right David; how that he hath
fought with sin, with death, and the devil, and overcome them: whereby
all men that were in bondage to sin, wounded with death, overcome of
the devil, are, without their own merits or deservings, loosed, justified,
restored to life and saved, brought to liberty and reconciled unto the
favour of God, and set at one with him again: which tidings as many as
believe laud, praise, and thank God; are glad, sing and dance for joy ...

Here ye see the nature of the law, and the nature of the Evangelion;
how the law is the key that bindeth and damneth all men, and the
Evangelion looseth them again. The law goeth before, and the Evangelion followeth. When a preacher preacheth the law, he bindeth all
consciences; and when he preacheth the gospel, he looseth them again.

Tyndale *A Pathway into the Holy Scripture*
(trans. from Luther's *Preface to the New Testament*)

27   O dreadful Justice, what a fright and terror
            Wast thou of old,
            When sin and error
      Did show and shape thy looks to me,
      And through their glass discolour thee!
He that did but look up, was proud and bold.

The dishes of thy balance seemed to gape,
            Like two great pits;
            The beam and scape
      Did like some torturing engine show:

Thy hand above did burn and glow,
Daunting the stoutest hearts, the proudest wits.

But now that Christ's pure veil presents the sight,
        I see no fears:
        Thy hand is white,
Thy scales like buckets, which attend
And interchangeably descend,
Lifting to heaven from this well of tears.

For where before thou still didst call on me,
        Now I still touch
        And harp on thee.
God's promises have made thee mine;
Why should I justice now decline?
Against me there is none, but for me much.

                              Herbert 'Justice' (II)

GRACE AND FREE WILL

28   Now wherever there is the express statement not to do this or that, and whenever the performance of the will is required to do or refrain from some action, in keeping with God's commandments, that is sufficient proof of the free choice of the will. Let no man, therefore, blame God in his heart whenever he sins, but let him impute the sin to himself. Nor does the fact that something is done in accordance with God's will transfer such an act from one's own will.

                              Augustine *Grace and Free Will* ii

29   I ask what merit can a man arrogate to himself if whatever, as a man, he is able to achieve by his natural intelligence and free choice, all this he owes to the one from whom he receives these powers? And yet God himself imputes this to our merit, that we do not turn our soul away from his grace, and that we apply our natural powers to simple obedience. And this surely goes to show that it is not wrong to say that man does something and yet attributes the sum of all that he does to God as its author, from whom it has come about that he was able to ally his own effort with the grace of God ... Thus to those who maintain that man can do nothing without the help of the grace of God, and conclude that therefore no works of men are good – to these we shall oppose a thesis to me much more probable, that there is nothing that man cannot do with the help of the grace of God, and that therefore all the works of man can be good.

                              Erasmus *On the Freedom of the Will* III

30   For my own part, I frankly confess that even if it were possible, I should not wish to have free choice given to me, or to have anything left in my own hands by which I might strive towards salvation. For, on the one hand, I should be unable to stand firm and keep hold of it amid so many adversities and perils and so many assaults of demons, seeing that even one demon is mightier than all men, and no man at all could be saved; and on the other hand, even if there were no perils or adversities or demons, I should nevertheless have to labour under perpetual uncertainty and to fight as one beating the air [I Cor. 9: 26], since even if I lived and worked to eternity, my conscience would never be assured and certain how much it ought to do to satisfy God. For whatever work might be accomplished, there would always remain an anxious doubt whether it pleased God or whether he required something more, as the experience of all self-justifiers proves, and as I myself learned to my bitter cost through so many years. But now, since God has taken my salvation out of my hands into his, making it depend on his choice and not mine, and has promised to save me, not by my own work or exertion but by his grace and mercy, I am assured and certain both that he is faithful and will not lie to me, and also that he is too great and powerful for any demons or any adversities to be able to break him or to snatch me from him ... So it comes about that, if not all, some and indeed many are saved, whereas by the power of free choice none at all would be saved, but all would perish together.

Luther *On the Bondage of the Will* VI

31   The condition of man after the fall of Adam is such, that he cannot turn and prepare himself, by his own natural strength and good works, to faith, and calling upon God: Wherefore we have no power to do good works pleasant and acceptable to God, without the grace of God by Christ preventing us [i.e. prevenient grace], that we may have a good will, and working with us, when we have that good will.

The Thirty-Nine Articles X 'Of Free Will'

32   Man in perfection of nature being made according to the likeness of his Maker resembleth him also in the manner of working; so that whatsoever we work as men, the same we do wittingly work and freely; neither are we according to the manner of natural agents any way so tied, but that it is in our power to leave the things we do undone ... To choose is to will one thing before another. And to will is to bend our souls to the having or doing of that which they see to be good. Goodness is seen with the eye of the understanding. And the light of that eye, is reason. So that two principal fountains there are of human action, knowledge and will; which will, in things tending towards any end, is termed choice.

Hooker *Of the Laws of Ecclesiastical Polity* I vi

33   By virtue of his wisdom God decreed the creation of angels and men as beings gifted with reason and thus with free will. At the same time he foresaw the direction in which they would tend when they used this absolutely unimpaired freedom. What then? Shall we say that God's providence or foreknowledge imposes any necessity upon them? Certainly not ... Nothing happens because God has foreseen it, but rather he

has foreseen each event because each is the result of particular causes which, by his decree, work quite freely and with which he is thoroughly familiar. So the outcome does not rest with God who forsees it, but only with the man whose action God foresees ... Divine foreknowledge definitely cannot itself impose any necessity, nor can it be set up as a cause, in any sense, of free actions. If it is set up in this way, then liberty will be an empty word, and will have to be banished utterly not only from religion but also from morality and even from indifferent matters. Nothing will happen except by necessity, since there is nothing God does not foresee.

Milton *Christian Doctrine* I iii

FAITH OPPOSED TO REASON

34   Where is the wise? where is the scribe? where is the disputer of this world? hath not God made foolish the wisdom of this world?

For after that in the wisdom of God the world by wisdom knew not God, it pleased God by the foolishness of preaching to save them that believe.

For the Jews require a sign, and the Greeks seek after wisdom:

But we preach Christ crucified, unto the Jews a stumblingblock, and unto the Greek foolishness;

But unto them which are called, both Jews and Greeks, Christ the power of God, and the wisdom of God.

Because the foolishness of God is wiser than men; and the weakness of God is stronger than men.

I Corinthians 1:20–5

35   What has Jerusalem to do with Athens, the Church with the Academy, the Christian with the heretic? Our principles come from the Porch of Solomon [i.e. not from the Stoic Porch], who had himself taught that the Lord is to be sought in simplicity of heart. I have no use for a Stoic or a Platonic or a dialectic Christianity. After Jesus Christ we have no need of speculation, after the Gospel no need of research. When we come to believe, we have no desire to believe anything else; for we begin by believing that there is nothing else which we have to believe.

Tertullian *The Prescriptions against the Heretics* vii

36   O false and treacherous probability,
Enemy of truth, and friend to wickedness;
With whose blear eyes opinion learns to see
Truth's feeble party here, and barrenness.
When thou hast thus misled humanity,
And lost obedience in the pride of wit,
With reason dar'st thou judge the deity,
And in thy flesh make bold to fashion it.
Vain thought, the Word of power a riddle is,
And till the veils be rent, the flesh new-born,

Reveals no wonders of that inward bliss,
Which but where faith is, everywhere finds scorn;
  Who therefore censures God with fleshly sprite,
  As well in time may wrap up infinite.

Greville *Caelica* ciii

RIGHT REASON AND NATURAL LAW

37   For when the Gentiles, which have not the law, do by nature the things contained in the law, these, having not the law, are a law unto themselves:
Which show the work of the law written in their hearts, their conscience also bearing witness, and their thoughts the mean while accusing or else excusing one another.

Romans 2:14–15

38   The general and perpetual voice of men is as the sentence of God himself. For that which all men have at all times learned, Nature herself must needs have taught; and God being the author of Nature, her voice is but his instrument. By her from him we receive whatsoever in such sort we learn. Infinite duties there are, the goodness whereof is by this rule sufficiently manifested, although we had no other warrant besides to approve them. The apostle St Paul having speech concerning the heathen saith of them, 'They are a law unto themselves.' His meaning is, that by force of the light of reason, wherewith God illuminateth every one which cometh into the world, men being enabled to know truth from falsehood, and good from evil, do thereby learn in many things what the will of God is; which will himself not revealing by any extraordinary means unto them, but they by natural discourse attaining the knowledge thereof, seem the makers of those laws which indeed are his, and they but only the finders of them out.

Hooker *Of the Laws of Ecclesiastical Polity* I viii

39   Further evidence for the existence of God is provided by the phenomenon of conscience, or right reason. This cannot be altogether asleep, even in the most evil men. If there were no God, there would be no dividing line between right and wrong. What was to be called virtue, and what vice, would depend upon mere arbitrary opinion. No one would try to be virtuous, no one would refrain from sin because he felt ashamed of it or feared the law, if the voice of conscience or right reason did not speak from time to time in the heart of every man, reminding him, however unwilling he may be to remember it, that a God does exist, that he rules and governs all things, and that everyone must one day render to him an account of his actions, good and bad alike.

Milton *Christian Doctrine* I ii

40   Abdiel rebukes Satan:
Unjustly thou deprav'st it with the name

Of servitude to serve whom God ordains,
Or nature; God and nature bid the same,
When he who rules is worthiest, and excels
Them whom he governs. This is servitude,
To serve the unwise, or him who hath rebelled
Against his worthier, as thine now serve thee,
Thy self not free, but to thy self enthralled.

Paradise Lost VI ll. 174–81

41 Michael to Adam:
                    Yet know withal,
Since thy original lapse, true liberty
Is lost, which always with right reason dwells
Twinned, and from her hath no dividual being:
Reason in man obscured, or not obeyed,
Immediately inordinate desires
And upstart passions catch the government
From reason, and to servitude reduce
Man till then free. Therefore since he permits
Within himself unworthy powers to reign
Over free reason, God in judgement just
Subjects him from without to violent lords.

Paradise Lost XII ll. 82–93

9 Humanism

The word 'humanism', used first in the nineteenth century, has acquired such a wide range of potential meanings and is often applied so carelessly that it has lost much of its original force. Its broad current meaning is a view of life which displaces God and puts man at the centre. The expression 'Renaissance humanism' needs to be used much more precisely if it is to have any value. Although 'humanism' was not a word current during the Renaissance, 'humanist' was. 'Humanist' is an anglicisation of the Italian *umanista*, meaning a Latin teacher, which in turn ultimately derives from Cicero's use of the word *humanitas*. The Latin *humanitas* (1) has a double meaning: first, mankind in a general sense (hence our word 'humanity'), second, as a translation of the Greek παιδεία (*paideia*), culture or liberal education which fully develops a man (this sense survives in the modern term 'humanities'). Renaissance humanism was primarily an educational movement which began in Italy in the early fourteenth century and reached England at the end of the fifteenth. A humanist was a classical scholar with two complementary aims: to recover the moral values of classical life, and to imitate the language and style of the classics as a means to that end. He hoped to unite wisdom (*sapientia*) and eloquence (*eloquentia*).

Cicero was the hero of the humanists for a variety of reasons (13, 14). As politician, orator and moralist he combined action and contemplation, public and private life, and hence was himself a model of the complete man. His literary style was for the humanists the embodiment of eloquence. His philosophical works, especially *Of Duties* (probably the most widely read classical work in the Renaissance), gave the humanists their ethics, while his rhetorical works, especially *On the Orator*, gave them their educational theory and in effect defined their role. Two rival systems of education coexisted in classical and Hellenistic Greece: the philosophical, going back to Plato, which provided a specialised and difficult intellectual training in mathematics, logic and metaphysics, and the rhetorical, going back to Isocrates, which was primarily literary in emphasis, taught the art of declamation, and prepared men for political life. In the Hellenistic world the emphasis was on rhetorical training, often conceived very narrowly. This was the kind of education that the Romans borrowed from the Greeks: it provided men with the skills necessary for success in public life, whether politics or the law courts. Cicero, who had experience of both kinds of Greek education, tried to bring them closer together and to transmit both traditions to Rome. In his philosophical works, such as *Tusculan Disputations*, *On the Nature of the Gods*, and *Of Duties*, Cicero paraphrased and popularised Greek moral philosophy and theology, while in his rhetorical works, such as *On the Orator* and *The Orator*, he adapted Greek rhetorical methods for Romans, at the same time attempting to widen the meaning of oratory (3). Cicero believed that the two kinds of education could not be separated without damage to both (4). Philosophy without oratory is sterile, while oratory without philosophy is dangerous. Eloquence and wisdom belong together. Yet in spite of this belief Cicero belongs ultimately in the camp of the rhetoricians. He has little interest in logical argument or philosophical problems for their own sake. For Cicero philosophy really means ethics, defining how men should behave, while oratory means persuading men to behave in the ways defined by ethics. The orator must himself be a good man. (This formulation was elaborated by Quintilian in *The Education of an Orator* [5, 6], and was repeatedly taken up in the Renaissance [21].) This belief in the moral and utilitarian function of education and in the social and political obligations of the man of letters (7) makes Cicero the heir of Isocrates and of the rhetorical tradition and the father of humanism.

In the medieval period the conflict between philosophy and rhetoric continued, now one and now the other dominating the educational system. The trivium (grammar, rhetoric and logic), the first part of the medieval system of the seven liberal arts, perpetuated both the classical literary and rhetorical tradition and the philosophical tradition that was temporarily to overthrow it in the thirteenth century. In France in the ninth and again in the early twelfth centuries we find the elements of humanism: the copying and reading of Latin poetry, philosophy and oratory. John of Salisbury, who studied at Chartres in the mid-twelfth century, had an enormous knowledge of available Latin literature. Yet this humanism was displaced late in the twelfth century and in the thirteenth by the increasing importance of the study of logic. In the thirteenth-century universities the arts course was a preliminary to the queen of the sciences, theology. In the intellectual system known as scholasticism which dominated medieval education, theology was joined with the more technical and abstract branches of philosophy – logic, epistemology and metaphysics. The principal classical author studied was Aristotle (the complete corpus of whose works was made available in translation via Arabic and directly from Greek by the end of the thirteenth century), but Aristotle the logician was given primacy over Aristotle the political theorist and rhetorician. To the schoolmen (as the later humanists disparagingly called the scholastic theologians) Aristotle was 'the Philosopher'; when the humanists attacked Aristotle it was the scholastic application of his work that they had in mind. Following a three-fold method of question, argument and conclusion (as exemplified in what was to be the most influential of scholastic works in succeeding centuries, the *Summa Theologiae* of Thomas Aquinas), scholastic writing ignored the rhetorical techniques of persuasion in favour of logical disputation.

It was against this abstract, rigorous and technical educational system, combining philosophy and theology, that the humanists rebelled. The beginnings of Renaissance humanism have been detected in Italy in the late thirteenth century, but the chief spokesman for the new attitudes was Petrarch in the mid-fourteenth century. Although Petrarch had much less access to classical literature than later humanists, and although he could not read Greek, nevertheless he established the principles and prepared the way for the development of humanism. The international language of learning in the West throughout the Middle Ages was Latin; it was a living, growing language, which had developed a sophisticated philosophical vocabulary. Petrarch repudiated medieval, scholastic Latin, and demanded a return to classical Latin, the language of Virgil and Horace in poetry and Cicero in prose, a language unable to accommodate medieval philosophy. For Petrarch medieval Europe had lost the values with the language and literature of the classical world, and he led the humanist attempt to revive them. The first step was to recover the texts of classical authors and to reintroduce the study of Greek in the West. Although humanists tended to exaggerate the extent to which classical literature was 'lost' during the medieval period (for if medieval monks had not copied classical manuscripts they would not have survived), nevertheless many important works ignored for hundreds of years were put into circulation again – for example, Aristotle's *Poetics* (available in Latin in the thirteenth century but not taught), Livy, Tacitus and the complete text of Quintilian. Knowledge of Greek established itself slowly during the fifteenth century, and reached its height with Ficino's translation of Plato and Plotinus into Latin. The invention of printing towards the end of the fifteenth century greatly helped the humanists in their task of disseminating classical literature, and some printers, for example Aldus Manutius of Venice, were themselves classical scholars. By the early sixteenth century the major Latin and Greek works of oratory, history, political and moral philosophy and poetry had been put into print by the humanists. Whereas scholasticism had developed in universities and had been the province of ecclesiastics, humanism was fostered by courts and princes. Logic, the art of disputation, had been the weapon of the schoolmen; rhetoric, the art of persuasion, was the weapon of the new class of humanist administrators. Learning, the humanists believed, must not be divorced from public life; the humanist regarded himself as a public servant. In this sense humanism can be regarded as a secularisation of learning.

But humanism was not at all an unchristian movement, although humanists (with important exceptions, such as the Florentine Neo-platonists) were on the whole indifferent to theology. Early Christian Fathers such as Jerome and Augustine had been ambivalent in their attitude to classical letters and the rhetorical tradition: in his famous Epistle 22 Jerome recounts the dream in which he is accused at the Judgement of being a Ciceronian, not a Christian, yet in Epistle 70 he defends the Christian use of classical learning with the biblical example of the taking of a captive wife (Deut. 21:10–13). Most humanists, beginning with Petrarch, attempted to harmonise classical ethics with the practical Christianity of the gospels (**13**). This Christian humanism flourished particularly in northern Europe, and the Dutch humanist Erasmus was its chief exponent. Erasmus, who was fond of referring to the schoolmen as 'barbarians', attacked scholasticism for its intellectu-alism, its method and its (to him) bad Latin. Christianity was for him a matter of conduct not of speculation, and he believed the pagan moralists, especially Cicero (**14**), to be closer to Christ than the scholastic theologians. The *philosophia Christi* (philosophy of Christ) that he taught was supported by the classics and the early Fathers, especially Jerome. Erasmus' radical act was to apply to the Scriptures the critical textual and philological methods the Italian humanists had been applying to classical literature. In 1516 he published the first edition of the New Testament in Greek, with a Latin translation that corrected the errors in the Vulgate. Erasmus saw himself above all as an educator in the Ciceronian sense: the pursuit of *bonae litterae* – 'good letters', otherwise known as 'the new learning' (the study of classical Latin and Greek, with Hebrew in addition) – would lead to the practice of the philosophy of Christ.

Erasmus, together with the younger Spanish humanist Vives, was the formative influence in the development of English humanism. English-men had travelled to Italy in the fifteenth century and taken an interest in Italian humanist scholarship, but the first important generation of English humanists was that of Colet and More in the early years of the reign of Henry VIII. Indeed the beginnings of English humanism can be dated from 1497 when Colet (who had studied in Italy and come under the influence of Ficino and Pico) began to lecture on St Paul's Epistles, applying the new critical methods without reference to scholastic commentaries. Erasmus, who formed the chief link between Italian and northern humanism by maintaining an enormous correspondence with fellow humanists and working in different humanist centres throughout Europe, paid three visits to England, the most important being from 1509 to 1514 on the accession of Henry VIII. Erasmus influenced three aspects of English humanism, educational, religious and political. Colet's foundation of the first English humanist school, St Paul's, in 1510 was the direct result of Erasmus' educational principles: dedicated to the child Jesus, the school aimed to lead its pupils through good letters to the good life (**15**). Erasmus' attacks on scholastic theology, monasticism and abuses in the church helped prepare the way for the English Reformation, though Erasmus himself was not a Protestant reformer (see Chapter 7). In addition, Erasmus helped to strengthen the orientation of English humanists towards the court and public life. Humanists, who had many enemies in the universities, looked to the courts for patronage; the accession of three new princes in the early sixteenth century, Henry VIII in 1509, Francis I of France in 1515, and the Emperor Charles V in 1518 seemed at first like a golden age for the new learning. In 1516 Erasmus was appointed a councillor to Charles, and addressed to him *The Education of a Christian Prince*, a handbook of political and moral behaviour which belongs in an old tradition of 'princes' mirrors' going back to Isocrates' *To Nicocles* (**9**). The English work following this tradition most closely is Sir Thomas Elyot's *Book named the Governor* (**16**). The humanists were anxious to educate a new generation of courtiers and politicians who would in turn mould their princes according to the humanist pattern. This idealism was to be severely tested in the course of the century. One of the important questions raised in Sir Thomas More's *Utopia* (1516) is whether the man of letters has any obligation to serve the prince, who is unlikely to follow his advice (**12**).

By the end of the sixteenth century the humanists had effected important changes in education. The universities were slow to respond (Milton was complaining about the scholastic curriculum at Cambridge in the 1620s), but several schools were established on humanist principles. Spenser at Merchant Taylors' under Mulcaster, Jonson at Westminster under Camden, Milton at St Paul's under Gill, all received a humanist training. The gentry were taking an increasing interest in education, and in this they were following court example. The three children of Henry VIII were themselves taught by notable humanists – Mary by Vives, Elizabeth by Ascham, Edward by Cheke.

Although humanism did not imply adherence to any particular philosophical or ethical system, nevertheless we can distinguish certain key concepts. The first is imitation (**19**). Humanist educators taught their pupils to imitate closely the style and language of classical authors – the method is described in Ascham's *The Schoolmaster* (**17**). At its worst this was an absurd and stultifying exercise (satirised in Erasmus' *Ciceronianus*), divorcing style and content; at its best imitation meant taking as a pattern not only the style but also the attitudes and conduct of the chosen model. The second concept is pragmatism. The humanists disapproved of abstract, theoretical knowledge; they valued knowledge as it could be used to promote the good life. They believed optimistically that education makes men better; Vives, Bacon and Milton (**18**) all express in different ways the view that education removes the consequences of the fall and restores man, a rational and fully developed creature, to his Creator. The humanists valued highly those classical ethical works, such as Aristotle's *Nicomachean Ethics* and Cicero's *Of Duties*, that represent man as a political being who perfects himself in society (Elyot's *Governor*, borrowing from *Of Duties* I, provided the earliest English account of the four classical cardinal virtues, justice, prudence, temperance and fortitude). The third key-concept of the humanists is duty. Plato's portrait of the education of the philosopher-king in *The Republic* V–VII tantalised the humanists: on the one hand it was an unattainable ideal, on the other hand it was an ideal that must be attempted. Hence the fascination of the relationship between philosophers or men of letters and rulers: Plato and Dionysius (**12**), Aristotle and Alexander, Plutarch and Trajan (though the last was not historical). Erasmus' relationship with Charles V and More's with Henry VIII were consciously in this tradition. Yet the humanist obligation to public service implied the acquiescence of the prince in his moral education, and princes were not so pliable. More's execution by Henry VIII in 1535 for refusing to compromise his 'good counsel' epitomises the tragic tensions inherent in humanism. Because of this tension the humanists felt strongly the temptation of the retired, contemplative life, of Horace's *otium* (leisure) as against Cicero's *negotium* (business); the garden often seemed a more fitting symbolic setting for the pursuit of wisdom than the court.

Although the humanists were above all concerned with classical literature, and although the international language of scholarship remained Latin (paradoxically, humanist insistence on Latin purity helped to render it a dead language), nevertheless humanist educational methods and attitudes had a profound effect on vernacular literature. One of the significant humanist achievements was to make the major works of classical literature available in English translation by the early seventeenth century: Shakespeare is the most obvious beneficiary. Humanism influenced the organisation of prose works: because of humanist distrust of abstract logical argument, digressive and anecdotal forms filled with moral examples were favoured, such as essays, dialogues, biography and history. Bacon's *Essays* and Greville's *Life of*

Sir Philip Sidney are examples. In addition, humanist educational methods affected the way poetry was written: thus Jonson told William Drummond that his master Camden taught him to write his poetry first as prose, and many of his poems are imitations, schoolboy exercises transformed. However, the most important influence was on the way the poet's role was conceived. Cicero's and Quintilian's portrait of the ideal orator underlay the humanist portrait of the ideal poet. Spenser in the letter to Ralegh defined the rhetorical purpose of *The Faerie Queene* as 'to fashion a gentleman or noble person in virtuous and gentle discipline' (Ch. **12.11**); on one level, the poem is a humanist handbook. Jonson, whose notebook *Discoveries* (**11, 21**) draws on Quintilian's *The Education of an Orator* (**5**) and Vives' *The Transmission of Knowledge* (**10**), succeeded best in realising humanist poetic theory. In this view the poem is an act of persuasion. The intention underlying Renaissance poems in praise of individuals (which may seem to modern readers very like flattery) is to provide their subjects with ideal portraits which they are encouraged to imitate and which will in turn make them worthy patterns for imitation; the poet offers the promise of fame as a reward. However, the humanist view of poetry needed a prince, a court and an agreed audience. We can see the conflict between the views of the poet as orator and the poet as prophet in Milton. Milton's pamphlet *Of Education* (**18**) is a humanist handbook in the tradition of Elyot, Ascham and Jonson, and in his early political works Milton perhaps accepted too easily the humanist assumption that the poet can persuade his audience to virtuous action, that his good counsel will be profitable. Milton's career can be interpreted in part as a search for the fit audience, and a testing of the roles of the orator, who must be heard for his speech to have meaning, and the prophet, who can speak the truth regardless of hearers.

'HUMANITAS'

1   Those who have spoken Latin and have used the language correctly do not give to the word *humanitas* the meaning which it is commonly thought to have, namely, what the Greeks call φιλανθρωπία [*philanthropia*], signifying a kind of friendly spirit and good-feeling towards all men without distinction; but they gave to *humanitas* about the force of the Greek παιδεία [*paideia*]; that is, what we call ... 'education and training in the liberal arts'. Those who earnestly desire and seek after these are most highly humanised. For the pursuit of that kind of knowledge, and the training given by it, have been granted to man alone of all the animals, and for that reason it is termed *humanitas*, or 'humanity'.

Aulus Gellius *The Attic Nights* XIII xvii

CLASSICAL DEFINITIONS OF RHETORIC AND THE ROLE OF THE
ORATOR

2   Rhetoric then may be defined as the faculty of discovering the possible
means of persuasion in reference to any subject whatever. This is the
function of no other of the arts, each of which is able to instruct and
persuade in its own special subject; thus, medicine deals with health and
sickness, geometry with the properties of magnitudes, arithmetic with
number, and similarly with all the other arts and sciences. But Rhetoric,
so to say, appears to be able to discover the means of persuasion in
reference to any given subject ... It is evident that, to be able to grasp [the
proofs of rhetoric], a man must be capable of logical reasoning, of
studying characters and the virtues, and thirdly the emotions – the nature
and character of each, its origin, and the manner in which it is produced.
Thus it appears that Rhetoric is as it were an offshoot of Dialectic and of
the science of Ethics, which may be reasonably called Politics.

Aristotle *Rhetoric* I ii

3   'Moreover,' [Crassus] continued, 'there is to my mind no more excellent
thing than the power, by means of oratory, to get a hold on assemblies
of men, win their good will, direct their inclinations wherever the speaker
wishes, or divert them from whatever he wishes. In every free nation, and
most of all in communities which have attained the enjoyment of peace
and tranquillity, this one art has always flourished above the rest and ever
reigned supreme. For what is so marvellous as that, out of the
innumerable company of mankind, a single being should arise, who
either alone or with a few others can make effective a faculty bestowed
by nature upon every man? ... For the one point in which we have our
very greatest advantage over the brute creation is that we hold converse
one with another, and can reproduce our thought in word ... To come,
however, at length to the highest achievements of eloquence, what other
power could have been strong enough either to gather scattered humanity
into one place, or to lead it out of its brutish existence in the wilderness
up to our present condition of civilisation as men and as citizens, or, after
the establishment of social communities, to give shape to laws, tribunals,
and civic rights? ... My assertion is this: that the wise control of the
complete orator is that which chiefly upholds not only his own dignity,
but the safety of countless individuals and of the entire State.'

Cicero *On the Orator* I viii

4   The older masters down to Socrates used to combine with their theory of
rhetoric the whole of the study and the science of everything that
concerns morals and conduct and ethics and politics; it was subsequently
... that the two groups of students were separated from one another, by
Socrates and then similarly by all the Socratic schools, and the
philosophers looked down on eloquence and the orators on wisdom, and
never touched anything from the side of the other study except what this
group borrowed from that one, or that one from this; whereas they would

have drawn from the common supply indifferently if they had been willing to remain in the partnership of early days.

On the Orator III xix

5   My aim, then, is the education of the perfect orator. The first essential for such a one is that he should be a good man, and consequently we demand of him not merely the possession of exceptional gifts of speech, but of all the excellences of character as well. For I will not admit that the principles of upright and honourable living should, as some have held, be regarded as the peculiar concern of philosophy. The man who can really play his part as a citizen and is capable of meeting the demands both of public and private business, the man who can guide a state by his counsels, give it a firm basis by his legislation and purge its vices by his decisions as a judge, is assuredly no other than the orator of our quest.

Quintilian *The Education of an Orator* I
Preface (compare **21**)

6   Cicero in several of his books and letters proclaims that eloquence has its fountain-head in the most secret springs of wisdom, and that consequently for a considerable time the instructors of morals and of eloquence were identical.... This exhortation of mine must not be taken to mean that I wish the orator to be a philosopher, since there is no other way of life that is further removed from the duties of a statesman and the tasks of an orator. For what philosopher has ever been a frequent speaker in the courts or won renown in public assemblies? Nay, what philosopher has ever taken a prominent part in the government of the state, which forms the most frequent theme of their instructions? None the less I desire that he, whose character I am seeking to mould, should be a 'wise man' in the Roman sense, that is, one who reveals himself as a true statesman, not in the discussions of the study, but in the actual practice and experience of life ...

The orator's duty is not merely to instruct, but also to move and delight his audience; and to succeed in doing this he needs a strength, impetuosity, and grace as well.

Education of an Orator XII ii

PUBLIC AND PRIVATE LIFE

7   There have been many and still are many who, while pursuing that calm of soul of which I speak, have withdrawn from civic duty and taken refuge in retirement. Among such have been found the most famous and by far the foremost philosophers and certain other earnest, thoughtful men who could not endure the conduct of either the people or their leaders; some of them, too, lived in the country and found their pleasure in the management of their private estates. Such men have had the same aims as kings – to suffer no want, to be subject to no authority, to enjoy their liberty, that is, in its essence, to live just as they please.... Perhaps

those men of extraordinary genius who have devoted themselves to learning must be excused for not taking part in public affairs; likewise, those who from ill-health or for some still more valid reason have retired from the service of the state and left to others the opportunity and the glory of its administration. But if those who have no such excuse profess a scorn for civil and military offices, which most people admire, I think that this should be set down not to their credit but to their discredit; for in so far as they care little, as they say, for glory and count it as naught, it is difficult not to sympathise with their attitude; in reality, however, they seem to dread the toil and trouble and also, perhaps, the discredit and humiliation of political failure and defeat ... Those whom Nature has endowed with the capacity for administering public affairs should put aside all hesitation, enter the race for public office, and take a hand in directing the government; for in no other way can a government be administered or greatness of spirit be made manifest.

Cicero *Of Duties* I xx–xxi

8   I regard as perfect, so far as men can be, those who are able to combine and mingle political capacity with philosophy; and I am inclined to think that these are secure in the possession of two things which are of the greatest good: a life useful to the world in their public position, and the calm and untroubled life in their pursuit of philosophy. For there are three forms of life, of which the first is the practical life, the second the contemplative life, and the third the life of enjoyment. The last, which is dissolute and enslaved to pleasure, is bestial and mean, but the contemplative life, which falls short in practice, is not useful, while the practical life, which has no portion in philosophy, is without culture or taste. One must try, then, as well as one can, both to take part in public life, and to lay hold of philosophy so far as the opportunity is granted.

Plutarch (?) *The Education of Children* viii

'GOOD COUNSEL'

9   Now as to each particular course of action, it is the business of those who are at the time associated with a king to advise him how he may handle it in the best way possible, and how he may both preserve what is good and prevent disaster; but as regards a king's conduct in general, I shall attempt to set forth the objects at which he should aim and the pursuits to which he should devote himself. Whether the gift when finished shall be worthy of the design, it is hard to tell at the beginning ... And yet the mere attempt is well worth while – to seek a field that has been neglected by others and lay down principles for monarchs; for those who educate men in private stations benefit them alone, but if one can turn those who rule over the multitude toward a life of virtue, he will help both classes, both those who hold positions of authority and their subjects; for he will give to kings a greater security in office and to the people a milder government.

Isocrates *To Nicocles* 6–8

10   You also understand how great is the similarity of gifts in princes and
learned men, so that these are not two different kinds of men, but they
are rather such as should be more friendly to each other and more closely
joined than they are. The one is made strong by the other; they are as it
were mutual helps. Both are given by God to states and peoples, that they
may have wise regard for the common good of the state; the learned by
their precepts; princes by their edicts and laws; both by their examples.
Learning requires freedom and leisure. This can be given by the royal
power. In return, princely power will receive counsel in dealing with the
difficult matters of business.

Vives *The Transmission of Knowledge* Dedicatory
Address to King John III of Portugal

11   Learning needs rest: sovereignty gives it. Sovereignty needs counsel:
learning affords it. There is such a consocation of offices, between the
prince, and whom his favour breeds, that they may help to sustain his
power, as he their knowledge ... A prince without letters, is a pilot
without eyes. All his government is groping ... The good counsellors to
princes are the best instruments of a good age. For though the prince
himself be of most prompt inclination to all virtue: yet the best pilots have
need of mariners.

Jonson *Discoveries* ll. 81–6, 1525–6, 1539–43

12   More addresses Raphael Hythloday:
'I must needs believe that you, if you be disposed and can find in your
heart to follow some prince's court, shall with your good counsels greatly
help and further the commonwealth. Wherefore there is nothing more
appertaining to your duty, that is to say to the duty of a good man. For
whereas your Plato judgeth that weal-publics shall by this means attain
perfect felicity, either if philosophers be kings, or else if kings give
themselves to the study of philosophy, how far, I pray you, shall
commonwealths then be from this felicity, if philosophers will vouchsafe
to instruct kings with their good counsel?'
'They be not so unkind,' quoth [Raphael], 'but they would gladly do
it, yea, many have done it already in books that they have put forth, if
kings and princes would be willing and ready to follow good counsel. But
Plato doubtless did well foresee, unless kings themselves would apply
their minds to the study of philosophy, that else they would never
thoroughly allow the counsel of philosophers, being themselves before,
even from their tender age, infected and corrupt with perverse and evil
opinions. Which thing Plato himself proved true in King Dionysius. If I
should propose to any king wholesome decrees, doing my endeavour to
pluck out of his mind the pernicious original causes of vice and
naughtiness, think you not that I should forthwith either be driven away
or else made a laughing-stock?'

More *Utopia* I

THE HUMANISTS' CICERO

13   I do not deny that I am delighted with Cicero's genius and eloquence, seeing that even Jerome – to omit countless others – was so fascinated by him that he could not free his own style from that of Cicero, not even under the pressure of the terrible vision [Epistle 22] ... If to admire Cicero means to be a Ciceronian, I am a Ciceronian. I admire him so much that I wonder at people who do not admire him ... However, when we come to think or speak of religion, that is, of supreme truth and true happiness, and of eternal salvation, then I am certainly not a Ciceronian, or a Platonist, but a Christian. I even feel sure that Cicero himself would have been a Christian if he had been able to see Christ and to comprehend his doctrine.

Petrarch *On his Own Ignorance and That of Many Others*

14   Perhaps the spirit of Christ is more widespread than we understand, and the company of saints includes many not in our calendar. Speaking frankly among friends, I can't read Cicero's *Of Old Age*, *Of Friendship*, *Of Duties*, *Tusculan Disputations* without sometimes kissing the book and blessing that pure heart, divinely inspired as it was.

Erasmus *The Godly Feast*

HUMANIST EDUCATIONAL THEORY

15   I would there were taught always the good literature, both Latin and Greek, and good authors such as have the very Roman eloquence joined with wisdom, specially Christian authors that wrote their wisdom with clean and chaste Latin, other in verse or in prose; for my intent is by this school specially to increase knowledge and worshipping of God and Our Lord Christ Jesu and good Christian life and manners in the children ... All barbary, all corruption, all Latin adulterate which ignorant blind fools brought into this world, and with that same hath disdained and poisoned the old Latin speech ... I say that filthiness and all such abusion which ... more rather may be called blotterature than literature, I utterly abanish and exclude out of this school and charge the masters that they teach always that is the best, and instruct the children in Greek and Latin in reading unto them such authors that hath with wisdom joined the pure chaste eloquence.

Colet *Statutes of Paul's School* 'What Shall Be Taught'

16   By the time that the child do come to seventeen years of age, to the intent his courage be bridled with reason, it were needful to read unto him some works of philosophy; specially that part that may inform him unto virtuous manners, which part of philosophy is called moral. Wherefore there would be read to him, for an introduction, two the first books of the work of Aristotle called *Ethicae*, wherein is contained the definitions and proper significations of every virtue; and that to be learned in Greek ...

Forthwith would follow the work of Cicero, called in Latin *De officiis*, whereunto yet is no proper English word to be given; but to provide for it some manner of exposition, it may be said in this form: 'Of the duties and manners appertaining to men.' But above all other, the works of Plato would be most studiously read when the judgement of a man is come to perfection, and by the other studies is instructed in the form of speaking that philosophers used. Lord God, what incomparable sweetness of words and matter shall he find in the said works of Plato and Cicero; wherein is joined gravity with delectation, excellent wisdom with divine eloquence, absolute virtue with pleasure incredible, and every place is so enfarced [stuffed] with profitable counsel joined with honesty, that those three books be almost sufficient to make a perfect and excellent governor.

Elyot The Governor I xi

17   Ye know not what hurt ye do to learning that care not for words but for matter and so make a divorce betwixt the tongue and the heart. For mark all ages, look upon the whole course of both the Greek and Latin tongue, and ye shall surely find that when apt and good words began to be neglected and properties of those two tongues to be confounded, then also began ill deeds to spring, strange manners to oppress good orders, new and fond opinions to strive with old and true doctrine, first in philosophy and after in religion, right judgement of all things to be perverted, and so virtue with learning is contemned and study left off.

Ascham The Schoolmaster II

18   The end then of learning is to repair the ruins of our first parents by regaining to know God aright, and out of that knowledge to love him, to imitate him, to be like him, as we may the nearest by possessing our souls of true virtue, which being united to the heavenly grace of faith makes up the highest perfection.

. . . . . .

I call therefore a complete and generous education that which fits a man to perform justly, skilfully and magnanimously all the offices both private and public of peace and war.

Milton Of Education (see also Prolusion III
'An Attack on the Scholastic Philosophy')

IMITATION

19   I know nothing can conduce more to letters, than to examine the writings of the ancients, and not to rest in their sole authority, or take all upon trust from them . . . For to all the observations of the ancients, we have our own experience: which, if we will use, and apply, we have better means to pronounce. It is true they opened the gates, and made the way, that went before us; but as guides, not commanders.

. . . . . .

The third requisite in our poet, or maker [after natural wit and exercise] is imitation, to be able to convert the substance, or riches of another poet, to his own use. To make choice of one excellent man above the rest, and so to follow him, till he grow very he: or, so like him, as the copy may be mistaken for the principal. Not, as a creature, that swallows, what it takes in, crude, raw, or indigested; but, that feeds with an appetite, and hath a stomach to concoct, divide, and turn all into nourishment.

Jonson *Discoveries* ll. 160–3, 166–71, 3056–65

HUMANIST POETICS

20   O blessed letters that combine in one
    All ages past, and make one live with all,
    By you we do confer with who are gone,
    And the dead living unto counsel call:
    By you the unborn shall have communion
    Of what we feel, and what doth us befall.
Soul of the world, knowledge, without thee,
    What hath the earth that truly glorious is?
    Why should our pride make such a stir to be,
    To be forgot? what good is like to this,
    To do worthy the writing, and to write
    Worthy the reading, and the world's delight?
    . . . . .
Power above powers, O heavenly eloquence,
    That with the strong rein of commanding words,
    Dost manage, guide, and master the eminence
    Of men's affections, more than all their swords:
    Shall we not offer to thy excellence
    The richest treasure that our wit affords?
Thou that canst do much more with one poor pen
    Than all the powers of princes can effect:
    And draw, divert, dispose, and fashion men
    Better than force or rigour can direct:
    Should we this ornament of glory then
    As the unmaterial fruits of shades, neglect?

Daniel *Musophilus* ll. 189–200, 939–50

21   I could never think the study of wisdom confined only to the philosopher: or of piety to the divine: or of state to the politic. But that he which can feign a commonwealth (which is the poet), can govern it with counsels, strengthen it with laws, correct it with judgements, inform it with religion, and morals; is all these. We do not require in him mere elocution; or an excellent faculty in verse; but the exact knowledge of all virtues, and their contraries; with ability to render the one loved, the other hated, by his proper embattling them . . .

The poet is the nearest borderer upon the orator, and expresseth all his virtues, though he be tied more to numbers; is his equal in ornament, and above him in his strengths.

> Jonson *Discoveries* ll. 1273–85, 3129–33 (compare **5**)

22   When the sword glitters o'er the judge's head,
And fear has coward churchmen silencèd,
Then is the poet's time, 'tis then he draws,
And single fights forsaken virtue's cause.
He, when the wheel of empire whirleth back,
And though the world's disjointed axle crack,
Sings still of ancient rights and better times,
Seeks wretched good, arraigns successful crimes.

> Marvell 'Tom May's Death' ll. 63–70 (May is rebuked
> in Elysium by the ghost of Jonson)

10 Biblical Exegesis and Typology

Biblical exegesis – the interpretation of the Bible – developed in different ways over the centuries as the Church came to terms with different problems, but ultimately it derives from the way the New Testament writers, particularly Paul, interpreted the Old Testament. Paul believed not only that the direct prophecies of the Messiah in the Old Testament were fulfilled in Christ, but that many of the events and persons and things of the Old Testament prefigure the life and teaching of Christ, even though this prefiguration was unknown to the characters of Old Testament history and the writers of the Old Testament books. Thus the Old Testament, though ostensibly a work of Jewish history and Jewish law, is really a Christian book, whose meaning is only revealed in the light of the events recorded in the New Testament. This idea is explained several times in Paul's Epistles, perhaps the most important sources being I and II Corinthians. For Christians, because of the gift of the gospel, the word of God is no longer veiled, as it was when Moses gave the Tables of the Law to the Israelites (Ch. **12.1**). In his mission to the gentiles Paul argued that Judaism was only a stepping-stone to Christianity, and that Jewish adherence to the letter of the law was blindness. 'The letter killeth, but the spirit giveth life' (II Cor. 3:6). 'But even unto this day, when Moses is read, the veil is upon their heart. Nevertheless when it shall turn to the Lord the veil shall be taken away' (II Cor. 3:15–16). The Epistle to the Hebrews (although not written by Paul) works out at length this relation between the two testaments.

This way of reading the Old Testament in terms of the New, which was developed by later Christian authors far beyond Paul's own practice, is known as typology. The word derives from the Greek τύπος (*typos*); the Latin equivalent is *figura*. Several English synonyms were in use in the sixteenth and seventeenth centuries: type, figure, sign, example (or ensample), shadow, foreshadowing, adumbration, similitude. (There is a problem for modern readers in that 'shadow' is sometimes used with a Platonic rather than a typological meaning.) A type is a person or event or thing in the Old Testament which prefigures a person or event or thing in the New Testament; the latter is the antitype. Type and antitype have a relationship in time: the antitype once and for all fulfils the type and reveals the meaning hidden in it. A type is not the same as a symbol (though in practice many Renaissance authors extended the term to include symbol – see Introduction **3**); thus light may be a symbol of God, or sunrise and spring may be symbols of the resurrection, but they are not properly speaking types. These are simple examples of types and antitypes: Jonah escaped from the whale's belly after three days; Christ rose from the dead on the third day (**1**). The Israelites were in the desert forty years; Christ fasted in the desert forty days. Moses struck the rock and water flowed; Christ's side was pierced and blood and water flowed (**3**). (Literal and spiritual refreshment are contrasted here.) Moses lifted up a brass serpent on a pole; Christ was lifted on the cross (**2**). Adam brought death into the world; the second Adam, Christ, brought life (Ch. **8.6**).

The early Christian Fathers worked out much more elaborate types and antitypes than are to be found in the New Testament. Just as Paul had spiritualised the Old Testament in his fight against Judaism, so the Fathers used the same method in their fight against rival religions: Judaism, paganism, Gnosticism, Manichaeism. They were partly concerned to counter any moral difficulties presented by aspects of the Old Testament story that might leave Christianity open to criticism. Augustine gives a detailed typological reading of Old Testament history in Books XV to XVII of *The City of God*. Sometimes well-established types are developed further; for example, the typology of Noah and the Flood which underlies the Epistles of Peter (Noah is a type of Christ, the Flood a type of baptism) is worked out in extraordinary detail by Augustine (*City of God* XV xxvi–vii): the ark is a type of the Church, and every aspect of its structure has typological significance. Sometimes new types are suggested; for example, Joshua, who was insignificant in earlier typology, becomes a type of Jesus in Origen's *Homily on Joshua*, because of his name and because unlike Moses he succeeded in reaching the Promised Land (**16**). The crossing of the Red Sea had for a long time been a type of baptism; Origen in his *Commentary on St John* similarly interpreted the crossing of the Jordan.

Both type and antitype have a historical existence. Typology implies a view of history as progressive revelation; the meaning of God's acts in the past becomes known through his acts in the present and future. However, this kind of historically based interpretation of the relation between the Old and New Testaments coexisted with another tradition, that of allegory (see Chapter 12): the Pentateuch (the five books of Moses) was allegorised by Philo, an Alexandrian Jew who lived at the time of Christ, in a series of works called *The Exposition of the Law*. Philo drew on the tradition of Greek allegory, developed from the fourth century BC particularly by the Stoics, through which Greek myth and literature could be defended against charges of immorality and made to reveal hidden meanings (see Chapter 2). Philo was not interested in history; he was interested in the timeless moral and philosophical meaning he could extract from a seemingly straightforward narrative. There is not much of this kind of allegorical interpretation in the New Testament, though there is a striking example in Galatians 4:21–31. Here Paul interprets the two sons of Abraham, Ishmael the son of the bondwoman Hagar, and Isaac the son of the freewoman Sarah, as allegories of law and gospel, Judaism and Christianity.

Philo's methods were taken up in the third century by the Christian Platonists of Alexandria, Clement and Origen, who were interested in bringing Christianity closer to Greek philosophy, and who wished to penetrate the shell of the scriptural text in order to reveal its kernel of meaning. This was to give a different weight to Paul's antithesis of letter and spirit. The emphasis was now not so much on the old and new covenants, on law and gospel (see Chapter 8), but on the literal (comparatively restricted and unimportant) meaning of the text, and the hidden spiritual meaning. The historical importance of the Old Testament was thus frequently undermined. Origen's exegetical method was sometimes twofold – the literal and the spiritual, and sometimes threefold – the literal, the moral and the spiritual. The literal was the least important level of meaning. Origen's *Commentary on the Song of Songs* (or Canticles), in which an erotic poem is allegorised as the yearning of the soul for God or of the Church for Christ, is an example of this kind of exegesis.

Although often criticised, this Alexandrian tradition of allegorical interpretation was extremely influential. In *Christian Instruction* Augustine provides general rules for allegorical interpretation (III x): 'In general, that method is to understand as figurative anything in Holy Scripture which cannot in a literal sense be attributed either to an upright character or to a pure faith.' Since 'Scripture commands only charity, and censures only lust', a passage of Scripture which does neither of these must be read allegorically (e.g. **4, 5**). Unlike Origen, Augustine did not undervalue the historical, literal meaning of Scripture, but he allowed that a passage could have several interpretations.

Thus typological and allegorical interpretation existed side by side. By the fifth century we find the beginnings of the fourfold exegetical method (**6**), which was systematised in the twelfth and thirteenth centuries, and which dominated interpretation of the Bible until the Reformation. The four senses in which the Bible could be understood were: (1) the literal sense (the historical narrative of events); (2) the allegorical sense (in which the whole Bible was interpreted as a book about Christ; this sense included typology); (3) the moral or tropological sense (concerned with the inner life of each Christian); (4) the anagogical sense (concerned with his hope of eternity). Through such a method of interpretation the Bible became a living book, existing in the past, present and future. Thus the exodus of the children of Israel from Egypt to the Promised Land could be read as (1) a historical narrative; (2) a prefiguration of the life of Christ; (3) the daily struggle of each Christian to achieve salvation; (4) a promise of the end of time (**8**). In order to prevent interpretation from proliferating irresponsibly Aquinas in the *Summa Theologiae* (I i 10) emphasised that all the senses are founded on the literal (**7**) and that 'nothing necessary for faith is contained under the spiritual sense which is not openly conveyed through the literal sense elsewhere'.

The Protestant reformers, because of their development of the Pauline theology of law and gospel and of the two covenants (see Chapter 8), and because of their historical, progressive interpretation of Christianity, rejected the Platonic Alexandrian method of allegory and the medieval tradition of fourfold interpretation. Calvinists and radical Puritans, through their interest in the establishment of godly Christian communities on earth, attached great importance to the historical meaning of Israel. But this does not mean that Protestants restricted Scripture to a simple literal meaning. On the contrary, Luther and especially Calvin particularly valued the typological interpretation of Scripture, but they denied that this involved them in a system of multiple meanings. For Luther, since the Old Testament is a book about Christ, the typological *is* the literal meaning (**9, 10**). It should be read with the clear eye of the gospel, not through the veil of the law. In his *Institutes of the Christian Religion* II Calvin provides just such a gospel interpretation of the Old Testament (**11**). In addition, the reformers were willing to allow some allegorisation of the literal sense as an aid in preaching.

For Protestants, therefore, typology took precedence over allegory. Typology was essential to their interpretation of Scripture and their understanding of history; allegory was, for some, a permissible aesthetic and moral device. In seventeenth-century England, Anglicans (**13**) were much more inclined to draw on the allegorical tradition than Puritans. In religious poetry a range of interpretation is evident, depending on the poet's intentions and religious affiliations. Milton's account of biblical exegesis in *Christian Doctrine* I xxx is strictly Protestant (**12**); he opposes multiple allegorical interpretation, and argues that the literal sense, which contains the typological, is perspicuous to the faithful reader. In *Paradise Lost* XI–XII Michael's account of the process of human history is based on typology (**16**). Herbert's biblical inter-pretation is more traditional than Milton's and allows more levels of allusion and meaning; for him the Bible is not only the record of God's acts in the past and the promise of his acts in the future, but also the journal of his own spiritual conflicts (**15**).

TYPOLOGY IN THE NEW TESTAMENT

1　　But he answered and said unto them, An evil and adulterous generation seeketh after a sign; and there shall no sign be given to it, but the sign of the prophet Jonas:

For as Jonas was three days and three nights in the whale's belly; so shall the Son of man be three days and three nights in the heart of the earth.

The men of Nineveh shall rise in judgement with this generation, and shall condemn it: because they repented at the preaching of Jonas; and, behold, a greater than Jonas is here.

(Matthew 12:39–41 (see also Luke 11:29–32)

2　　And as Moses lifted up the serpent in the wilderness, even so must the Son of man be lifted up:

That whosoever believeth in him should not perish, but have eternal life.

John 3:14–15

3　　Moreover, brethren, I would not that ye should be ignorant, how that all our fathers were under the cloud, and all passed through the sea;

And were all baptized unto Moses in the cloud and in the sea;

And did all eat the same spiritual meat;

And did all drink the same spiritual drink: for they drank of that spiritual Rock that followed them: and that Rock was Christ.

. . . . . .

Now these things were our examples, to the intent we should not lust after evil things, as they also lusted.

. . . . . .

Now all these things happened unto them for ensamples: and they are written for our admonition, upon whom the ends of the world are come.

I Corinthians 10:1–4, 6, 11

PATRISTIC ALLEGORY

4　Augustine comments on the following passage:

Thy teeth are like a flock of sheep that are even shorn, which came up from the washing: whereof every one bear twins, and none is barren among them.

Song of Solomon 4:2

5　　I find more delight in considering the saints when I regard them as the teeth of the Church. They bite off men from their heresies and carry them over to the body of the Church, when their hardness of heart has been softened as if by being bitten off and chewed. With very great delight I look upon them also as shorn sheep that have put aside worldly cares, as if they were fleece. Coming up from the washing, that is, the baptismal font, all bear twins, that is, the two precepts of love, and I see no one destitute of that holy fruit.

Augustine *Christian Instruction* II vi

THE FOURFOLD METHOD

6   *Littera gesta docet, quid credas allegoria,*
     Moralis quid agas, quo tendas anagogia.
(The literal sense teaches you the narrative, the allegorical what to believe, the moral how to behave, and the anagogical where you are going.)

Augustine of Dacia (?)

7   That first meaning whereby the words signify things belongs to the sense first-mentioned, namely the historical or literal. That meaning, however, whereby the things signified by the words in their turn also signify other things is called the spiritual sense; it is based on and presupposes the literal sense. Now this spiritual sense is divided into three ... The allegorical sense is brought into play when the things of the Old Law signify the things of the New Law; the moral sense when the things done in Christ and in those who prefigured him are signs of what we should carry out; and the anagogical sense when the things that lie ahead in eternal glory are signified.

Thomas Aquinas *Summa Theologiae* I i 10

8   One must realise that the meaning of this work [*The Divine Comedy*] is not simple, but is rather to be called polysemous, that is, having many meanings. The first meaning is the one obtained through the letter; the second is the one obtained through the things signified by the letter. The first is called literal, the second allegorical or moral or anagogical. In order that this manner of treatment may appear more clearly, it may be applied to the following verses: 'When Israel went out of Egypt, the house of Jacob from a people of strange language; Judah was his sanctuary, and Israel his dominion' [Psalms 114:1–2]. For if we look to the letter alone, the departure of the children of Israel from Egypt in the time of Moses is indicated to us; if to the allegory, our redemption accomplished by Christ is indicated to us; if to the moral sense, the conversion of the soul from the woe and misery of sin to a state of grace is indicated to us; if to the anagogical sense, the departure of the consecrated soul from the slavery of this corruption to the liberty of eternal glory is indicated. And though these mystic senses may be called by various names, they can all generally be spoken of as allegorical, since

they are diverse from the literal or historical.

Dante *Letter to Can Grande della Scala*

PROTESTANT EXEGESIS

9   The Holy Spirit is the plainest writer and speaker in heaven and earth, and therefore his words cannot have more than one, and that the very simplest, sense, which we call the literal, ordinary, natural, sense. That the things indicated by the simple sense of his simple words should signify something further and different, and therefore one thing should always signify another, is more than a question of words or of language. For the same is true of all other things outside the Scriptures, since all of God's works and creatures are living signs and words of God, as St Augustine and all the teachers declare. But we are not on that account to say that the Scriptures or the Word of God have more than one meaning.

Luther *Answer to Goat Emser*

10   If you would interpret well and confidently, set Christ before you, for he is the man to whom it [the Old Testament] all applies, every bit of it.

Luther *Preface to the Old Testament*

11   The same inheritance was appointed for them [the patriarchs] and for us, but they were not yet old enough to be able to enter upon it and manage it. The same church existed among them, but as yet in its childhood. Therefore, keeping them under this tutelage, the Lord gave, not spiritual promises unadorned and open, but ones foreshadowed, in a measure, by earthly promises. When, therefore, he adopted Abraham, Isaac, Jacob, and their descendants into the hope of immortality, he promised them the Land of Canaan as an inheritance. It was not to be the final goal of their hopes, but was to exercise and confirm them, as they contemplated it, in hope of their true inheritance, an inheritance not yet manifested to them ... He adds the promise of the land, solely as a symbol of his benevolence and as a type of the heavenly inheritance.

Calvin *Institutes of the Christian Religion* II xi 2

12   Each passage of Scripture has only a single sense, though in the Old Testament this sense is often a combination of the historical and the typological ... No inferences should be made from the text, unless they follow necessarily from what is written. This precaution is necessary, otherwise we may be forced to believe something which is not written instead of something which is, and to accept human reasoning, generally fallacious, instead of divine doctrine, thus mistaking the shadow for the substance.

Milton *Christian Doctrine* I xxx

13   My God, my God, thou art a direct God, may I not say a literal God, a God that wouldst be understood literally and according to the plain sense of all that thou sayest? but thou art also (Lord, I intend it to thy glory, and

let no profane misinterpreter abuse it to thy diminution), thou art a figurative, a metaphorical God too; a God in whose words there is such a height of figures, such voyages, such peregrinations to fetch remote and precious metaphors, such extensions, such spreadings, such curtains of allegories, such third heavens of hyperboles, so harmonious elocutions, so retired and so reserved expressions, so commanding persuasions, so persuading commandments, such sinews even in thy milk, and such things in thy words, as all profane authors seem of the seed of the serpent that creeps, thou art the Dove that flies ... Neither art thou thus a figurative, a metaphorical God in thy word only, but in thy works too. The style of thy works, the phrase of thine actions, is metaphorical. The institution of thy whole worship in the old law was a continual allegory; types and figures overspread all, and figures flowed into figures, and poured themselves out into farther figures; circumcision carried a figure of baptism, and baptism carries a figure of that purity which we shall have in perfection in the new Jerusalem. Neither didst thou speak and work in this language only in the time of thy prophets; but since thou spokest in thy Son it is so too. How often, how much more often, doth thy Son call himself a way, and a light, and a gate, and a vine, and bread, than the Son of God, or of man? How much oftener doth he exhibit a metaphorical Christ, than a real, a literal?

Donne *Devotions* Expostulation xix

TYPOLOGY IN POETRY

14   Man, dream no more of curious mysteries,
As what was here before the world was made,
The first man's life, the state of Paradise,
Where Heaven is, or Hell's eternal shade,
    For God's works are like him, all infinite;
    And curious search but crafty sin's delight.

The flood that did, and dreadful fire that shall,
Drown, and burn up the malice of the earth,
The divers tongues, and Babylon's downfall,
Are nothing to the man's renewed birth;
    First, let the Law plough up thy wicked heart,
    That Christ may come, and all these types depart.

When thou hast swept the house that all is clear,
When thou the dust hast shaken from thy feet,
When God's all might doth in thy flesh appear,
Then seas with streams above thy sky do meet;
    For goodness only doth God comprehend,
    Knows what was first, and what shall be the end.

Greville *Caelica* lxxxviii

15 Joy, I did lock thee up: but some bad man
    Hath let thee out again:
 And now, methinks, I am where I began
   Seven years ago: one vogue and vein,
   One air of thoughts usurps my brain.
 I did toward Canaan draw; but now I am
 Brought back to the Red Sea, the sea of shame.

 For as the Jews of old by God's command
    Travelled and saw no town:
 So now each Christian hath his journeys spanned:
   Their story pens and sets us down.
   A single deed is small renown.
 God's works are wide, and let in future times;
 His ancient justice overflows our crimes.

 Then have we too our guardian fires and clouds;
    Our Scripture-dew drops fast:
 We have our sands and serpents, tents and shrouds;
   Alas! our murmurings come not last.
   But where's the cluster? where's the taste
 Of mine inheritance? Lord, if I must borrow,
 Let me as well take up their joy, as sorrow.

 But can he want the grape who hath the wine?
    I have their fruit and more.
 Blessed be God, who prospered Noah's vine,
   And made it bring forth grapes good store:
   But much more him I must adore,
 Who of the Law's sour juice sweet wine did make,
 Even God himself, being pressèd for my sake.
       Herbert 'The Bunch of Grapes' (compare **3**;
       see also 'The Holy Scriptures' and 'Aaron')

16 Michael prophesies to Adam:
 God from the mount of Sinai, whose grey top
 Shall tremble, he descending, will himself
 In thunder lightning and loud trumpets' sound
 Ordain them laws; part such as appertain
 To civil justice, part religious rites
 Of sacrifice, informing them, by types
 And shadows, of that destined seed to bruise
 The serpent, by what means he shall achieve
 Mankind's deliverance. But the voice of God
 To mortal ear is dreadful; they beseech
 That Moses might report to them his will,
 And terror cease; he grants what they besought
 Instructed that to God is no access
 Without mediator, whose high office now

Moses in figure bears, to introduce
One greater, of whose day he shall foretell,
And all the prophets in their age the times
Of great Messiah shall sing.
. . . . .
So law appears imperfect, and but given
With purpose to resign them in full time
Up to a better Covenant, disciplined
From shadowy types to truth, from flesh to spirit,
From imposition of strict laws, to free
Acceptance of large grace, from servile fear
To filial, works of law to works of faith.
And therefore shall not Moses, though of God
Highly beloved, being but the minister
Of law, his people into Canaan lead;
But Joshua whom the gentiles Jesus call,
His name and office bearing, who shall quell
The adversary serpent, and bring back
Through the world's wilderness long wandered man
Safe to eternal paradise of rest.

Milton *Paradise Lost* XII ll. 227–44, 300–14

11 Theories of Poetry

A number of different theories about the nature of poetry and the poet
coexisted in the Renaissance. In their formulation of these theories
Renaissance poets and critics drew on certain key classical texts, but
modified them in the light of their Christian beliefs. Aristotle's *Poetics*
(scarcely known in the Middle Ages) and Horace's *The Art of Poetry*
were the most important of these. A group of works on the nature of
oratory, rhetoric, and on the role of the orator contributed directly to
poetic theory: Aristotle's *Rhetoric*, Cicero's *Orator* and *On the Orator*,
and Quintilian's *Education of an Orator*. Plato was generally influential
as reinterpreted by the Neoplatonists, but three works dealing directly
or indirectly with poetic theory, *Ion*, *Phaedrus* and *Republic* X, were
read in their own right. The educational theory of poetry was influenced
by a minor essay of Plutarch, *How the Young Man Should Study Poetry*.
There was a large body of Renaissance Italian criticism drawing on
classical sources, but with important exceptions this went unread by
English critics.

Unlike their modern counterparts, Renaissance critics were on the
whole less concerned with the sources of poetry than with its function.
In terms of its sources and its relation to reality, poetry was variously
regarded as inspiration, madness, imaginative creation or imitation. In
terms of its function, its effect on the individual or on society, it was
regarded as a civilising force, an educational instrument, a means to
action or a key to secret knowledge. The poet, depending on which view
of poetry the critic was adopting, was a madman, priest, prophet,
craftsman, teacher, orator or social critic. Poetry was often treated as
part of what was considered a larger, more important, subject, usually
theology, philosophy or rhetoric.

The Muses are the mythological embodiment of the ancient belief
that the poet is inspired by a force outside himself to write of subjects
beyond his normal reach. The daughters of Zeus and Memory, each of
the nine Muses patronised a different art: Clio (history), Euterpe
(music), Thalia (comedy), Melpomene (tragedy), Terpsichore (dancing), Erato (lyric poetry), Polyhymnia (song and rhetoric), Calliope
(epic poetry), Urania (astronomy). Their leader was Apollo, and the
mountains of Helicon and Parnassus were sacred to them. Homer,
Hesiod (1) and Pindar speak of themselves as inspired by the Muses,

and invocation of the Muses to help the poet became a traditional formula of epic and heroic poetry. Although in Renaissance poetry reference to the Muses is often simply elaboration of a convention, or a device whereby the poet personifies an aspect of himself (as in Sidney's famous outburst in *Astrophel and Stella* i: '"Fool!" said my Muse to me, "Look in thy heart and write"'), it can also be a serious embodiment of the tension between classical and Christian images and vocabularies, heroic inspiration by the Muses sometimes fusing and sometimes contrasting with prophetic inspiration by angels or apostolic inspiration by the Holy Ghost. Milton appears to differentiate completely between the two traditions; in *The Reason of Church Government* he says the writing of a poem is not 'to be obtained by the invocation of Dame Memory and her Siren daughters [i.e. the Muses], but by devout prayer to that eternal Spirit who can enrich with all utterance and knowledge, and sends out his Seraphim with the hallowed fire of his altar to touch and purify the lips of whom he pleases'. (This identification of the Christian poet with the prophet Isaiah (6:6–7) is also made in the 'Nativity Ode'.) Yet in *Paradise Lost*, while ostensibly maintaining this distinction, Milton in fact incorporates the classical tradition: he repudiates Calliope, the epic Muse, but the Spirit which supports and teaches him is Urania, the 'heavenly Muse', 'the meaning, not the name' (2). He distinguishes the idea of true Christian from false classical inspiration while retaining the classical form.

Closely allied to the idea of inspiration is that of poetic madness or frenzy (*furor poeticus*). The most elaborate classical statement of this idea is in Plato's *Ion* 534. Plato clearly intends to belittle the irrational, capricious knowledge of the poet in comparison with the rational, earned knowledge of the philosopher, but Renaissance Neoplatonism transforms poetic madness into a term of approval. In this view the poet becomes a priest (Latin *vates*) with a sacred office; he is a mediator, a chosen instrument by means of which divine truth propagates itself; although he cannot exercise rational control over his own utterances, he has involuntary access to a truth above reason. The poet-priest's divine knowledge is sometimes paradoxically associated with a significant physical disability: the seer is blind. In *Paradise Lost* III ll. 1–55 the blind Milton, invoking light, identifies himself with the blind poets and prophets of antiquity, Homer and Teiresias. A criticism of the idea of poetic inspiration may be contained in the episode in *The Faerie Queene* VI x in which Colin Clout's vision of the dancing Graces is interrupted and broken by the knight Calidore, who tries to share in it. Spenser perhaps means that though the poet may apprehend an other-worldly perfection he can neither control it nor transmit it, hence he cannot mediate between the celestial and mundane worlds.

The idea that the poet is divinely inspired was widespread in the Renaissance. However, the poet's divine nature was sometimes interpreted in a more daring way. Just as God, the creator of the world, is a maker, a poet, so the poet, the creator of his own world, is a god. The idea of God as a maker is both Platonic and Christian. In Plato's *Timaeus* 29–30 the Demiurge makes the world as a copy of perfect Form. The analogy between the creator and the craftsman, and between the world and a work of art, is continued by Plotinus (*Ennead* V viii). Deriving from these and from similar biblical images (God is a potter in Isaiah 29:16) the idea of God as an artist becomes a Renaissance commonplace, usefully summed up by Browne in *Religio Medici*: 'All things are artificial; for nature is the art of God.' God is regarded as the author of two books, the Book of Works, or nature, and the Book of Words, or Scripture. Augustine compares God's ordering of human history with the principle of poetic antithesis: 'There is a beauty in the composition of the world's history arising from the antithesis of contraries – a kind of eloquence in events, instead of in words' (*City of God* XI xviii). Theology, according to Boccaccio in the *Life of Dante* xxii, is the poetry of God; and in Scripture God uses poetic devices. It is a logical though bold step to turn the analogy around. Theology is poetry, says Boccaccio, and poetry is theology; the poet is a theologian. The most interesting Renaissance accounts linking God and the poet through their common creative capacity are those of Sidney in *An Apology for Poetry* (3) and Tasso in *Discourses on the Heroic Poem* (4). The poet is like God because he creates a second nature which is not based on existing nature but which is made out of nothing, out of his own imagination (5). His world is like God's world because it is controlled by the same principle of discordant concord (*concordia discors*), or unity through variety (4; Ch. 6.9, 10). The design of a work of art is like the design of the universe not because the poet imitates God's design but because he creates on the same principles as God (see Chapter 13).

This Renaissance idea of the poet as creator represents a radical departure from the various traditional definitions of the poet as imitator of nature. The most important theory of poetry as imitation or mimesis is expounded in Aristotle's *Poetics*. Aristotle rebuts the theory of imitation put forward by Plato in *Republic* X 595–602, that a work of art is at two removes from reality because the artist imitates a natural object which is itself an imitation of ideal Form. For Aristotle, on the contrary, imitation is not the copying of the particulars of the natural world but the revelation of its essence. Poetry is concerned not with the factual but the probable; thus 'poetry is something more philosophical and more worthy of serious attention than history; for while poetry is concerned with universal truths, history treats of particular facts' (*Poetics* IX, translated by T. S. Dorsch). Important though this theory is, it does not appear to have been properly understood in Renaissance England. Some of the assumptions of the theory of imitation were accepted: the idea that the poet imitates a known, external reality was far more orthodox than the idea that he creates a new reality. The term 'imitation' is frequently to be found in Renaissance theorists, but in a different sense from Aristotle's. It means the imitation not of nature but of literary forms, genres and other poets. Imitation in this sense is an important humanist concept, and it implies a view of the poet not as inspired priest but as responsible craftsman (see Chapter 9).

Theories about the sources of poetry – divine inspiration, creation from the poet's imagination, imitation of nature – were much less debated than theories about its effects. These theories were largely moralistic, but a number of approaches can be distinguished. In *The Art of Poetry* Horace gives a brief sketch of the history of poetry; poets were the ancient law-givers and educators, the founders of civilisation. As examples he mentions the myths of Orpheus, who tamed wild men and beasts with his music, and Amphion, who charmed the stones of Thebes to build themselves (**8**). In the Renaissance Orpheus and Amphion became standard symbols of the artist's ability to impose harmony on chaos, to bring about through the means of aesthetic enchantment some socially beneficial end. Yet the myth of Orpheus (which seems particularly to have fascinated Milton), though it contains the theory of the civilising power of poetry, also suggests the precariousness of civilisation, and perhaps the destructive capacities of inspiration. Ovid tells the story in *Metamorphoses* XI ll. 1–55. Orpheus, the gentle singer and tamer of beasts and men and even inanimate objects, was torn apart by Maenads, themselves inspired female followers of Dionysus, who was incensed at Orpheus' refusal to worship him. His mother Calliope, the epic Muse, could do nothing to save him, as Milton laments in *Lycidas* ll. 58–63 and *Paradise Lost* VI ll. 31–9 (**2**).

The myth of Orpheus is a complex and suggestive account of the social effects of poetry and the relation between the poet and society. But the Renaissance critic's account of these effects is often much cruder. Horace's view that the best poet both pleases and teaches (*Art of Poetry* 1. 343) contains the germ of the widely held Renaissance idea (also derived from Lucretius) that the function of poetry is essentially didactic, that it is a way of introducing philosophical ideas, disguised with the pleasures of metre, rhyme and fable, to intellects too feeble to digest philosophy unadorned (**10**). Poetry is a sugared pill, or, in Lucretius' image, honey on the rim of a cup of medicine (**7**). In *How the Young Man Should Study Poetry* Plutarch regards the reading of poetry as a stepping-stone to the serious adult study of philosophy. This idea is taken up in the Renaissance, for example, by Harington in his preface to *Orlando Furioso*: poetry is an introduction for untutored minds to the more important subject of theology (9).

This belittling and patronising theory of poetry as a sugared pill is by no means the only didactic theory held in the Renaissance; it can be found coexisting with or incorporated into theories that in some respects contradict it. Two other didactic theories illustrate this process: the humanist theory of poetry as rhetoric, and the allegorical theory of poetry. In the simplest didactic theory poetry is a means of conveying moral knowledge. In the humanist view poetry does not simply teach; it moves men to action, it makes them better, it causes them to imitate the moral ideal embodied in the poem. Humanist theory regards poetry as having an important political function. Thus whereas the sugared pill theory is concerned with the intellectually feeble reader, the fool, as Harington describes him, humanist theory is concerned with the socially and politically conspicuous reader. Both are to be transformed through poetry; the fool will become wise, the conspicuous man will become a moral example. Though the humanist theory is based on classical rhetorical theory it represents an important Renaissance innovation. (For further discussion see Chapter 9.)

The allegorical theory of poetry, which persisted from antiquity through the Middle Ages, but which was given prominence by Renaissance Neoplatonists, assumes three different classes of reader. The first, the most superficial, reads only the fable and does not penetrate beyond it. The second (the swallower of the sugared pill) learns from the fable simple moral truths. The third, most important reader penetrates the veil of fable to acquire secret philosophical or religious knowledge which cannot be expressed otherwise than through fable. For the second class of reader poetry is less serious than philosophy, for the third class it is more serious. (For further discussion see Chapter 12.)

The most interesting English Renaissance critics of poetry were themselves poets who repeatedly tested their own ideas in their poems, Sidney, Spenser, Jonson and Milton being the chief examples. Much interesting speculation about the nature and ends of poetry can be found not in prose treatises but in the poems themselves: in Sidney's *Astrophel and Stella*, for example, or Herbert's *The Temple*. But modern readers applying Renaissance theory to Renaissance poems should be cautious. A good deal of lyric poetry simply slips through the net of social and moral theory, yet almost no Renaissance critic (the Italian Castelvetro is an exception) was prepared to allow that the chief function of poetry might be to give delight.

THE INSPIRED POET

1   The Muses once taught Hesiod to sing
    Sweet songs, while he was shepherding his lambs
    On holy Helicon; the goddesses
    Olympian, daughters of Zeus who holds
    The aegis, first addressed these words to me:
    'You rustic shepherds, shame: bellies you are,
    Not men! We know enough to make up lies
    Which are convincing, but we also have
    The skill, when we've a mind, to speak the truth.'
    So spoke the fresh-voiced daughters of great Zeus
    And plucked and gave a staff to me, a shoot
    Of blooming laurel, wonderful to see.
    And breathed a sacred voice into my mouth
    With which to celebrate the things to come
    And things which were before. They ordered me
    To sing the race of blessed ones who live
    Forever, and to hymn the Muses first
    And at the end.

                            Hesiod *Theogony* ll. 22–34

2   Descend from heaven Urania, by that name
    If rightly thou art called, whose voice divine
    Following, above the Olympian hill I soar,
    Above the flight of Pegasean wing.
    The meaning, not the name I call: for thou
    Nor of the Muses nine, nor on the top
    Of old Olympus dwell'st, but heavenly born,
    Before the hills appeared, or fountain flowed,
    Thou with eternal wisdom didst converse,
    Wisdom thy sister, and with her didst play
    In presence of the almighty Father, pleased
    With thy celestial song.

    . . . . . . Still govern thou my song,
    Urania, and fit audience find, though few.
    But drive far off the barbarous dissonance
    Of Bacchus and his revellers, the race
    Of that wild rout that tore the Thracian bard [i.e. Orpheus]
    In Rhodope, where woods and rocks had ears
    To rapture, till the savage clamour drowned
    Both harp and voice; nor could the Muse defend
    Her son. So fail not thou, who thee implores:
    For thou art heavenly, she an empty dream.

                        Milton *Paradise Lost* VII ll. 1–12, 30–9

THE POET AS CREATOR

3   Only the poet, disdaining to be tied to any such subjection, lifted up with
       the vigour of his own invention, doth grow in effect into another nature,
       in making things either better than Nature bringeth forth, or, quite anew,
       forms such as never were in Nature, as the heroes, demigods, Cyclops,
       Chimeras, Furies, and such like: so as he goeth hand in hand with Nature,
       not enclosed within the narrow warrant of her gifts, but freely ranging
       only within the zodiac of his own wit.
            Nature never set forth the earth in so rich tapestry as divers poets have
       done; neither with pleasant rivers, fruitful trees, sweet-smelling flowers,
       nor whatsoever else may make the too much loved earth more lovely. Her
       world is brazen, the poets only deliver a golden . . .
            Neither let it be deemed too saucy a comparison to balance the highest
       point of man's wit with the efficacy of Nature; but rather give right
       honour to the heavenly Maker of that maker, who having made man to
       his own likeness, set him beyond and over all the works of that second
       nature: which in nothing he showeth so much as in poetry, when with the
       force of a divine breath he bringeth things forth far surpassing her doings,
       with no small argument to the incredulous of that first accursed fall of
       Adam: since our erected wit maketh us know what perfection is, and yet
       our infected will keepeth us from reaching unto it.

                                                       Sidney *An Apology for Poetry*

4   Just as in this marvellous domain of God called the world we behold the
       sky scattered over and adorned with such variety of stars, and as we
       descend from realm to realm, we marvel at the air and the sea full of birds
       and fish, and the earth host to so many animals wild and tame, with
       brooks, springs, lakes, meadows, fields, forests, and mountains, here
       fruits and flowers, there glaciers and snow, here dwellings and ploughed
       fields, there desert and wilderness; yet for all this, the world that contains
       in its womb so many diverse things is one, its form and essence one, and
       one the bond that links its many parts and ties them together in discordant
       concord, and nothing is missing, yet nothing is there that does not serve
       for necessity or ornament; just so, I judge, the great poet (who is called
       divine for no other reason than that as he resembles the supreme Artificer
       in his workings he comes to participate in his divinity) can form a poem
       in which, as in a little world, one may read here of armies assembling,
       here of battles on land or sea, here of conquests of cities, skirmishes and
       duels, here of jousts, here descriptions of hunger and thirst, here
       tempests, fires, prodigies, there of celestial and infernal councils, there
       seditions, there discord, wanderings, adventures, enchantments, deeds of
       cruelty, daring, courtesy, generosity, there the fortunes of love, now
       happy, now sad, now joyous, now pitiful. Yet the poem that contains so
       great a variety of matters none the less should be one, one in form and
       soul; and all these things should be so combined that each concerns the
       other, corresponds to the other, and so depends on the other necessarily
       or verisimilarly that removing any one part or changing its place would

destroy the whole. And if that is true, the art of composing a poem resembles the plan of the universe, which is composed of contraries, as that of music is.

Tasso *Discourses on the Heroic Poem* III

5   A poet is as much to say as a maker. And our English name well conforms with the Greek word, for of ποιεῖν [*poiein*], to make, they call a maker *poeta*. Such as (by way of resemblance and reverently) we may say of God; who without any travail to his divine imagination made all the world of nought, nor also by any pattern or mould, as the Platonics with their Ideas do fantastically suppose. Even so the very poet makes and contrives out of his own brain both the verse and matter of his poem, and not by any foreign copy or example ... It is therefore of poets thus to be conceived, that if they be able to devise and make all these things of themselves, without any subject of verity, that they be (by manner of speech) as creating gods.

Puttenham *The Art of English Poesy* I i

6   The use of this feigned history [i.e. poetry] hath been to give some shadow of satisfaction to the mind of man in those points wherein the nature of things doth deny it, the world being in proportion inferior to the soul; by reason whereof there is, agreeable to the spirit of man, a more ample greatness, a more exact goodness, and a more absolute variety, than can be found in the nature of things. Therefore, because the acts or events of true history have not that magnitude which satisfieth the mind of man, poesy feigneth acts and events greater and more heroical. Because true history propoundeth the successes and issues of actions not so agreeable to the merits of virtue and vice, therefore poesy feigns them more just in retribution, and more according to revealed providence. Because true history representeth actions and events more ordinary and less interchanged, therefore poesy endueth them with more rareness, and more unexpected and alternative variations. So as it appeareth that poesy serveth and conferreth to magnanimity, morality, and to delectation. And therefore it was ever thought to have some participation of divineness, because it doth raise and erect the mind, by submitting the shows of things to the desires of the mind; whereas reason doth buckle and bow the mind unto the nature of things.

Bacon *The Advancement of Learning* II iv

THE POET AS EDUCATOR

7   My art is not without a purpose. Physicians, when they wish to treat children with a nasty dose of wormwood, first smear the rim of the cup with a sweet coat of yellow honey. The children, too young as yet for foresight, are lured by the sweetness at their lips into swallowing the bitter draught. So they are tricked but not trapped, for the treatment restores them to health. In the same way our doctrine often seems

unpalatable to those who have not sampled it, and the multitude shrink from it. That is why I have tried to administer it to you in the dulcet strains of poesy, coated with the sweet honey of the Muses. My object has been to engage your mind with my verses while you gain insight into the nature of the universe and the pattern of its architecture.

Lucretius *The Nature of the Universe* I ll. 935–50

8   While men still roamed the woods, Orpheus, the holy prophet of the gods, made them shrink from bloodshed and brutal living; hence the fable that he tamed tigers and ravening lions; hence too the fable that Amphion, builder of Thebes's citadel, moved stones by the sound of his lyre, and led them whither he would by his supplicating spell. In days of yore, this was wisdom, to draw a line between public and private rights, between things sacred and things common, to check vagrant union, to give rules for wedded life, to build towns, and grave laws on tables of wood; and so honour and fame fell to bards and their songs, as divine.

Horace *The Art of Poetry* ll. 391–401

9   Tasso in his excellent work of *Jerusalem Liberata* likeneth poetry to the physic that men give unto little children when they are sick . . . speaking to God with a pretty prosopopeia [personification],

Thou knowst, the wanton worldlings ever run
To sweet Parnassus' fruits, how otherwhile
The truth well sauced with pleasant verse hath won
Most squeamish stomachs with the sugared style:
So the sick child that potions all doth shun
With comfits and with sugar we beguile,
And cause him take a wholesome sour receipt:
He drinks, and saves his life with such deceit.

This is then that honest fraud in which (as Plutarch saith) he that is deceived is wiser than he that is not deceived, and he that doth deceive is honester than he that doth not deceive.

Harington Preface to *Orlando Furioso*

10   I say the philosopher teacheth, but he teacheth obscurely, so as the learned only can understand him; that is to say, he teacheth them that are already taught. But the poet is the food for the tenderest stomachs, the poet is indeed the right popular philosopher . . . He beginneth not with obscure definitions, which must blur the margent with interpretations, and load the memory with doubtfulness; but he cometh to you with words set in delightful proportion, either accompanied with, or prepared for, the well enchanting skill of music; and with a tale forsooth he cometh unto you, with a tale which holdeth children from play, and old men from the chimney corner. And, pretending no more, doth intend the winning of the mind from wickedness to virtue: even as the child is often brought to take more wholesome things by hiding them in such other as have a pleasant taste: which, if one should begin to tell them the nature of aloes or

rhubarb they should receive, would sooner take their physic at their ears than at their mouth.

Sidney *An Apology for Poetry*

12 Allegory

The term allegory (Greek ἀλληγορία) comes from classical rhetoric, and means literally saying one thing to mean another. Plutarch says in *How the Young Man Should Study Poetry* (19e) that it replaced an older term: *hyponoia (ὑπονοία)*, or deep meaning. It was defined in classical times and in the Renaissance primarily as a trope, a figure of speech. Quintilian states: 'Allegory ... either presents one thing in words and another in meaning, or else something absolutely opposed to the meaning of the words. The first type is generally produced by a series of metaphors' (*Education of an Orator* VIII vi 44). The idea that allegory is a continued metaphor is a Renaissance commonplace; for example, Henry Peacham in *The Garden of Eloquence* compares metaphor to a star, and allegory to a constellation of stars. However, although allegory is a rhetorical term, it should not be regarded solely or even chiefly as a matter of technique. Despite the traditional rhetorical definition it has much wider implications. Allegory has its origins in a religious frame of mind, which sees nature and history as charged with hidden divine meanings that can be revealed to the diligent seeker, and it manifests itself both as a method of interpreting texts and as a method of writing. The tendency to see allegory simply as a technical device has resulted in some attempts to elevate symbolism at the expense of allegory. C. S. Lewis's definition in *The Allegory of Love* of symbolism as a mode of thought and allegory as a mode of expression reflects this tendency. But allegory is much more flexible than this definition suggests. On the one hand it is associated with general terms like myth, symbol, parable and fable, and on the other with more restricted terms like metaphor, conceit and emblem.

Allegory was first practised in antiquity not as a method of writing but as a method of reading texts. Stoic and, later, Neoplatonic philosophers allegorised the myths narrated by Greek and Roman poets so that they revealed a variety of meanings (this process is described in Chapter 2). This can be described as imposed allegory, since there is no reason to suppose that Virgil or Homer would have recognised some of the meanings read into their works. Allegory can be imposed on authors for different reasons. On a simple level this can be a schoolmasterly attempt to make dangerous authors respectable, and there is something of this tendency in the allegorisation of Homer in the Hellenistic period, Ovid in the Middle Ages, and Ariosto in the Renaissance. More seriously, allegory can be imposed because the interpreter believes that the text he is studying contains significant hidden truths which have escaped careless readers. Both Homer and Virgil were repeatedly allegorised from late antiquity to the Renaissance for this reason. The fifteenth-century Italian humanist Landino in allegorising the *Aeneid* emphasised its moral meaning: Aeneas' journey from Troy to Italy guided by Venus is the voyage of man away from passion towards the contemplative life guided by celestial love. Such allegory might even be imposed subsequently by an author himself, as Tasso did in his 'Account of the Allegory' of *Jerusalem Delivered*. However, some Renaissance readers were sceptical of imposed allegory. In the Prologue to *Gargantua* Rabelais satirises the allegorising reader in the image of a dog trying to lick marrow out of a bone: he regards the Neoplatonising of Homer and the Christianising of Ovid as equally implausible.

The other important text in the development of the tradition of allegorical interpretation is the Bible (**1–3**). (The biblical tradition is described in Chapter 10.) Critics disagree as to how far the fourfold method of exegesis used in reading the Bible was applied to the interpretation or affected the writing of medieval secular literature. In the *Letter to Can Grande* Dante suggests that *The Divine Comedy* should be read in the same way as the Bible (Ch. **10.8**), but in the *Convivio* (or *Banquet*) II i he distinguishes the allegory practised by poets from that practised by theologians. From the literary point of view the great importance of the biblical tradition of allegorisation is that it reinforced the habit of reading and thinking allegorically. Readers expected literary works to be 'polysemous' in Dante's phrase, that is, to have multiple meanings.

Although it is helpful to distinguish allegorical interpretation from allegorical writing, Renaissance theorists of allegory (mythographers and poets rather than rhetoricians) were not particularly concerned with this distinction. Their interest was rather in the function of allegory, in the relation between the work and its audience, and in the kinds of meaning it contained (**7–10**). We can isolate three explanations as to why a work of literature contains multiple meanings and why these meanings are not spelt out directly. These explanations use three different kinds of image to express the relationship between allegorical form and meaning. The first explanation is simple, the other two more complex. The first is didactic: allegorical fiction conveys moral truths in a pleasing form. There is nothing secret or obscure about this moral level of meaning; allegory simply makes it more acceptable to its readers. The image here is of the sugared pill or honey on the medicine-cup (see Chapter 11). The second explanation is that far from being a means of making clear ideas available, allegory conceals ideas from the vulgar and reveals them only to the deserving. An allegorical work will therefore function in different ways for different readers according to their capacities. Reading allegory becomes a kind of intellectual test: serious readers will identify themselves through the act of reading. Superficial readers will only see the surface meaning; serious readers must work hard to extract or unlock the hidden meaning from the work. Their reward will be religious or philosophical meanings available only to the few. The relevant image here is of the rind and the fruit (**7, 10**), or the nut and the kernel (Rabelais' marrow-bone is a parody version). The third explanation is the most interesting. Allegory is regarded as a means of saying things that would otherwise be inexpressible. The image here is that of the veil: the cloud veiling the sun (**6, 8**), or the veil with which Moses covered his face when he came down from Sinai with the Tables of the Law (**1**). Through the veil readers can penetrate to the light beyond, which otherwise would dazzle them (**12**). Thus an allegorical work is not self-contained, but is part of an incomplete process. This process is only completed when its readers fully intuit the meanings which the author himself can only partly express. The question of whether the meanings are consciously intended by the author becomes irrelevant.

The relation between clarity and obscurity in allegory can be seen to be a complicated one. Spenser called *The Faerie Queene* a 'dark conceit' (**11**); this phrase should perhaps be understood in two different ways. The 'darkness' of allegory may refer to the author's attempt to conceal his meanings from the many and reveal them to the few; the work is thus obscure for some readers and clear for others. Or the 'darkness' may refer to the author's attempt to filter the light of truth through the dark glass of allegorical form; obscurity is thus paradoxically a means of achieving clarity.

Only the simplest kind of didactic allegory with a single level of meaning (sometimes referred to as 'naive' allegory) is susceptible of paraphrase. A late but useful example is the House of the Interpreter in Bunyan's *Pilgrim's Progress*: the Interpreter presents Christian with dramatic emblems, and then paraphrases their doctrinal meaning. Complex, polysemous allegory cannot be paraphrased in this way, though readers can distinguish kinds of meaning, the most important being moral, political and historical, religious and philosophical. A complex allegory is not necessarily to be read continuously on several levels of meaning. The allegory may be intermittent; different levels may be present in different parts of the work, or rarely they may be present simultaneously. These levels can all be illustrated from *The*

Faerie Queene (**11–14**). Moral allegory is usually concerned with conflict between virtues and vices in the individual; an early example is the *Psychomachia* (war in the soul) of the fourth-century Christian Latin poet Prudentius. The best example of this kind of moral allegory in *The Faerie Queene* is the quest of Sir Guyon, the Knight of Temperance, in Book II; guided by his palmer, representing reason, he defeats excess and chooses the path of the mean. The allegory of the House of Alma (the temperate body and soul) in II ix is didactic like Bunyan's. (The Neoplatonic theorist Henry Reynolds in *Mythomystes* objected to such moral allegory precisely because its meaning was obvious.) Political and historical allegory is likely to matter less to modern readers than the other levels of meaning, but it deserves to be taken seriously, and not regarded simply as a key to historical events and characters. Spenser includes a good deal of specific historical allegory: Book V deals among other topics with the execution of Mary Queen of Scots and the revolt of the Netherlands against Spain. But it is the overall tendency of the historical allegory that is important. Just as in Aeneas' search for the new Troy Virgil both celebrates and exhorts Augustus, so in Prince Arthur's search for the Faerie Queene Gloriana Spenser both celebrates and exhorts Elizabeth (see Chapter 5). He makes more sparing use of religious and philosophical allegory, though these levels are more memorable because more universal. The Garden of Adonis in III vi, perhaps the most striking passage in the poem, is philosophical allegory of the kind that reaches clarity through obscurity: no reader can pin down the logic of Spenser's argument about the relation of mutability to eternity, but every reader who grasps the implications of the allegory has found the heart of the poem. Overtly religious allegory is largely confined to Book I. On the whole *The Faerie Queene* is a worldly, secular poem, concerned with the problems of living this life, but in Book I, the legend of the Red Cross Knight, or Holiness, Spenser explores the central subject of great medieval allegories like *The Divine Comedy* and *Piers Plowman*, the search of the soul for salvation. In fact readers can profitably apply the medieval fourfold method of biblical exegesis to this book (see Chapter 10): the adventure of Red Cross and Una is the story of a knight who kills a dragon and wins a princess; it is also the search of the individual Christian for the true faith, the history of the true Church culminating in the English Reformation under Elizabeth, and the return of redeemed man to paradise by means of Christ's victory over Satan.

Allegory may take several literary forms. It may be progressive narrative (Spenser's 'continued allegory') or static description. Typical forms are the quest (deriving both from medieval romance and from allegorised epic such as the *Odyssey*); the dream vision (Plato's Myth of Er and Cicero's Dream of Scipio, the latter subsequently allegorised by Macrobius, are classical examples; *Piers Plowman* and *The Pilgrim's Progress* are both dream allegories); the progress, triumph, pageant or masque (deriving from classical and Renaissance forms of public ceremonial; there are several instances in *The Faerie Queene*, but Jonson's court masques are the most highly developed examples); the debate (perhaps deriving from classical and medieval educational disciplines; the debate between Milton's Comus and the Lady draws on this method of public disputation); the emblem (a pictorial allegory accompanied by an explanation in verse; Francis Quarles's *Emblems* was a very popular example of the fashion for emblem books, which was initiated in the sixteenth century by the Italian Alciati).

Modern readers must learn how to read an allegory. They must discern the kind of allegory it is, and the levels of meaning it contains; they must recognise allegory when it is there, and avoid imposing it falsely when it is not. They face two different dangers: of neglecting or undervaluing allegorical meanings that are present in a work, and of inventing meanings that are inappropriate to it. Sometimes non-existent clues are picked up; sometimes the author's provocation of the reader is deliberately ironic. Marvell is an example of an author who has been badly served by modern readers clumsily misapplying techniques of allegorical interpretation; a poem like 'Upon Appleton House' plays delicately with the idea of allegory, yet it has had weighty political and religious meanings tactlessly forced on it. On the whole, however, allegorical works provide their readers with enough clues about their nature to provoke them into the appropriate allegorical interpretation.

BIBLICAL PRECEDENTS FOR ALLEGORY AND THEIR USE

1   And it came to pass, when Moses came down from mount Sinai with the two tables of testimony in Moses' hand ... that Moses wist not that the skin of his face shone while he talked with [God].

And when Aaron and all the children of Israel saw Moses, behold, the skin of his face shone; and they were afraid to come nigh him.
......
And till Moses had done speaking with them, he put a veil on his face.

But when Moses went in before the Lord to speak with him, he took the veil off, until he came out. And he came out, and spake unto the children of Israel that which he was commanded.

And the children of Israel saw the face of Moses, that the skin of

Moses' face shone: and Moses put the veil upon his face again, until he
went in to speak with him.

Exodus 34:29–30, 33–5

2   And the disciples came, and said unto him, Why speakest thou unto
them in parables?

He answered and said unto them, Because it is given unto you to know
the mysteries of the kingdom of heaven, but to them it is not given.

For whosoever hath, to him shall be given, and he shall have more
abundance: but whosoever hath not, from him shall be taken away even
that he hath.

Therefore speak I to them in parables: because they seeing see not; and
hearing they hear not, neither do they understand.

Matthew 13:10–13

3   For we know in part, and we prophesy in part.

But when that which is perfect is come, then that which is in part shall
be done away.

When I was a child, I spake as a child, I understood as a child, I thought
as a child: but when I became a man, I put away childish things.

For now we see through a glass [i.e. in a mirror], darkly: but then face
to face: now I know in part; but then shall I know even as also I am
known.

I Corinthians 13:9–12

4   But to go higher, did not our Saviour himself speak in parables? as that
divine parable of the sower, that comfortable parable of the prodigal son,
that dreadful parable of Dives and Lazarus, though I know of this last
many of the fathers hold that it is a story indeed and no parable. But in
the rest it is manifest that he [that] was all holiness, all wisdom, all truth,
used parables, and even such as discreet poets use, where a good and
honest and wholesome allegory is hidden in a pleasant and pretty fiction;
and therefore for that part of poetry of imitation, I think nobody will
make any question but it is not only allowable, but godly and
commendable, if the poet's ill handling of it do not mar and pervert the
good use of it.

Harington Preface to *Orlando Furioso*

5   Solidity, indeed becomes the pen
Of him that writeth things divine to men;
But must I needs want solidness, because
By metaphors I speak; was not God's laws,
His Gospel-laws in olden time held forth
By types, shadows, and metaphors?
. . . . . .
Be not too forward therefore to conclude
That I want solidness, that I am rude:
All things solid in show not solid be;
All things in parables despise not we

Lest things most hurtful lightly we receive;
And things that good are, of our souls bereave.
    My dark and cloudy words they do but hold
The truth, as cabinets enclose the gold.
    The prophets usèd much by metaphors
To set forth truth: yea, who so considers
Christ, his Apostles too, shall plainly see,
That truths to this day in such mantles be.
    Am I afraid to say that Holy Writ,
Which for its style and phrase puts down all wit,
Is everywhere so full of all these things,
(Dark figures, allegories), yet there springs
From that same book that lustre and those rays
Of light that turns our darkest nights to days.

Bunyan *The Pilgrim's Progress* 'The Author's
Apology for his Book'

6   Through that pure Virgin-shrine
That sacred veil drawn o'er thy glorious noon
That men might look and live as glow-worms shine,
        And face the moon:
    Wise Nicodemus saw such light
    As made him know his God by night.

        Most blest believer he!
Who in that land of darkness and blind eyes
Thy long expected healing wings could see,
        When thou didst rise,
    And what can never more be done,
    Did at midnight speak with the sun!

. . . . . .
        There is in God (some say)
A deep, but dazzling darkness; As men here
Say it is late and dusky, because they
        See not all clear;
    O for that night! where I in him
    Might live invisible and dim.

Vaughan 'The Night' ll. 1–12, 49–54

(Vaughan habitually uses the veil as an image of the Incarnation.)

SOME THEORIES OF ALLEGORY

7   It is obvious that anything that is gained with fatigue seems sweeter than
         what is acquired without any effort. The plain truth, since it is quickly
         understood with little difficulty, delights us and passes from the mind.
         But, in order that it may be more pleasing, because acquired with labour,

and therefore be better retained, the poets hide the truth beneath things apparently quite contrary to it. For that reason they produce fables, rather than some other covering, because their beauty attracts those whom neither philosophical demonstrations nor persuasions would have been able to allure. What then shall we say about the poets? Shall we hold that they are madmen, as their senseless adversaries, saying they know not what, have thought them? Certainly not; on the contrary they employ in their productions the most profound thought, which is equivalent to everything hidden in the fruit, and admirable and splendid language, which corresponds to the rind and the leaves.

Boccaccio *The Life of Dante* xxii

8   When things perfectly clear seem obscure, it is the beholder's fault. To a half-blind man, even when the sun is shining its brightest, the sky looks cloudy. Some things are naturally so profound that not without difficulty can the most exceptional keenness in intellect sound their depths; like the sun's globe, by which, before they can clearly discern it, strong eyes are sometimes repelled. On the other hand, some things, though naturally clear perhaps, are so veiled by the artist's skill that scarcely anyone could by mental effort derive sense from them; as the immense body of the sun when hidden in clouds cannot be exactly located by the eye of the most learned astronomer. That some of the prophetic poems are in this class, I do not deny.

Yet not by this token is it fair to condemn them; for surely it is not of the poet's various functions to rip up and lay bare the meaning which lies hidden in his inventions. Rather where matters truly solemn and memorable are too much exposed, it is his office by every effort to protect as well as he can and remove them from the gaze of the irreverent, that they cheapen not by too common familiarity. So when he discharges this duty and does it ingeniously, the poet earns commendation, not anathema.

Wherefore I again grant that poets are at times obscure, but invariably explicable if approached by a sane mind; for these cavillers view them with owl eyes, not human. Surely no one can believe that poets invidiously veil the truth with fiction, either to deprive the reader of the hidden sense, or to appear the more clever; but rather to make truths which would otherwise cheapen by exposure the object of strong intellectual effort and various interpretation, that in ultimate discovery they shall be more precious.

Boccaccio *Genealogy of the Pagan Gods* XIV xii

9   Parables have been used in two ways, and (which is strange) for contrary purposes. For they serve to disguise and veil the meaning, and they serve also to clear and throw light upon it.... In the old times, when the inventions and conclusions of human reason (even those that are now trite and vulgar) were as yet new and strange, the world was full of all kinds of fables, and enigmas, and parables, and similitudes: and these were used not as a device for shadowing and concealing the meaning, but

as a method of making it understood; the understandings of men being then rude and impatient of all subtleties that did not address themselves to the sense, – indeed scarcely capable of them. For as hieroglyphics came before letters, so parables came before arguments.

Bacon *Of the Wisdom of the Ancients*

10   The ancient poets have indeed wrapped as it were in their writings divers and sundry meanings, which they call the senses or mysteries thereof. First of all for the literal sense (as it were the utmost bark or rine [i.e. rind]) they set down in manner of an history the acts and notable exploits of some persons worthy memory: then in the same fiction, as a second rine and somewhat more fine, as it were nearer to the pith and marrow, they place the moral sense profitable for the active life of man, approving virtuous actions and condemning the contrary. Many times also under the selfsame words they comprehend some true understanding of natural philosophy, or sometimes of politic government, and now and then of divinity: and these same senses that comprehend so excellent knowledge we call the allegory, which Plutarch defineth to be when one thing is told, and by that another is understood ... The men of greatest learning and highest wit in the ancient times did of purpose conceal these deep mysteries of learning, and, as it were, cover them with the veil of fables and verse for sundry causes: one cause was that they might not be rashly abused by profane wits, in whom science is corrupted, like good wine in a bad vessel; another cause why they wrote in verse was conservation of the memory of their precepts, as we see yet the general rules almost of every art, not so much as husbandry, but they are oftener recited and better remembered in verse than in prose; another, and a principal cause of all, is to be able with one kind of meat and one dish (as I may so call it) to feed divers tastes. For the weaker capacities will feed themselves with the pleasantness of the history and sweetness of the verse, some that have stronger stomachs will as it were take a further taste of the moral sense, a third sort, more high conceited than they, will digest the allegory: so as indeed it hath been thought by men of very good judgement, such manner of poetical writing was an excellent way to preserve all kind of learning from that corruption which now it is come to since they left that mystical writing of verse.

Harington Preface to *Orlando Furioso*

ALLEGORY IN 'THE FAERIE QUEENE'

11   Sir, knowing how doubtfully all allegories may be construed, and this book of mine, which I have entitled *The Faerie Queene*, being a continued allegory, or dark conceit, I have thought good, as well for avoiding of jealous opinions and misconstructions, as also for your better light in reading thereof (being so by you commanded), to discover unto you the general intention and meaning, which in the whole course thereof

I have fashioned, without expressing of any particular purposes, or by accidents, therein occasioned. The general end therefore of all the book is to fashion a gentleman or noble person in virtuous and gentle discipline: Which for that I conceived should be most plausible and pleasing, being coloured with an historical fiction, the which the most part of men delight to read, rather for variety of matter than for profit of the ensample, I chose the history of King Arthur . . .

To some, I know, this method will seem displeasant, which had rather have good discipline delivered plainly in way of precepts, or sermoned at large, as they use, than thus cloudily enwrapped in allegorical devices. But such, me seem, should be satisfied with the use of these days, seeing all things accounted by their shows, and nothing esteemed of, that is not delightful and pleasing to common sense.

Spenser Letter to Sir Walter Ralegh
(appended to *The Faerie Queene*)

12   And thou, O fairest Princess under sky!
      In this fair mirror mayest behold thy face,
      And thine own realms in land of Faery,
      And in this antique image thy great ancestry.

      The which O! pardon me thus to enfold
      In covert veil, and wrap in shadows light,
      That feeble eyes your glory may behold,
      Which else could not endure those beamès bright,
      But would be dazzled with exceeding light.

Spenser *The Faerie Queene* Proem to Book II stanzas 4–5

13   And if ought else, great bards beside,
      In sage and solemn tunes have sung,
      Of tourneys and of trophies hung;
      Of forests, and enchantments drear,
      Where more is meant than meets the ear.

Milton *Il Penseroso* ll. 116–20

14   Spenser in what he saith hath a way of expression peculiar to himself; he bringeth down the highest and deepest mysteries that are contained in human learning to an easy and gentle form of delivery – which showeth he is master of what he treateth of, he can wield it as he pleaseth. And he hath done this so cunningly that if one heed him not with great attention, rare and wonderful conceptions will unperceived slide by him that readeth his works, and he will think he hath met with nothing but familiar and easy discourses; but let one dwell awhile upon them and he shall feel a strange fullness and roundness in all he saith. The most generous wines tickle the palate least, but they are no sooner in the stomach but by their warmth and strength there, they discover what they are; and those streams that steal away with least noise are usually deepest and most dangerous to pass over.

Kenelm Digby 'Concerning Spenser'

13 Numerology

Numerology, or the science of the symbolic meaning of numbers, was applied in the Renaissance to three different subjects: the cosmos, the Bible and the work of art. God was believed to have created the world on numerical principles and to have given the Bible an additional layer of meaning by filling it with symbolic numbers. The initiate into the mysteries of numerology could 'read' both God's books, the Book of Works (the universe) and the Book of Words (the Bible). The artist could imitate the divine process of creation by organising his work on numerical principles; the harmonious construction of the work would thus reflect the harmony of the universe not because it was an imitation in a simple sense but because it was created by the same method.

The idea that the basis of the world is number derives from the Pythagorean and Platonic tradition. Our knowledge of the beliefs of Pythagoras, a Greek philosopher and mathematician of the sixth century BC who founded a religious community in southern Italy, is entirely second-hand: it comes from a hostile critic, Aristotle (1), and from sympathisers such as Plato and the Neoplatonists. Because the Pythagoreans expressed numbers spatially, as groups of points, they came to think of numbers as having concrete existence. The two most important groups of numbers are the Tetrad (4) and the Decad (10). The Tetrad can be expressed geometrically: 1 as a point, 2 as a line, 3 as a triangle, 4 as a pyramid. The Tetrad is the basis of the Decad because $10 = 1 + 2 + 3 + 4$. This relationship is expressed in the Tetractys, which consists of the points of the Decad arranged triangularly: $\therefore\therefore$. Each number in the Decad has a particular meaning, which is not merely symbolic. Pythagoras discovered that the musical scale can be expressed in terms of numerical proportion, and this discovery led to the belief that everything in the universe can be similarly expressed: things are numbers (1). The opposition between odd and even numbers was regarded as underlying all contraries: limit and the unlimited, male and female, light and dark, good and bad. The monad (1) represents unity, the dyad (2) excess or defect, the triad (3) reconciliation of opposites, the tetrad (4) equilibrium and justice (hence, for example, the emphasis in antiquity on 4 humours, 4 elements, 4 virtues). The numerical and musical theories in Pythagoreanism are closely linked: there is an underlying harmony between man and the cosmos, the microcosm and macrocosm, which can be expressed in terms of both number and music (for these theories see Chapter 6).

Some Pythagorean ideas were taken up and elaborated by Plato. The importance Plato attached to mathematics can be judged from the educational scheme he designed for his Guardians, the ruling class in the *Republic*, who are required to study this subject from the age of 20 to that of 30 (**2**). Numbers have aesthetic and moral significance. The *Timaeus* (31–6) describes how God first created the world's body as a geometrically perfect sphere (**3**), and then created its soul in arithmetical and musical proportions according to a design known as the Platonic Lambda (because it resembles the Greek letter l):

$$
\begin{array}{cc}
 & 1 \\
2 & 3 \\
2^2 = 4 & 9 = 3^2 \\
2^3 = 8 & 27 = 3^3
\end{array}
$$

Thus universal harmony can be measured. There was an extremely influential application of this idea by the Roman architect Vitruvius. Vitruvius argues in *On Architecture* III i that the proportions of the perfect human body can be calculated mathematically, and that a man with arms and legs outspread exactly fits a circle and a square. These principles can then be applied to the design of buildings (**4**). Thus the mathematical proportions on which micro- and macrocosm are constructed become an objective aesthetic standard.

In the Pythagorean and Platonic tradition the first ten numbers are especially significant; in the biblical tradition, which goes back to Babylonian astrology, certain numbers assume meanings because of their associations. Some significant numbers in the Old Testament are 7 (God's day of rest after the Creation), 10 (the Commandments), 12 (the tribes of Israel), 40 (the years spent by the Israelites in the desert), 70 (the number of the patriarchs). Numbers in the New Testament which echo significant numbers in the Old Testament form a system of numerical typology (on the functioning of typology see Chapter 10). Thus the 40 years in the desert typify Christ's 40 days of fasting, the 70 patriarchs typify the 70 disciples appointed by Christ to assist the 12 Apostles (themselves typified by the 12 tribes). With the beginnings of Biblical exegesis in Alexandria Pythagorean and Platonic methods were introduced by Philo Judaeus to help interpret biblical numbers. In the hands of Augustine numerical exegesis became a sophisticated technical skill (**5**, **6**). Augustine associated the divine geometer of *Timaeus* with the Christian God; the statement in the Apocryphal Book of Wisdom 11:20 'thou hast ordered all things in measure and number and weight' became the basis of the view that God had created the world by number. Numerical exegesis went far beyond interpretation of the obviously significant biblical numbers. Every number used in the Bible in however seemingly trivial a context was scrutinised for its meaning. In Books XI and XII of *The City of God* we can see how far this process was taken. A single number could be interpreted in many different ways, according to how it was divided. The Pythagorean Decad acquired new Christian connotations, and numbers not necessarily stressed in the Bible became significant, for example 3 (the Trinity – a non-biblical doctrine perhaps influenced by Pythagorean-ism), 4 (the gospels), 33 (the years of Christ's life).

The Pythagorean and Platonic tradition of number symbolism was also transmitted independently from biblical numerical exegesis by the encyclopedists of late antiquity and the early Middle Ages. The more influential works are Macrobius' *Commentary on the Dream of Scipio*, Boethius' *The Principles of Arithmetic*, Martianus Capella's *The Marriage of Philology and Mercury* (Book VII), and Isidore's *On Number*. Some of these works are arithmological, that is they expound the meaning and powers of specific numbers in the Decad. Thus Macrobius (I vi) discusses at length the significance of the number 7. The impetus behind these works was pedagogical, the desire to transmit the traditions of classical culture; thus they simplified and passed on to generations of readers a basic knowledge of the principles of numerology. The classical attitude to number was perpetuated in the medieval curriculum of the Seven Liberal Arts, the elementary Trivium (three ways) consisting of literary studies, grammar, rhetoric and dialectic, and the advanced Quadrivium (four ways) consisting of mathematical studies, arithmetic, geometry, astronomy and music. Boethius (who first gave the Quadrivium its name) regarded arithmetic as the basis of the other sciences; in this he was following a tradition going back to Pythagoras.

In the Renaissance numerology was approached rather differently. The encyclopedic tradition of late antiquity and the Middle Ages was concerned with expounding the basic principles. Renaissance writers on numerology, most of them Neoplatonists, regarded it as a mystery whose secrets were the property of the initiated. (This esoteric attitude had been characteristic of the early Pythagorean community.) Renaissance numerologists combined traditional sources – Pythagorean/Platonic and exegetical texts – with sources which were acquiring new interest – the Jewish Cabala, the Orphic and Hermetic writings (**8**, **9**). Significant Italian numerological works include Pico's *Heptaplus* (a sevenfold interpretation of the seven days of creation), Giorgio's *Harmony of the World* and Bongo's *On the Mystery of Numbers*. It is difficult to assess the knowledge or acceptance of the Italian Neoplatonist numerological tradition in England. Donne's attitude in *Essays in Divinity* is revealing. He refers to Giorgio as 'that transcending wit', yet he seems embarrassed by the excessive application of Pythagorean number symbolism to the Bible (**7**). Three seventeenth-century authors, Henry Reynolds, Sir Thomas Browne and Henry More, seem to have accepted it wholeheartedly. In *Religio Medici* Browne describes God as 'a skilful geometrician', and he sees man's task as the unravelling of God's difficult designs in nature, the Bible and history. Browne performs an elaborate piece of numerological detective work in *The Garden of Cyrus*, identifying the repeated uses of the number 5 in nature and art. Reynolds, following Pico, makes an impassioned plea in *Mythomystes* for the mysteries of number to be properly studied, yet the defensive tone of the work suggests that he felt his position to be an unpopular one (**9**).

Numerology was more than a means of interpreting the universe and the Bible; it was a principle of artistic composition. Biblical number symbolism was used in the construction of Gothic cathedrals, and in the Renaissance architects like Alberti and Palladio, following Vitruvius, designed their churches to reflect on the one hand the proportions of the human body and on the other the proportions of the universe. Italian humanist architectural theory, made available in England in the early seventeenth century by Inigo Jones and Sir Henry Wotton, is reflected not only in English Palladian architecture but in country house poetry. Numerology was used as a principle of literary organisation by Augustine; *The City of God*, for example, has 22 books, reflecting the number of letters in the Hebrew alphabet. Augustine thus expounded the principles of number symbolism in his text, and illustrated them in his structure. The numerological organisation of a literary work enables a writer to express meaning through form; it is in effect a kind of allegory. The most important practitioner of numerical composition in the Middle Ages was Dante. Both *The New Life* and *The Divine Comedy* have complex numerical structures, the most important numbers being 3 and 9. *The Divine Comedy* has 3 books (symbolising the Trinity) and 100 cantos (one is introductory, leaving 99). Nine is the number associated with Beatrice; it is divisible by 3, thus indicating her divine nature. Dante's numerical structures, though difficult to unravel, are not secret; Dante constantly draws attention to how his poems are composed and to be read (e.g. *The New Life* xxx), comparing his methods with those of divine creation.

To what extent were such numerological methods of composition used by English Renaissance poets, and how can we identify them? Two kinds of poetic numerology have been distinguished: 'substantive', in which number symbols are themselves the subject of a work, and are expounded and illustrated by the poet, and 'formal', in which the symbols are contained in the structure, so that the numbers of lines in a stanza or stanzas in a poem have symbolic meaning. The first kind of numerology is usually self-explanatory; the second is more difficult to detect. Readers are faced with the question of whether numerological composition was a habitual or an esoteric practice. Poets conversant with Neoplatonism, such as Spenser, Chapman (**14**), Milton and Henry More, were certainly familiar with numerological theory and are the likeliest practitioners of numerological composition. Some aspects of numerology were common knowledge among educated men, and were often explored in poetry: for example, the ideas of God as a geometer creating by number, of the proportion between the human body and the cosmos, of the circle, the most valued geometric form, representing both physical and moral perfection. God in Cowley's *Davideis* I (Ch. **6.21**) and in *Paradise Lost* VII (**10**) creates the world according to geometrical and musical proportion. Country house poems such as Marvell's 'Upon Appleton House' stress the correspondence between the good man and the architectural proportions of his estate (**12**). Jonson took a broken compass and an incomplete circle as his motto (thereby indicating his awareness of his own moral limitations), and in his celebratory poems, such as the ode on Henry Morison, used the describing of a circle as an image of moral perfection (**11**). In addition to such allusions to the theory of numerology, we find 'substantive' number symbolism in many poems (**13**, **14**), the best example being *The Faerie Queene*. Thus in Book I Spenser uses the Pythagorean system of contraries in his pairing of opposite characters such as Una and Duessa; sometimes these opposites appear as triads, such as Fidelia, Speranza and Charissa (Faith, Hope and Charity), the opposites of Sansfoy, Sansloy and Sansjoy (Faithless, Lawless and Joyless).

Such geometrical and numerical patterns are evident to patient readers, and would not have seemed mysterious in the Renaissance. 'Formal' numerology is another matter. Critics have only recently begun to investigate 'formal' numerological composition, by counting word, line or stanza totals to discover whether there is a correspondence between the symbolic meaning of these numbers and the poem's content. This procedure is fraught with difficulties, one being that the critics may read meanings into the numbers they arrive at, another being that three different systems of number symbolism were available to the poet, Pythagorean, Biblical and temporal (the ways in which time could be divided, for example 24 hours, 7 days, 52 weeks, 12 months, 365 days). Thus the number 4 might represent justice, or the gospels, or the seasons; the context would confirm which meaning if any was intended. Two poems which have been convincingly shown to use 'formal' numerology are Spenser's *Epithalamion* and Milton's 'Nativity Ode'. Spenser uses temporal symbolism; his poem illustrates through its stanza and line numbers the passing of the 24 hours of the day and 365 days of the year. Milton's numbers are biblical and Platonic: the ode's introduction has seven-line stanzas, the 'Hymn' eight-line, indicating the transition from time to eternity, from discord to harmony. Indeed it has been argued that the basis of the poem's numerical organisation is the Platonic Lambda. Such complex schemes are probably meant to be secret, to be legible only by God, the poet and the initiate, as with the highest level of allegory. Mundane readers can appreciate the formal symmetry of a poem without realising that the symmetry itself expresses the poem's meaning. 'Formal' numerology is thus an enigma; the danger for modern readers is that they may be so teased that they will track down numerical composition where it was never intended.

PYTHAGOREAN/PLATONIC NUMEROLOGY

1   The so-called Pythagoreans applied themselves to mathematics, and were the first to develop this science; and through studying it they came to believe that its principles are the principles of everything. And since *numbers* are by nature first among these principles, and they fancied that they could detect in numbers, to a greater extent than in fire and earth and water, many analogues of what is and comes into being – such and such a property of number being *justice*, and such and such *soul* or *mind*, another *opportunity*, and similarly, more or less, with all the rest – and since they saw further that the properties and ratios of the musical scales are based on numbers, and since it seemed clear that all other things have their whole nature modelled upon numbers, and that numbers are the ultimate things in the whole physical universe, they assumed the elements of numbers to be the elements of everything, and the whole universe to be a proportion of number.

Aristotle *Metaphysics* I v

2   Number is the subject of the whole art of calculation and of the science of number; and since the properties of number appear to have the power of leading us towards reality, these must be among the studies we are in search of. The soldier must learn them in order to marshal his troops; the philosopher, because he must rise above the world of change and grasp

true being, or he will never become proficient in the calculations of reason. Our Guardian is both soldier and philosopher; so this will be a suitable study for our law to prescribe. Those who are to take part in the highest functions of state must be induced to approach it, not in an amateur spirit, but perseveringly, until, by the aid of pure thought, they come to see the real nature of number. They are to practise calculation, not like merchants or shopkeepers for purposes of buying and selling, but with a view to war and to help in the conversion of the soul itself from the world of becoming to truth and reality.

Plato *Republic* VII 524

3   Now anything that has come to be must be corporeal, visible, and tangible: but nothing can be visible without fire, nor tangible without solidity, and nothing can be solid without earth. So god, when he began to put together the body of the universe, made it of fire and earth. But it is not possible to combine two things properly without a third to act as a bond to hold them together. And the best bond is one that effects the closest unity between itself and the terms it is combining; and this is best done by a continued geometrical proportion ... So god placed water and air between fire and earth, and made them so far as possible proportional to one another, so that air is to water as water is to earth; and in this way he bound the world into a visible and tangible whole. So by these means and from these four constituents the body of the universe was created to be at unity owing to proportion; in consequence it acquired concord, so that having once come together in unity with itself it is indissoluble by any but its compounder.

Plato *Timaeus* 31–2

4   The planning of temples depends upon symmetry: and the method of this architects must diligently apprehend. It arises from proportion (which in Greek is called *analogia*). Proportion consists in taking a fixed module, in each case, both for the parts of a building and for the whole, by which the method of symmetry is put into practice. For without symmetry and proportion no temple can have a regular plan; that is, it must have an exact proportion worked out after the fashion of the members of a finely-shaped human body ... Now the navel is naturally the exact centre of the body. For if a man lies on his back with hands and feet outspread, and the centre of a circle is placed on his navel, his fingers and toes will be touched by the circumference. Also a square will be found described within the figure, in the same way as a round figure is produced. For if we measure from the sole of the foot to the top of the head, and apply the measure to the outstretched hands, the breadth will be found equal to the height, just like sites which are squared by rule. Therefore if Nature has planned the human body so that the members correspond in their proportions to its complete configuration, the ancients seem to have had reason in determining that in the execution of their works they should

observe an exact adjustment of the several members to the general pattern of the plan.

Vitruvius *On Architecture* II i 1–4

NUMERICAL BIBLICAL EXEGESIS

5   The works of Creation are described as being completed in six days, the same formula for a day being repeated six times. The reason for this is that six is the number of perfection. It is not that God was constrained by the intervals of time, as if he could not have created all things simultaneously, and have made them afterwards conform to temporal succession by appropriate movements. No, the reason was that the completion or perfection of the works is expressed by the number six. For six is the first number which is the sum of its parts, that is of its fractions, the sixth, the third, and the half, for one, two and three added together make six ... Hence the theory of number is not to be lightly regarded, since it is made quite clear, in many passages of the holy Scriptures, how highly it is to be valued. It was not for nothing that it was said in praise of God, 'Thou hast ordered all things in measure and number and weight' [Wisdom 11:20].

Augustine *The City of God* XI xxx

6   The significance of 40 days of fasting:
It is composed of four times ten; as it were, the knowledge of all things joined together by time. The course of the day and year are accomplished through the number four; the days are carried through in intervals of hours: morning, noon, evening, and night; the years, by the spring, summer, autumn, and winter months. But, while we are living in time, we must abstain and fast from all pleasure in time because of the eternity in which we hope to live; although, by the passage of time, that very doctrine of despising temporal things and striving for eternal goods is recommended to us. Further, the number ten symbolises the knowledge of the Creator and the creature. For a trinity is present in the Creator, while the number seven signifies the creature, by reason of his life and body. In the case of his life, there are three commandments to love God with our whole heart, our whole soul, and our whole mind; with regard to the body, there are four very discernible elements of which it is composed. So, while the number ten is being impressed upon us in the sense of time, that is, multiplied by four, we are being instructed to live virtuously and temperately, free from the delights of time – in other words, to fast for forty days.

Augustine *Christian Instruction* II xvi

7   In a few words we will consider, whether any mystery reside in that chosen number [70]; the rather because very many remarkable things, and passages in history, seem to me to have been limited in that number, which therefore seems more periodic than any other. But because any

over-curious and mysterious consideration of this number 70, though it
be composed of the two greatest numbers (for ten cannot be exceeded,
but that to express any further number you must take a part of it again;
and seven is ever used to express infinite), be too Cabalistic and
Pythagoric for a vulgar Christian ... because I am one, and in a low
degree, of the first and vulgar rank, and write but to my equals, I will
forbear it, as misinterpretable; since to some palates it may taste of
ostentation; but to some, of distraction from better contemplations, and
of superstition to others: yet, we may, as well with reverence to the things,
as respect to the number, rest a little upon those works of God, or his
servants, which this number, at least, reduces to our memory. First
therefore, those fathers of the world, to whom God affords a room by
name in the 10th of Gen. from whom are derived all nations ... are
reckoned there to be 70 ... And in that great captivity of Babylon ... the
chosen people of God were trodden down 70 years. To which foreign
sojourning, for many concurrences, and main circumstances, many have
assimilated and compared the Roman Church's straying into France, and
being impounded in Avignon 70 years ... Then, those disciples, suppliers
and fellow-workers with the Apostles ... whom our most blessed Saviour
instituted, were also of this number, 70. And so having refreshed to your
memory, upon this occasion of the number 70, these stories out of the
Bible, we will end with this observation, that when God moved
Ptolomeus to a desire of having the Bible translated [from Hebrew into
Greek], he accited from Jerusalem 72, for that glorious and mystic work;
and these, though they were 72, either for affection to conform
themselves to a number so notorious, or for some true mystery in it, or
for what else, God knows, have ever retained the name of Septuagint [i.e.
70].

> Donne *Essays in Divinity* II 'Variety in the Number'

RENAISSANCE ATTITUDES TO NUMEROLOGY

8   The ancient system of philosophising through numbers ... was held to by
the early theologians, by Pythagoras in particular, by Aglaophamus, by
Philolaus, by Plato and the early Platonists. But in this age, this doctrine,
like other famous ones, has so passed out of use by the negligence of
posterity, that scarcely any traces of it are to be found. Plato writes in the
Epinomis that among all liberal arts and theoretical sciences the science
of numbering is chief and most divine. Again, asking why man is the
wisest animal, he answers that it is because he knows how to number ...
These things could not in any way be true if they had understood by the
art of numbering that art at which now the merchants are expert above
all. Plato also witnesses this, warning us in a loud voice not to confuse
this divine arithmetic with mercantile arithmetic.

> Pico della Mirandola *On the Dignity of Man* (compare **2**)

9   Now, from this means that the first ancients used of delivering their
knowledges thus among themselves by word of mouth, and by successive
reception from them down to after ages, that art of mystical writing by
numbers, wherein they couched under a fabulous attire those their verbal
instructions, was after called *scientia Cabalae*, or the science of reception
– *Cabala* among the Hebrews signifying no other than the Latin *receptio*:
a learning by the ancients held in high estimation and reverence, and not
without great reason; for if God (as the excellent John Picus rehearses)
... did nothing by chance, but through his wisdom disposed all things as
in weight and measure, so likewise in number; and which taught the
ingenious Salluste [du Bartas] to say that:

> Sacred harmony
> And law of number did accompany
> The Almighty most, when first his ordinance
> Appointed earth to rest and heaven to dance, [trans. Sylvester]

well might Plato consequently affirm that, among all the liberal arts and
contemplative sciences, the chiefest and most divine was the *scientia
numerandi* ... And I am fully of opinion ... that the ignorance of this art,
and the world's maim in the want or not understanding of it, is insinuated
in the poets' generally-sung fable of Orpheus, whom they feign to have
recovered his Euridice from hell with his music, that is, truth and equity
from darkness of barbarism and ignorance with his profound and
excellent doctrines; but that in the thick caliginous way to the upper earth
she was lost again, and remains lost to us that read and understand him
not, for want merely of the knowledge of that art of numbers that should
unlock and explain his mystical meanings to us.

Henry Reynolds Mythomystes

GOD AS GEOMETER

10   Silence, ye troubled waves, and thou deep, peace,
Said then the omnific Word, your discord end:
    Nor stayed, but on the wings of cherubim
Uplifted, in paternal glory rode
Far into chaos, and the world unborn;
For chaos heard his voice: him all his train
Followed in bright procession to behold
Creation, and the wonders of his might.
Then stayed the fervid wheels, and in his hand
He took the golden compasses, prepared
In God's eternal store, to circumscribe
This universe, and all created things:
One foot he centred, and the other turned
Round through the vast profundity obscure,
And said, Thus far extend, thus far thy bounds,

This be thy just circumference, O world.

Milton *Paradise Lost* VII ll. 216–31

PROPORTION AS MORAL PERFECTION

11   All offices were done
      By him, so ample, full, and round,
      In weight, in measure, number, sound,
      As though his age imperfect might appear,
      His life was of humanity the sphere.

Jonson 'To the Immortal Memory and Friendship of that
Noble Pair, Sir Lucius Cary and Sir H. Morison' ll. 48–52

12   Within this sober frame expect
      Work of no foreign architect,
      That unto caves the quarries drew,
      And forests did to pastures hew,
      Who of his great design in pain
      Did for a model vault his brain,
      Whose columns should so high be raised
      To arch the brows that on them gazed.
      . . . . . .
      But all things are composèd here
      Like Nature, orderly and near:
      In which we the dimensions find
      Of that more sober age and mind,
      When larger-sizèd men did stoop
      To enter at a narrow loop;
      As practising, in doors so strait,
      To strain themselves through heaven's gate.
      . . . . . .
      Humility alone designs
      Those short but admirable lines,
      By which, ungirt and unconstrained,
      Things greater are in less contained.
      Let others vainly strive to immure
      The circle in the quadrature!
      These holy mathematics can
      In every figure equal man.

Marvell 'Upon Appleton House' stanzas 1, 4, 6

'SUBSTANTIVE' NUMBER SYMBOLISM IN POETRY

13   Upon this primrose hill,
        Where, if heaven would distill
      A shower of rain, each several drop might go

To his own primrose, and grow manna so;
And where their form, and their infinity
    Make a terrestrial galaxy,
    As the small stars do in the sky:
I walk to find a true love; and I see
That 'tis not a mere woman, that is she,
But must, or more, or less than woman be.

    Yet know I not, which flower
    I wish; a six, or four;
For should my true love less than woman be,
She were scarce anything; and then, should she
Be more than woman, she would get above
    All thought of sex, and think to move
    My heart to study her, and not to love;
Both these were monsters; since there must reside
Falsehood in woman, I could more abide,
She were by art, than nature falsified.

    Live primrose then, and thrive
    With thy true number five;
And women, whom this flower doth represent,
With this mysterious number be content;
Ten is the farthest number; if half ten
    Belong unto each woman, then
    Each woman may take half us men;
Or if this will not serve their turn, since all
Numbers are odd, or even, and they fall
First into this, five, women may take us all.
                Donne 'The Primrose' (a true love is a flower with four
                or six petals; the primrose has five petals; five, the
                number of marriage, is assumed to be the number of
                women, and ten the number of men)

14   The marriage of Hymen and Eucharis:
                Next before her [Eucharis] went
Five lovely children decked with ornament
Of her sweet colours, bearing torches by;
  . . . . . .
The odd disparent number they did choose,
To show the union married loves should use,
Since in two equal parts it will not sever,
But the midst holds one to rejoin it ever,
As common to both parts: men therefrom deem
That equal number gods do not esteem,
Being authors of sweet peace and unity,
But pleasing to the infernal empery,

Under whose ensigns wars and discords fight,
Since an even number you may disunite
In two parts equal, nought in middle left
To reunite each part from other reft;
And five they hold in most especial prize,
Since 'tis the first odd number that doth rise
From the two foremost numbers' unity,
That odd and even are: which are two and three,
For one no number is, but thence doth flow
The powerful race of number.

Chapman *Hero and Leander* Sestiad V ll. 317–19, 323–40

A Note on the Division
of Historical Periods

For the reader's convenience I give below a list of standard labels, some of which are used in this book, together with the approximate historical periods to which they refer.

1 *Antiquity*: used loosely to cover the entire period of ancient Greek and Roman history.

Pre-classical or Homeric Greece: before 800 BC. *Classical Greece*: c. 800 BC to 323 BC (death of Alexander the Great). *The Hellenistic Period*: 322 BC to 30 BC (conquest of Egypt by Rome).

Republican Rome: 753 BC (traditional date of foundation of Rome) to 30 BC (triumph of Octavian, later Augustus). *The Roman Empire*: 27 BC (government of Augustus) to AD 410 (sack of Rome) or 476 (last emperor of western empire deposed).

2 *The Middle Ages*: used loosely to cover the period from the supremacy of Christianity in the Roman empire (the first ecumenical council of the Church was held at Nicaea 325) or the fall of Rome in the fifth century to the fourteenth or fifteenth centuries. The close of the Middle Ages is dated differently for individual countries. *The Early Middle Ages*: the fifth to the eleventh centuries (the earlier part of this period used to be referred to as the *Dark Ages*). *The High Middle Ages*: the eleventh to the thirteenth centuries. *The Later Middle Ages*: the fourteenth and fifteenth centuries in northern Europe; in Italy this period is designated as the Renaissance.

3 *The Renaissance*: used differently according to which country (e.g. Italy, France, England) or which field (e.g. literature, art, diplomacy, economics) is being discussed. At its broadest it can cover the late thirteenth to the late seventeenth centuries. The term is also applied to two earlier periods, the *Carolingian Renaissance* (ninth century) and the *Renaissance of the Twelfth Century* in France. In Italy, the *Early Renaissance* refers to the fourteenth century, the *High Renaissance* to the fifteenth and first half of the sixteenth centuries. In this book the *Renaissance in England* refers to the sixteenth and first three-quarters of the seventeenth century.

Abbreviations

EL	Everyman's Library (London and New York)
FC	The Fathers of the Church (Washington, D.C.)
GR	Greece and Rome (Oxford)
LCC	Library of Christian Classics (Philadelphia and London)
LLA	Library of Liberal Arts (Indianapolis and New York)
Loeb	Loeb Classical Library (Cambridge, Mass., and London)
ML	Muses' Library (London)
Norton	Norton Critical Editions (New York)
PC	Penguin Classics (Harmondsworth)
PEL	Penguin English Library (Harmondsworth)
PEP	Penguin English Poets (Harmondsworth)
PM	Past Masters (Oxford)
TT	Tudor Translations (London)
WC	World's Classics (Oxford)

References

References for extracts are arranged alphabetically by author. Readers can thus use the references in two ways: to follow up an extract in the work from which it is taken, or as an index, to trace all the extracts from a particular author through the book. Page references are preceded by the relevant chapter and extract number in bold type. (Where appropriate book, chapter and line references are given immediately below each extract in the text, thus enabling readers to refer to more than one edition of a work.) All texts have been modernised, and punctuation and capitalisation of modernised texts have in some cases been simplified. Titles given below extracts have been modernised and shortened, but the spelling of the editions used has been retained for titles in this index. Both Latin and English titles are given where I consider that this will help readers to identify a work.

Aquinas, St Thomas, *Summa Theologiae* (otherwise *Theologica*), vol. I, trans. T. Gilby (London and New York, 1964), **10.7** pp. 37–9

Ariosto, Ludovico, *Orlando Furioso*, trans. Sir J. Harington, ed. G. Hough (London, 1962), **1.14** p. 67 (see also Harington)

Aristotle, *The 'Art' of Rhetoric*, trans. J. H. Freese (Loeb, 1947), **9.2** pp. 15, 17, 19

Aristotle, *On the Heavens (De Caelo)*, trans. W. K. C. Guthrie (Loeb, 1939), **6.4** pp. 23–5; **6.12** pp. 193–5

Aristotle, *Metaphysics*, trans. H. Tredennick (2 vols, Loeb, 1933), **6.5** II pp. 145, 147, 149; **13.1** I p. 33

Ascham, Roger, *The Schoolmaster*, ed. L. V. Ryan (Ithaca, 1967), **9.17** p. 115

Augustine, *Christian Instruction (De Doctrina Christiana)*, trans. J. Gavigan (FC, 1966), **10.5** pp. 65–6; **13.6** p. 84

Augustine, *Concerning the City of God against the Pagans (De Civitate Dei)*, trans. H. Bettenson (PC, 1972), **1.9** p. 590; **4.7** p. 348; **5.11** pp. 48; **5.12** pp. 593, 596; **5.13** p. 1091; **8.1** p. 523; **13.5** p. 465

Augustine, *Confessions and Enchiridion (or Handbook)*, trans. A. C. Outler (LCC, 1955), **8.7** pp. 404–5

Augustine, *The Teacher, The Free Choice of the Will, Grace and Free Will*, trans. R. P. Russell (FC, 1968), **8.28** p. 255

Augustine of Dacia (?), cited in D. W. Robertson, Jr, *A Preface to Chaucer* (Princeton, 1962), **10.6** p. 293

Bacon, Francis, *The Advancement of Learning*, ed. T. Case (W C, London, 1960) **11.6** pp. 96–7

Bacon, Francis, *Of the Wisdom of the Ancients (De Sapientia Veterum)*, trans.

J. Spedding, in *Works*, ed. J. Spedding, R. L. Ellis and D. D. Heath, vol. VI (London, 1878), **12.9** p. 698

The Bible, the Authorised Version

The Acts of the Apostles **5.8** 1:6–7

Colossians **8.24** 2:13–14

I Corinthians **8.6** 15:21–2; **8.34** 1:20–5; **10.3** 10:1–4, 6, 11; **12.3** 13:9–12

Daniel **5.7** 7:17–18, 23–7

Ecclesiastes **6.32** 1:4–5

Ephesians Intro. **4** 6:13

Exodus **1.7** 3:7–8; **12.1** 34:29–30, 33–5

Galatians **8.11** 3:10–13; **8.23** 3:23–9

Genesis **1.6** 2:8–10

Isaiah **1.8** 11:6–9

James **8.14** 1:27

John **10.2** 3:14–15

Joshua **6.30** 10:12–13

Matthew **10.1** 12:39–41; **12.2** 13:10–13

II Peter **5.9** 3:3–8, 10, 13

Psalms **5.6** 90:1–2, 4; **6.31** 93:1

Revelation **5.10** 20:1–4

Romans **8.5** 5:19–21; **8.10** 3:19–24, 28; **8.17** 8:28–31; **8.18** 9:13–16, 19–21; **8.22** 8:14–15; **8.37** 2:14–15

Song of Solomon (otherwise Song of Songs or Canticles) **10.4** 4:2

The Bible, the Authorised Version, Preface, in A. W. Pollard, *Records of the English Bible* (London, 1911), **7.9** p. 349

The Bible, the Geneva Bible, Preface, in A.W. Pollard, *Records of the English Bible* (London, 1911), **7.8** pp. 279–80

Boccaccio, Giovanni, *Genealogy of the Pagan Gods* XIV and XV (*Genealogia Deorum Gentilium*), trans. C. G. Osgood as *Boccaccio on Poetry* (LLA, 1956), **12.8** pp. 59–60

Boccaccio, Giovanni, *The Life of Dante*, trans. A. H. Gilbert, in A. H. Gilbert, *Literary Criticism: Plato to Dryden* (New York, 1940), **12.7** p. 211

Boethius, *The Principles of Music*, trans. C. M. Bower (George Peabody College Ph.D., 1966), **6.13** pp. 44, 46–7

The Book of Common Prayer, 'Of Ceremonies' **7.15** (see also The Thirty-Nine Articles)

The Book of Homilies, i.e. *Certain Sermons or Homilies appointed to be read in Churches* . . . (Oxford, 1822), **7.4** p. 10; **7.7** pp. 14–16; **7.11** pp. 60–1; **8.13** p. 30

Browne, Sir Thomas, *The Major Works*, ed. C. A. Patrides (PEL, 1977), Intro. **3** pp. 375–6; **4.10** p. 115; **6.19** pp. 149–50; **6.24** pp. 103–4; **6.34** p. 75; **7.13** p. 64

Bruno, Giordano, *On the Infinite Universe and Worlds*, trans. D. W. Singer, in D. W. Singer, *Giordano Bruno: His Life and Thought* (New York, 1950), **6.28** pp. 245–6

Bunyan, John, *The Pilgrim's Progress*, ed. R. Sharrock (PEL 1965), **12.5** p. 34

Calvin, John, *Institutes of the Christian Religion*, trans. F. L. Battles (2 vols,

LCC 1960), **8.2** I pp. 251–2; **8.20** II p. 931; **10.11** I p. 451

Campion, Thomas, *The Works*, ed. W. R. Davis (London, 1969), **4.11** p. 43

Castiglione, Baldassare, *The Book of the Courtier*, trans. Sir T. Hoby (EL, 1928), **3.4** p. 319

Chapman, George, *Hero and Leander*, in Christopher Marlowe, *The Complete Poems and Translations*, ed. S. Orgel (PEP, 1971), **13.14** p. 75

Cicero, *The Nature of the Gods (De Natura Deorum)*, trans. H. C. P. McGregor (PC, 1972), **2.2** p. 152

Cicero, *De Officiis (Of Duties)*, trans. W. Miller (Loeb, 1913), **9.7** pp. 71, 73–5

Cicero, *De Oratore (On the Orator)*, trans. E. W. Sutton and H. Rackham (2 vols, Loeb, 1948), **9.3** I pp. 23–7; **9.4** II p. 59

Cicero, *De Re Publica (The Republic)*, trans. C. W. Keyes (Loeb, 1928), **6.6** pp. 269–71

Cleveland, John, *The Poems*, ed. B. Morris and E. Withington (Oxford, 1967), **3.13** pp. 54–5

Colet, John, *Statutes of Paul's School*, in E. M. Nugent, ed., *The Thought and Culture of the English Renaissance* (Cambridge, 1956), **9.15** pp. 40–1

Comes, Natalis, *Mythologiae . . . Libri Decem (Ten Books of Mythology)* (2 vols, Frankfurt, 1584), **2.11** p. 707 (trans. I. Rivers)

Copernicus, *On the Revolutions of the Celestial Spheres (De Revolutionibus Orbium Celestium)*, vol. I, trans. J. F. Dobson and S. Brodetsky, in T. S. Kuhn, *The Copernican Revolution* (Cambridge, Mass., 1957), **6.27** pp. 179–80

Cowley, Abraham, *Poems*, ed. A. R. Waller (Cambridge, 1905), **6.21** p. 253

Crashaw, Richard, *The Verse in English* (New York, 1949), **7.26** pp. 210–11

Daniel, Samuel, *Poems and A Defence of Ryme*, ed. A. C. Sprague (Chicago, 1965), **4.12** p. 117; **9.20** pp. 74, 96

Dante, *Letter to Can Grande della Scala*, trans. A. H. Gilbert, in A. H. Gilbert, *Literary Criticism: Plato to Dryden* (New York, 1940), **10.8** pp. 202–3

Digby, Kenelm, 'Concerning Spenser that I wrote at Mr May's Desire', in P. J. Alpers, ed., *Edmund Spenser* (Penguin Critical Anthologies, 1969), **12.14** p. 60

Donne, John, *The Complete English Poems*, ed. A. J. Smith (PEP, 1973). **3.12** pp. 55–6; **6.25** pp. 310–11; **6.35** p. 277; **6.36** pp. 294–5; **7.20** p. 316; **13.13** p. 74

Donne, John, *Devotions upon Emergent Occasions* (Ann Arbor, Michigan, 1959), **8.3** p. 148; **10.13** pp. 124–5

Donne, John, *Essays in Divinity*, ed. E. M. Simpson (Oxford, 1952), **13.7** pp. 59–61

Drayton, Michael, *Poems*, ed. J. Buxton (2 vols, ML, 1953), **1.19** I pp. 123–4

Du Bartas, *His Diuine Weekes and Workes*, trans. J. Sylvester (London, 1641), **6.23** p. 52; **6.33** pp. 2–3

Elyot, Sir Thomas, *The Book Named The Governor* (EL, 1962), **6.14** pp. 3–4; **9.16** p. 39

Empedocles, trans. J. E. Raven, in G. S. Kirk and J. E. Raven, *The Presocratic Philosophers* (Cambridge, 1962), **6.8** p. 327

Epictetus, *The Discourses as reported by Arrian, The Manual, and Fragments,* trans. W. A. Oldfather (2 vols, Loeb, 1925), **4.2** II p. 483; **4.3** II p. 491

Erasmus, 'An exhortacion to the diligent studye of scripture' (*Paraclesis*), (trans. W. Roy), in *The New Testament in Englishe* (trans. W. Tyndale) (London, 1550), **7.6** sig. + ii verso

Erasmus, *On the Freedom of the Will*, trans. E. G. Rupp, in Luther and Erasmus, *Free Will and Salvation*, ed. E. G. Rupp and P. S. Watson (LCC, 1969), **8.29** pp. 84–5

Erasmus, *The Godly Feast (Convivium Religiosum)*, trans. C. R. Thompson, in *Ten Colloquies* (LLA, 1957), **9.14** p. 155

Fanshawe, Sir Richard, in *The Oxford Book of Seventeenth-Century Verse*, ed. H. J. C. Grierson and G. Bullough (Oxford, 1934), **1.17** p. 449

Fletcher, Giles, *Christ's Triumph over Death*, in Giles and Phineas Fletcher, *Poetical Works*, ed. F. S. Boas, vol. I (Cambridge, 1908), **8.8** p. 61

Fletcher, Phineas, *The Purple Island*, in Giles and Phineas Fletcher, *Poetical Works*, ed. F. S. Boas, vol. II (Cambridge, 1909), **6.17** p. 21

Foxe, John, *The First Volume of the Ecclesiasticall History, contayning the Actes & Monumentes of thinges passed in euery Kinges time, in this Realme, especially in the Churche of England* (London, 1576), **5.14** sig. * ij verso

Galileo Galilei, *Dialogue Concerning the Two Chief World Systems – Ptolemaic and Copernican*, trans. S. Drake (Berkeley and Los Angeles, 1962), **6.29** pp. 50–1

Gellius, Aulus, *The Attic Nights*, trans. J. C. Rolfe (3 vols, Loeb, 1948), **9.1** II p. 457

Greville, Fulke, *Selected Poems*, ed. T. Gunn (London, 1968), **8.4** pp. 127–8; **8.36** pp. 133–4; **10.14** p. 119

Hall, Joseph, *Heaven upon Earth*, in *The Works*, ed. P. Wynter, vol. VI (New York, 1969, rev. edn, first pub. Oxford, 1863), **4.9** pp. 6–7

Harington, Sir John, *A Preface, or rather a Briefe Apologie of Poetrie*, in G. G. Smith, ed., *Elizabethan Critical Essays*, vol. II (Oxford, 1904), **11.9** p. 199; **12.4** pp. 205–6; **12.10** pp. 201–3 (see also Ariosto)

Heraclitus, trans. G. S. Kirk, in G. S. Kirk and J. E. Raven, *The Presocratic Philosophers* (Cambridge, 1962), **6.7** p. 191

Herbert, George, *The English Poems*, ed. C. A. Patrides (EL, 1974), Intro. **2** p. 60; **6.26** p. 106; **7.21** pp. 122–3; **8.27** pp. 150–1; **10.15** pp. 139–40

Hesiod, *Theogony, Works and Days*, trans. D. Wender (PC, 1973), **1.1** p. 62; **11.1** pp. 23–4

Homer, *The Odyssey*, trans. E. V. Rieu (PC, 1946), **1.2** p. 79

Hooker, Richard, *Of the Laws of Ecclesiastical Polity*, ed. C. Morris, vol. I (EL, 1965), **7.5** pp. 281–2; **7.12** pp. 421–2; **8.32** pp. 169–70; **8.38** pp. 176–7

Horace, *Satires, Epistles, and Ars Poetica (The Art of Poetry)*, trans. H. R. Fairclough (Loeb, 1966), **11.8** p. 483

Ignatius Loyola, St, *The Spiritual Exercises*, trans. W. H. Longridge (rev. edn, London, 1930), **7.23** pp. 57–8

Isocrates, trans. G. Norlin (3 vols, Loeb, 1954), **9.9** I pp. 43–5

Jonson, Ben, *The Complete Poems*, ed. G. Parfitt (PEP, 1975), Intro. **4** p. 193; **1.21** p. 82; **4.14** p. 69; **5.17** p. 67; **9.11** pp. 376–7, 411; **9.19** pp. 378–9, 448 (line missing from Penguin text restored); **9.21** pp. 405, 450; **13.11** p. 213

Jonson, Ben, 'The Mind of the Front', in Sir Walter Ralegh, *The Historie of the World* (London, 1614), **5.18** (compare the slightly different version in *The Complete Poems*, ed. G. Parfitt, p. 161)

Laud, William, *A Speech Delivered in the Star Chamber ... at the Censure of John Bastwick, Henry Burton, and William Prynne*, in P. E. More and F. L. Cross, eds, *Anglicanism* (London, 1957), **7.17** pp. 607–8

Lipsius, Justus, *Two Bookes of Constancie*, trans. J. Stradling (London, 1595), **4.6** p. 78

Livy, *The Early History of Rome: Books I–V of The History of Rome*, trans. A. de Sélincourt (PC, 1960), **5.4** p. 34

Lovelace, Richard, in *Minor Poets of the Seventeenth Century*, ed. R. G. Howarth (EL, 1953), **1.22** p. 328; **4.15** pp. 259–60

Lucretius, *On the Nature of the Universe (De Rerum Natura)*, trans. R. Latham (PC, 1951), **11.7** pp. 54–5

Luther, Martin, 'Answer before the Emperor and the Diet of Worms', trans. E. G. Rupp and B. Drewery, in *Martin Luther*, ed. E. G. Rupp and B. Drewery (London, 1970), **7.2** p. 60

Luther, Martin, *Answer to the Superchristian, Superspiritual, and Superlearned Book of Goat Emser*, in H. T. Kerr, Jr, ed., *A Compend of Luther's Theology* (Philadelphia, 1943), **10.9** pp. 18–19

Luther, Martin, 'Autobiographical Fragment', trans. E. G. Rupp and B. Drewery, in *Martin Luther*, ed. E. G. Rupp and B. Drewery (London, 1970), **8.12** p. 6

Luther, Martin, *On the Bondage of the Will*, trans. P. S. Watson, in Luther and Erasmus, *Free Will and Salvation*, ed. E. G. Rupp and P. S. Watson (LCC, 1969), **8.30** pp. 328–9

Luther, Martin, *To the Christian Nobility of the German Nation*, trans. C. M. Jacobs, rev. J. Atkinson, in *Selected Writings*, vol. I, ed. T. G. Tappert (Philadelphia, 1967), **7.1** pp. 263, 265, 271

Luther, Martin, *The Freedom of a Christian* (otherwise *Treatise on Christian Liberty* or *On the Liberty of a Christian Man*), trans. W. A. Lambert, rev. H. J. Grimm, in *Selected Writings*, vol. II, ed. T. G. Tappert (Philadelphia, 1967), **8.25** pp. 20, 25, 29

Luther, Martin, Preface to the Old Testament, trans. C. M. Jacobs, rev. E. T. Bachmann, in *Selected Writings*, vol. IV. ed. T. G. Tappert (Philadelphia, 1967), **10.10** p. 387

Marcus Aurelius, *Meditations*, trans. M. Staniforth (PC, 1964), **4.1** p. 51

Marvell, Andrew, *The Complete Poems*, ed. E. S. Donno (PEP, 1972), **1.18** p. 85; **1.20** p. 116; **2.16** pp. 184–5; **3.10** pp. 103–4; **5.19** p. 130; **9.22** pp. 59–60; **13.12** pp. 75–6

Milton, John, *Christian Doctrine (De Doctrina Christiana)*, trans. J. Carey, in *Complete Prose Works of John Milton*, ed. D. M. Wolfe, vol. VI (New Haven, 1973), **8.21** p. 190; **8.33** p. 164; **8.39** p. 132; **10.12** pp. 581, 583

Milton, John, *The Poems*, ed. J. Carey and A. Fowler (Longman's Annotated English Poets, London, 1968). Intro. **4** pp. 1160–3; **1.10** pp. 626–9; **1.11** p. 1023; **1.12** pp. 1055–6; **1.13** p. 1166; **2.13** pp. 1163–4; **2.18** pp. 111–12; **3.9** pp. 199–200; **5.20** p. 1123; **6.18** pp. 605–6; **6.20** p. 159; **6.37** pp. 817–18,

824; **7.22** pp. 411–12; **8.9** pp. 576–7; **8.40** p. 737; **8.41** p. 1032; **10.16** pp. 1038–9, 1042; **11.2** pp. 774–5, 777; **12.13** p. 144; **13.10** pp. 787–8

Milton, John, *Selected Prose*, ed. C. A. Patrides (PEL, 1974), **2.19** pp. 234–5; **7.19** p. 99; **9.18** pp, 182, 185

Montaigne, *The Essayes of Michael Lord of Montaigne*, trans. J. Florio (3 vols, W C, London, 1904–6), **4.8** II pp. 367–8

More, Thomas, *Utopia*, trans. R. Robinson (EL, 1951), **9.12** pp. 39–40

Ovid, *The Metamorphoses*, trans. M. M. Innes (PC, 1955), **1.5** pp. 31–2; **2.6** pp. 244–5; **2.15** p. 210; **6.3** p. 29; **6.9** p. 40; **6.10** pp. 339, 341

Petrarch, *On his Own Ignorance and That of Many Others (De sui ipsius et multorum ignorantia)*, trans. H. Nachod, in *The Renaissance Philosophy of Man*, ed. E. Cassirer *et al.* (Chicago, 1956), **9.13** pp. 114–15

Pico della Mirandola, *Heptaplus*, trans. D. Carmichael, in *On the Dignity of Man, On Being and the One, Heptaplus* (LLA, 1965), **6.22** p. 135

Pico della Mirandola, *On the Dignity of Man*, trans. C. G. Wallis, in *On the Dignity of Man, On Being and the One, Heptaplus* (LLA, 1965), **13.8** pp. 25–6

Pico della Mirandola, *A Platonick Discourse*, trans. T. Stanley, in T. Stanley, *The History of Philosophy* (2nd edn, London, 1687), **3.3** p. 203

Plato, *Gorgias*, trans. W. Hamilton (PC, 1960), **6.1** pp. 117–18

Plato, *Phaedo*, in *The Last Days of Socrates*, trans. H. Tredennick (PC, 1959), **3.7** pp. 135–6

Plato, *The Republic*, trans. F. M. Cornford (Oxford, 1941), **2.1** pp. 68–9; **3.6** p. 226; **6.11** p. 346; **13.2** p. 236

Plato, *The Symposium*, trans. W. Hamilton (PC, 1951), **3.1** pp. 93–4

Plato, *Timaeus*, trans. H. D. P. Lee (PC, 1965), **6.2** p. 45; **13.3** pp. 43–4

Plotinus, *Enneads*, trans. A. H. Armstrong (7 vols, Loeb, 1966–88), **3.2** I pp. 255–9

Plutarch (?), *The Education of Children*, in *Moralia*, vol. I, trans. F. C. Babbit (Loeb, 1949), **9.8** p. 37

Plutarch, *Isis and Osiris*, in *Moralia*, vol. V, trans. F. C. Babbit (Loeb, 1957), **2.3** pp. 155–7; **2.17** pp. 121, 131

Polybius, *The Histories*, trans. W. R. Paton (6 vols, Loeb, 1922–7), **5.2** I p. 11; **5.3** I p. 99

Puttenham, George, *The Arte of English Poesie*, in G. G. Smith, ed., *Elizabethan Critical Essays*, vol. II (Oxford, 1904), **11.5** pp. 3–4

Quintilian, *Institutio Oratoria (Education of an Orator)*, trans. H. E. Butler (4 vols, Loeb, 1921–2), **9.5** I pp. 9–11; **9.6** IV pp. 385, 389

Reynolds, Henry, *Mythomystes*, in J. E. Springarn, ed., *Critical Essays of the Seventeenth Century*, vol. I (London, 1908), **13.9** pp. 158–9

Ross, Alexander, *Mystagogus Poeticus or the Muses Interpreter* (2nd edn, London, 1648), **2.5** p. 5; **2.7** p. 6; **2.12** p. 169

Sallustius, *On the Gods and the World*, trans. G. Murray, in G. Murray, *Five Stages of Greek Religion* (Oxford, 1925), **2.4** pp. 242–3

Sandys, George, *Ovid's Metamorphosis Englished, Mythologiz'd, and Represented in Figures* (Oxford, 1632), **2.8** p. 367; **2.14** p. 322

Seneca, *De Providentia (On Providence), De Constantia Sapientis (On the Firmness of the Wise Man)*, in *Moral Essays*, vol. I, trans. J. W. Basore

(Loeb, 1928), **4.4** pp. 55–7; **4.5** pp. 43–5

Shakespeare, William, *Venus and Adonis*, in *The Poems*, ed. F. T. Prince (The Arden Shakespeare, London, 1960), **2.9** pp. 60–2

Sidney, Sir Philip, *An Apology for Poetry*, ed. G. Shepherd (London, 1965), **11.3** pp. 100–1; **11.10** pp. 109, 113

Sidney, Sir Philip, *Astrophel and Stella*, in *Silver Poets of the Sixteenth Century*, ed. G. Bullett (EL, 1947), **3.11** p. 174

Smith, John, *The Excellency and Nobleness of True Religion*, in G. R. Cragg, ed., *The Cambridge Platonists* (New York, 1968), **3.8** pp. 97–8

Southwell, Robert, *The Poems*, ed. J. H. McDonald and N. P. Brown (Oxford, 1967), **7.24** pp. 18–19

Spenser, Edmund, *The Faerie Queene* (2 vols, EL, 1910), Intro. **1** I p. 151; **1.16** I p. 237; **2.10** I pp. 419–20; **5.15** I p. 142; **5.16** II p. 454; **6.15** II pp. 119–20; **6.16** II pp. 452–3; **12.11** I pp. 1–2; **12.12** I p. 170

Spenser, Edmund, *Minor Poems*, ed. E. de Sélincourt (Oxford, 1910), **3.5** p. 447

Tacitus, *The Annals of Imperial Rome*, trans. M. Grant (rev. edn, PC, 1975), **5.5** p. 150

Tasso, Torquato, *Discourses on the Heroic Poem*, trans. M. Cavalchini and I. Samuel (Oxford, 1973), **11.4** pp. 77–8

Tasso, Torquato, *Jerusalem Delivered*, trans. E. Fairfax, ed. J. C. Nelson (New York, 1963), **1.15** p. 316

Taylor, Jeremy, Preface to *An Apology for Authorised and Set Forms of Liturgy*, in P. E. More and F. L. Cross, eds, *Anglicanism* (London, 1957), **7.14** p. 170

Teresa of Avila, St, *The Life of Teresa of Jesus*, trans. E. A. Peers (New York, 1960), **7.25** pp. 273–4

Tertullian, *The Prescriptions against the Heretics*, in *Early Latin Theology*, trans. S. L. Greenslade (LCC, 1956), **8.35** p. 36

The Thirty-Nine Articles, i.e. 'Articles of Religion', in The Book of Common Prayer **7.3** VI; **7.10** XXVIII; **7.16** XXXIV; **8.16** XIII; **8.19** XVII; **8.31** X

Thucydides, *The Peloponnesian War*, trans. R. Warner (PC 1954), **5.1** pp. 24–5

Travers, Walter, *A Full and Plain Declaration of Ecclesiastical Discipline*, trans. T. Cartwright, in E. H. Emerson, *English Puritanism from John Hooper to John Milton* (Durham, N.C., 1968), **7.18** pp. 88–9

Tyndale, William, *Doctrinal Treatises and Introductions to Different Portions of the Holy Scriptures*, ed. H. Walter (Cambridge, 1848), **8.15** p. 493; **8.26** pp. 8–9, 21

Vaughan, Henry, *The Complete Poems*, ed. A. Rudrum (PEP, 1976). Intro. **3** pp. 172–3; **12.6** pp. 289–90

Virgil, *The Aeneid*, trans. W. F. Jackson Knight (PC, 1956), **1.4** p. 171

Virgil, *The Pastoral Poems (Eclogues)*, trans. E. V. Rieu (PC, 1949), **1.3** pp. 53–5

Vitruvius, *On Architecture*, trans. F. Granger (2 vols, Loeb, 1931), **13.4** I pp. 159–61

Vives, Juan Luis, *The Transmission of Knowledge (De Tradendis Disciplinis)*, trans. F. Watson, in F. Watson, *Vives: On Education* (Cambridge, 1913), **9.10** p. 5

Wotton, Sir Henry, in *The Oxford Book of Seventeenth-Century Verse*, ed. H. J. C. Grierson and G. Bullough (Oxford, 1934), **4.13** pp. 77–8

Further Reading

These lists, which are arranged under chapter headings, are not intended as complete bibliographies of the subjects concerned. Instead, they provide briefly annotated selections of books dealing with a number of different aspects of each subject and ranging from the introductory to the specialised. Easier works are asterisked, and students unfamiliar with the subject are advised to start with these. Many contain useful bibliographies. For works on specific non-English authors the Bibliographical Appendix should be consulted. Some works on individual English poets are listed here in cases where these are particularly relevant.

INTRODUCTION

Three books which cover similar ground to this one and which students will find useful are A. G. Dickens *et al.*, *Background to the English Renaissance** (London, 1974), a series of introductory lectures; C. S. Lewis, *The Discarded Image: An Introduction to Medieval and Renaissance Literature** (Cambridge, 1964); J. R. Mulder, *The Temple of the Mind: Education and Literary Taste in Seventeenth-Century England** (New York, 1969). On the classical tradition see R. R. Bolgar. *The Classical Heritage and its Beneficiaries* (Cambridge, 1958, first pub. 1954). Two more difficult works which discuss in different ways the influences of classical on later literature are E. R. Curtius, *European Literature and the Latin Middle Ages*, trans. W. R. Trask (London, 1953, first pub. 1948), and F. Kermode, *The Classic* (London, 1975).

A comprehensive guide with helpful bibliographies is provided by C. A. Patrides and R. B. Waddington, eds, *The Age of Milton: Backgrounds to Seventeenth-Century Literature** (Manchester, 1980). W. Kerrigan and G. Braden, *The Idea of the Renaissance* (Baltimore, 1991), is a lively introduction with chapters on Italian thinkers.

1 THE GOLDEN AGE AND THE GARDEN OF EDEN

The classical texts on the golden age are collected by A. O. Lovejoy and G. Boas, *Primitivism and Related Ideas in Antiquity* (New York, 1965, first pub. 1935). For Renaissance uses of classical motifs see A. B. Giamatti, *The Earthly Paradise and the Renaissance Epic* (Princeton, 1966); H. Levin, *The Myth of the Golden Age in the Renaissance* (New York, 1972, first pub. 1969); F. A. Yates, *Astraea* (London, 1975). N. Frye is extremely illuminating on the idea of paradise in 'The Mythos of Summer: Romance', in *Anatomy of Criticism* (New York, 1969, first pub. 1957), and *Five Essays on Milton's Epics**

(London, 1966). What sixteenth-century theologians thought about paradise is set out by A. Williams, *The Common Expositor: An Account of the Commentaries on Genesis 1527–1633* (Chapel Hill, 1948). The early chapters of R. Williams, *The Country and the City* (London, 1973) are highly critical of the use of golden age motifs in seventeenth-century poetry. S. Stewart, *The Enclosed Garden* (Madison, 1966), is useful for Herbert and Marvell.

T. Comito, *The Idea of the Garden in the Renaissance* (Hassocks, 1978), is wide ranging and suggestive. Literary developments are traced in H. Cooper, *Pastoral: Mediaeval into Renaissance* (Ipswich, 1977). A Low, *The Georgic Revolution* (Princeton, 1985), explores the emphasis on work in sixteenth- and seventeenth-century rural poetry.

2 THE PAGAN GODS

For the myths, consult H. J. Rose, *A Handbook of Greek Mythology** (London, 1958, first pub. 1928). R. Graves, *The Greek Myths* (2 vols, Harmondsworth, 1955), is detailed but eccentric in interpretation. M. Grant, *Myths of the Greeks and Romans** (London, 1962), is an attractive introduction which compares literary uses. G. S. Kirk, *The Nature of Greek Myths** (Harmondsworth, 1974), is a good introduction to theory. On the Christian absorption of classical educational methods see H. I. Marrou, *A History of Education in Antiquity*, trans. G. Lamb (New York, 1964, first English edn 1956). The most important book on the continuity of the gods is J. Seznec, *The Survival of the Pagan Gods*, trans. B. Sessions (New York, 1961, first pub. 1940). On myth in English Renaissance literature see D. C. Allen, *Mysteriously Meant: The Rediscovery of Pagan Symbolism and Allegorical Interpretation in the Renaissance* (Baltimore, 1970), especially ch. VIII; D. Bush, *Mythology and the Renaissance Tradition in English Poetry* (Minneapolis, 1932); D. T. Starnes and E. W. Talbert, *Classical Myth and Legend and Renaissance Dictionaries* (Westport, Conn., 1973, first pub. 1955); H. G. Lotspeich, *Classical Mythology in the Poetry of Edmund Spenser* (New York, 1965, first pub. 1932); C. G. Osgood, *The Classical Mythology of Milton's English Poems* (New York, 1900). On the gods in Renaissance painting see E. Panofsky, *Studies in Iconology* (New York, 1962, first pub. 1939); E. Wind, *Pagan Mysteries in the Renaissance* (London, 1958, rev. 1967).

L. Barkan, *The Gods Made Flesh: Metamorphosis and the Pursuit of Paganism* (New Haven, 1986), explores Ovidian motifs in Renaissance poetry.

3 PLATONISM AND NEOPLATONISM

A good introduction to Plato is J. E. Raven, *Plato's Thought in the Making** (Cambridge, 1965). On pagan Neoplatonism see A. H. Armstrong, *An Introduction to Ancient Philosophy* (London, 1947), and F. Copleston, *A History of Philosophy* I: *Greece and Rome* (2nd edn rev., New York, 1962). On Florentine Neoplatonism see E. Cassirer, P. O. Kristeller and J. H. Randall, Jr, eds, *The Renaissance Philosophy of Man* (Chicago, 1967); S. Jayne, 'Ficino and the Platonism of the English Renaissance', *Comparative Literature*, IV

(1952), 214–38; P. O. Kristeller, *Eight Philosophers of the Italian Renaissance** (London, 1965), *Renaissance Thought** (New York, 1961), *Renaissance Thought* II* (New York, 1965); J. C. Nelson, *Renaissance Theory of Love* (New York, 1958); N. A. Robb, *Neoplatonism of the Italian Renaissance* (London, 1935); D. P. Walker, *The Ancient Theology* (London, 1972); E. Wind, *Pagan Mysteries in the Renaissance* (London, 1958, rev. 1967). Studies of Neoplatonism and English poets include R. Ellrodt, *Neoplatonism in the Poetry of Spenser* (Geneva, 1960); W. Nelson, 'Love Creating', in *The Poetry of Edmund Spenser** (New York, 1971); E. Welsford, *Spenser: Fowre Hymns, Epithalamion* (Oxford, 1967); I. Samuel, *Plato and Milton* (Ithaca, 1947). On the Cambridge Platonists see E. Cassirer, *The Platonic Renaissance in England* (London, 1953), and the anthology edited by G. R. Cragg, *The Cambridge Platonists* (New York, 1968).

For a fuller introduction to Plato see *The Cambridge Companion to Plato*, ed. R. Kraut (Cambridge, 1992). On pagan Neoplatonism see also R. T. Wallis, *Neo-Platonism* (London, 1972). On Florentine Neoplatonism see a further survey by P. O. Kristeller, *Renaissance Thought and its Sources* (New York, 1979), and two very detailed histories: A. Field, *The Origins of the Platonic Academy of Florence* (Princeton, 1988), and J. Hankins, *Plato in the Italian Renaissance*, 2 vols (Leiden, 1990), especially the Introduction and Pt 4. Modern scholars are warned not to overemphasise the importance of Plato in C. B. Schmitt, *Aristotle and the Renaissance* (Cambridge, Mass., 1983).

4 STOICISM

A good introduction is F. H. Sandbach, *The Stoics** (London, 1975); see also A. H. Armstrong, *An Introduction to Ancient Philosophy* (London, 1947). E. V. Arnold, *Roman Stoicism* (Cambridge, 1911), is detailed but rather old-fashioned; J. M. Rist, *Stoic Philosophy* (Cambridge, 1969), is altogether more demanding. On Renaissance Stoicism see J. L. Saunders, *Justus Lipsius: The Philosophy of Renaissance Stoicism* (New York, 1955), and R. Kirk's introduction to *Two bookes of constancie written in Latine by Iustus Lipsius; Englished by Sir John Stradling* (New Brunswick, 1939). Jonson's Stoicism is discussed by I. Rivers, *The Poetry of Conservatism, 1600–1745* (Cambridge, 1973); that of the Cavaliers by M. -S. Røstvig, *The Happy Man* I (rev. edn, Oslo, 1962), and E. Miner, *The Cavalier Mode from Jonson to Cotton* (Princeton, 1971).

There is a revised edition of F. H. Sandbach, *The Stoics** (Bristol, 1989). See also A. A. Long, *Hellenistic Philosophy: Stoics, Epicureans, Sceptics* (2nd edn, London, 1986, first pub. 1974). The tension between Stoicism and Christianity in the Renaissance is explored in W. J. Bouwsma, 'The Two Faces of Humanism: Stoicism and Augustinianism in Renaissance Thought', *The Usable Past* (Berkeley, 1990). The political influence of Lipsius' Stoicism is traced in G. Oestreich, *Neostoicism and the Early Modern State*, trans. D. McLintock (Cambridge, 1982). For the translation and diffusion of Stoic texts in England see G. Monsarrat, *Light from the Porch: Stoicism and English Renaissance Literature* (Paris, 1984).

5 VIEWS OF HISTORY

There is a brief but provocative contrast between classical and Christian views of history in R. G. Collingwood, *The Idea of History* (London, 1970, first pub. 1946). On classical historians see J. B. Bury, *The Ancient Greek Historians* (London, 1909), and M. L. W. Laistner, *The Greater Roman Historians* (Berkeley, 1947). C. A. Patrides, *The Grand Design of God** (London, 1972), gives a survey of Christian views and has useful bibliographical notes. See also C. R. North, *The Old Testament Interpretation of History* (London, 1946); R. L. P. Milburn, *Early Christian Interpretations of History* (London, 1954); and a more specialised work, R. A. Markus, *Saeculum: History and Society in the Theology of St Augustine* (Cambridge, 1970). N. Cohn, *The Pursuit of the Millennium* (rev. edn, London, 1970, first pub. 1957), is an excellent history of millenarianism, though concentrating on the Middle Ages. On changing attitudes to history in the Renaissance P. Burke, *The Renaissance Sense of the Past** (London, 1969), is a useful introduction for students; the first two chapters of W. K. Ferguson, *The Renaissance in Historical Thought* (Cambridge, Mass., 1948), are indispensable. For English historiography in general see F. J. Levy, *Tudor Historical Thought* (San Marino, 1967). A superb account of the Protestant view is W. Haller, *Foxe's Book of Martyrs and the Elect Nation* (London, 1963). Sir Charles Firth, *Essays Historical and Literary* (Oxford, 1968, first pub. 1938), includes essays on the histories of Ralegh and Milton. For changing treatments of the Matter of Britain see T. D. Kendrick, *British Antiquity* (London, 1950), and R. F. Brinkley, *Arthurian Legend in the Seventeenth Century* (Baltimore, 1932). F. Kermode, *The Classic* (London, 1975), discusses poetic use of classical ideas of empire. For the views of history of specific poets see E. A. Greenlaw, *Studies in Spenser's Historical Allegory* (Baltimore, 1932); F. Kermode, *Renaissance Essays* (London, 1973), on Spenser; M. Fixler, *Milton and the Kingdoms of God* (London, 1964); J. A. Mazzeo, *Renaissance and Seventeenth-Century Studies* (New York, 1964), on Marvell.

G. W. Trompf, *The Idea of Historical Recurrence in Western Thought: From Antiquity to the Reformation* (Berkeley, 1979), questions the traditional contrast between Judeo-Christian linear and Greco-Roman cyclical views. A. G. Dickens and J. Tonkin, *The Reformation in Historical Thought* (Oxford, 1985), is a parallel volume to that by W. K. Ferguson (see above). Changes in historical consciousness are explored by A. B. Ferguson, *Clio Unbound: Perception of the Social and Cultural Past in Renaissance England* (Durham, N.C., 1979). K. R. Firth, *The Apocalyptic Tradition in Reformation Britain 1530–1645* (Oxford, 1979), is an interesting corrective to W. Haller (see above). For further studies of the views of specific poets see D. Norbrook, *Poetry and Politics in the English Renaissance* (London, 1984), on Spenser and Milton; M. O'Connell, *Mirror and Veil: The Historical Dimension of Spenser's 'Faerie Queene'* (Chapel Hill, 1977); E. W. Tayler, *Milton's Poetry: Its Development in Time* (Pittsburgh, 1979).

6 COSMOLOGY

Two very helpful general histories of science are S. Toulmin and J. Goodfield, *The Fabric of the Heavens** (London, 1961), on cosmology, and *The Architecture of Matter** (London, 1962), on physics. R. G. Collingwood, *The Idea of Nature* (Oxford, 1965, first pub. 1945), is brief and provocative. For a clear introduction to Greek science see S. Sambursky, *The Physical World of the Greeks** (London, 1956): J. H. Randall, Jr, *Aristotle* (New York, 1960), covers all aspects of his work. For post-Greek science A. C. Crombie, *Augustine to Galileo* (2 vols, 2nd edn, London, 1961), is clear and systematic with a good bibliography. A good detailed account of the old cosmology is J. L. E. Dreyer, *A History of Astronomy from Thales to Kepler* (2nd edn rev., New York, 1953). For Renaissance science and astronomy an excellent introduction is M. Boas, *The Scientific Renaissance** (London, 1962); see also T. S. Kuhn, *The Copernican Revolution* (Cambridge, Mass., 1975, first pub. 1957), the most thoughtful account; A. Koyré, *From the Closed World to the Infinite Universe* (Baltimore, 1957), on the development of the idea of infinity and the plurality of worlds; A. Koestler, *The Sleepwalkers** (London, 1959), a very readable account of Copernicus, Tycho, Kepler and Galileo; F. R. Johnson, *Astronomical Thought in Renaissance England* (New York, 1968, first pub. 1937), which stresses the importance of Recorde, Dee and T. Digges.

For cosmological ideas in literature two good introductions are C. S. Lewis, *The Discarded Image** (Cambridge, 1964), and E. M. W. Tillyard, *The Elizabethan World Picture** (London, 1956, first pub. 1943). A very scholarly, well-documented account is S. K. Heninger, Jr, *Touches of Sweet Harmony: Pythagorean Cosmology and Renaissance Poetics* (San Marino, 1974). A. O. Lovejoy, *The Great Chain of Being* (New York, 1960, first pub. 1936), is important but difficult. For cosmic music see L. Spitzer, *Classical and Christian Ideas of World Harmony* (Baltimore, 1963), and J. Hollander, *The Untuning of the Sky: Ideas of Music in English Poetry* (Princeton, 1961). For astrology see D. C. Allen, *The Star-Crossed Renaissance* (New York, 1966, first pub. 1941). P. H. Kocher, *Science and Religion in Elizabethan England* (San Marino, 1953), covers a useful range of topics. Specific literary studies include M. H. Nicolson, *The Breaking of the Circle: Studies in the Effect of the 'New Science' upon Seventeenth-Century Poetry** (rev. edn. New York, 1960), and *Science and Imagination* (Ithaca, 1962, first pub. 1956), chs I–IV; C. M. Coffin, *John Donne and the New Philosophy* (New York, 1937); C. A. Patrides, *Milton and the Christian Tradition* (Oxford, 1966), ch. 3; K. Svendsen, *Milton and Science* (Cambridge, Mass., 1956); J. A. Mazzeo, 'Metaphysical Poetry and the Poetic of Correspondence', in *Renaissance and Seventeenth-Century Studies* (New York, 1964).

A. G. Debus, *Man and Nature in the Renaissance** (Cambridge, 1978), stresses both the mystical-occult tradition and the new mathematical–observational approach to nature, and has an annotated bibliography. B. Vickers, ed., *Occult and Scientific Mentalities in the Renaissance* (Cambridge, 1984), is more detailed (and critical of Debus). The range of cosmological thought in the Renaissance is clearly explained and beautifully illustrated in

S. K. Heninger, Jr, *The Cosmographical Glass: Renaissance Diagrams of the Universe* (San Marino, 1977).

7 REFORMATION AND COUNTER-REFORMATION

For reference consult F. L. Cross and E. A. Livingstone, eds, *The Oxford Dictionary of the Christian Church* (2nd edn, London, 1974). O. Chadwick, *The Reformation* * (rev. edn, Harmondsworth, 1972; vol. III of *The Pelican History of the Church*), and A. G. Dickens, *Reformation and Society in Sixteenth-Century Europe* * (London, 1966), are useful general introductions. A. G. Dickens, *The English Reformation* (rev. edn, London, 1973), is excellent. H. Bettenson, ed., *Documents of the Christian Church* (2nd edn, London, 1963), contains much relevant material. A lively biography of Luther which forms an excellent introduction to the Reformation as a whole is R. H. Bainton, *Here I Stand* * (New York, 1950). A useful summary account of English Bible translation is C. R. Thompson, 'The Bible in English 1525–1611',* in L. B. Wright and V. A. La Mar, eds, *Life and Letters in Tudor and Stuart England* (Ithaca, 1962). See also *The Cambridge History of the Bible*, vol. III, ed. S. L. Greenslade (Cambridge, 1963), especially chs I, II and IV; and A. W. Pollard, *Records of the English Bible* (London, 1911). C. C. Butterworth, *The Literary Lineage of the King James Bible 1340–1611* (Philadelphia, 1941), provides passages for comparison. For liturgy and ceremonies see especially H. Davies, *Worship and Theology in England*, vol. I, *From Cranmer to Hooker* (Princeton, 1970), vol. II, *From Andrewes to Baxter and Fox* (Princeton, 1975); the same author's *The Worship of the English Puritans* (London, 1948) is more detailed. F. Proctor and W. H. Frere, *A New History of the Book of Common Prayer* (rev. edn. London, 1901) is factual. A full anthology of Anglican writers, but with a High Church emphasis, is P. E. More and F. L. Cross, eds, *Anglicanism* (London, 1957, first pub. 1935). A much slighter anthology of Puritan writers is E. H. Emerson, ed., *English Puritanism from John Hooper to John Milton* (Durham, N.C., 1968). J. F. H. New, *Anglican and Puritan* (London, 1964), is a brief but far from easy account of their differences. Detailed histories of Puritanism are M. M. Knappen, *Tudor Puritanism* (Chicago, 1970, first pub. 1939), and P. Collinson, *The Elizabethan Puritan Movement* (London, 1967), for the sixteenth century; W. Haller, *The Rise of Puritanism* (New York, 1957, first pub. 1938), for the seventeenth century. For the Counter-Reformation, A. G. Dickens, *The Counter Reformation* * (London, 1968), is a general historical introduction; H. O. Evennett, *The Spirit of the Counter-Reformation* (Cambridge, 1968), is much more theoretical. L. L. Martz, *The Poetry of Meditation* (rev. edn, New Haven, 1962), explores the influence of Catholic devotion on English poets, especially Southwell, Donne and Herbert; L. B. Campbell, *Divine Poetry and Drama in Sixteenth-Century England* (Cambridge, 1959), explores the turning of the Bible into English literature.

Parts of A. G. Dickens, *The English Reformation*, were considerably rewritten for the second edition (1989). On the English Bible see also G. Hammond, *The Making of the English Bible* (Manchester, 1982), and D.

Norton, *A History of the Bible as Literature*, vol. I, *From Antiquity to 1700* (Cambridge, 1993). There is much disagreement on the causes and meaning of the English Reformation: see R. O'Day, *The Debate on the English Reformation** (London, 1986), and C. Haigh, ed., *The English Reformation Revised* (Cambridge, 1987), Introduction and ch. I, which challenges A. G. Dickens and the 'Foxe version'. The characteristics of Puritanism are briefly outlined in P. Collinson, *English Puritanism** (London, 1983); his *The Religion of Protestants: The Church in English Society 1559–1625* (Oxford, 1982) is much fuller but very lively and readable. Two works which emphasise the importance and popularity of late medieval Catholicism are J. Bossy, *Christianity in the West 1400–1700** (Oxford, 1985), and E. Duffy, *The Stripping of the Altars: Traditional Religion in England c. 1400–c. 1580* (New Haven, 1992). On the Counter-Reformation see J. Delumeau, *Catholicism between Luther and Voltaire*, trans. J. Moiser (London, 1977), with an introduction by J. Bossy. On the impact of the reformed churches in Europe see M. Prestwich, ed., *International Calvinism 1541–1715* (Oxford, 1985). Religious differences in seventeenth-century England are explored in different ways by J. S. McGee, *The Godly Man in Stuart England: Anglicans, Puritans and the Two Tables 1620–1670* (New Haven, 1976); N. Tyacke, *Anti-Calvinists: The Rise of English Arminianism c. 1590–1640* (Oxford, 1987); and H. Trevor-Roper, *Catholics, Anglicans and Puritans* (London, 1989, first pub. 1987). J. E. Booty et al., *The Godly Kingdom of Tudor England: Great Books of the English Reformation* (Wilton, Conn., 1981), provides accounts of the Great Bible, Erasmus' Paraphrases, the Book of Homilies, and the Book of Common Prayer. See also R. Zim, *English Metrical Psalms: Poetry as Praise and Prayer 1535–1601* (Cambridge, 1987). Two very thorough studies of literature and the Reformation are J. N. King, *English Reformation Literature: The Tudor Origins of the Protestant Tradition* (Princeton, 1982), and its sequel, *Spenser's Poetry and the Reformation Tradition* (Princeton, 1990). Two idiosyncratic, controversial accounts of the responses of specific poets to religious upheaval are J. Carey, *John Donne: Life, Mind and Art* (London, 1981) and C. Hill, *Milton and the English Revolution* (London, 1977). N. H. Keeble, *The Literary Culture of Nonconformity in Later Seventeenth-Century England* (Leicester, 1987), is a very full and sympathetic account of the later stages of Puritanism.

8 PROTESTANT THEOLOGY

For accounts of the thought of specific authors see P. Brown, *Augustine of Hippo* (London, 1967); P. S. Watson, *Let God be God!* (London, 1947), on Luther; F. Wendel, *Calvin*, trans. P. Mairet (London, 1965, first pub. in France, 1950). More general accounts include C. H. and K. George, *The Protestant Mind of the English Reformation* (Princeton, 1961), a book that tends to blur distinctions, and J. T. McNeill, *The History and Character of Calvinism* (New York, 1954). P. Miller, *The New England Mind: The Seventeenth Century* (Cambridge, Mass., 1963, first pub. 1939), a very detailed account of American Puritan thought, is also useful for England. For the Arminian revolt against

Calvinism see A. W. Harrison, *Arminianism** (London, 1937). For Anglican thought with its particular emphasis on reason see H. Baker, *The Dignity of Man* (Cambridge, Mass., 1947) and *The Wars of Truth* (London, 1952); J. S. Marshall, *Hooker and the Anglican Tradition* (London, 1963); H. R. McAdoo, *The Spirit of Anglicanism* (London, 1965), chs I–IV; J. Tulloch, *Rational Theology and Christian Philosophy in England in the Seventeenth Century* (2 vols, Edinburgh, 1872); R. Hoopes, *Right Reason in the English Renaissance* (Cambridge, Mass., 1962), which has chapters on Spenser and Milton. C. A. Patrides, *Milton and the Christian Tradition* (Oxford, 1966), is thorough and helpful.

For very clear general introductions to Protestant thought and its antecedents see S. Ozment, *The Age of Reform 1250–1550: An Intellectual and Religious History of Late Medieval and Reformation Europe** (New Haven, 1980), and A. McGrath, *The Intellectual Origins of the European Reformation** (Oxford, 1987) and *Reformation Thought: An Introduction** (Oxford, 1988). A. McGrath, *Luther's Theology of the Cross* (Oxford, 1985), is a detailed account of his doctrine of justification. For the development of predestinarian theology in England see D. D. Wallace, Jr, *Puritans and Predestination: Grace in English Protestant Theology, 1525–1695* (Chapel Hill, 1982), and R. T. Kendall, *Calvin and English Calvinism to 1649* (Oxford, 1979). The conflict between Calvinist and Arminian views in mid-seventeenth-century England is summarised by I. Rivers, *Reason, Grace, and Sentiment*, vol. I (Cambridge, 1991), ch. I. The following studies interpret seventeenth-century poets in the context of Protestant theology: B. K. Lewalski, *Protestant Poetics and the Seventeenth-Century Religious Lyric* (Princeton, 1979); R. Strier, *Love Known: Theology and Experience in George Herbert's Poetry* (Chicago, 1983); M. A. Radzinowicz, *Toward Samson Agonistes* (Princeton, 1978), Pt 5; H. MacCallum, *Milton and the Sons of God* (Toronto, 1986).

9 HUMANISM

Useful general introductions include F. B. Artz, *Renaissance Humanism 1300–1550** (Kent, Ohio, 1966); P. O. Kristeller, *Renaissance Thought** (New York, 1961), ch. I and *Renaissance Thought II** (New York, 1965), chs I–III; J. A. Mazzeo, *Renaissance and Revolution* (New York, 1965), ch. I; W. H. Woodward, *Studies in Education during the Age of the Renaissance 1400–1600* (Cambridge, 1906); M. P. Gilmore, *The World of Humanism 1453–1517* (New York, 1962, first pub. 1952), chs VII and VIII. For the transmission of the classics see R. P. Bolgar, *The Classical Heritage and its Beneficiaries* (Cambridge, 1958, first pub. 1954), and L. D. Reynolds and N. G. Wilson, *Scribes and Scholars** (rev. edn, Oxford, 1974, first pub. 1968). For classical education see H. I. Marrou, *A History of Education in Antiquity* (New York, 1964, first English edn, 1956). For a general introduction to scholasticism see D. Knowles, *The Evolution of Medieval Thought** (London, 1962). M. M. Phillips, *Erasmus and the Northern Renaissance** (London, 1949), is a helpful introduction. E. H. Harbison, *The Christian Scholar in the Age of the*

Reformation (New York, 1956), is an interesting work on the literary scholarship of Christian thinkers. Works on aspects of English humanism include F. Caspari, *Humanism and the Social Order in Tudor England* (Chicago, 1954); J. M. Major, *Sir Thomas Elyot and Renaissance Humanism* (Lincoln, Neb., 1964); G. K. Hunter, *John Lyly: The Humanist as Courtier* (London, 1962), ch. I. D. Bush, *The Renaissance and English Humanism* (Toronto, 1956, first pub. 1939), is general in its terms and polemical. For humanist educational practice see J. Simon, *Education and Society in Tudor England* (Cambridge, 1966), and D. L. Clark, *John Milton at St Paul's School* (New York, 1948). E. M. Nugent, ed., *The Thought and Culture of the English Renaissance* (Cambridge, 1956), is a useful anthology for the early sixteenth century.

L. D. Reynolds and N. G. Wilson, *Scribes and Scholars**, has been revised (3rd edn, Oxford, 1991), as has M. M. Phillips, *Erasmus and the Northern Renaissance** (rev. edn, Woodbridge, 1981). There is a clear summary by P. O. Kristeller, 'Humanism',* *The Cambridge History of Renaissance Philosophy*, ed. C. B. Schmitt *et al.* (Cambridge, 1988). The impact of printing on literature is explored by E. L. Eisenstein, *The Printing Revolution in Early Modern Europe* (Cambridge, 1983). A. Grafton and L. Jardine, *From Humanism to the Humanities* (London, 1986), describes changes in educational practice. For classical rhetoric and its influence see B. Vickers, *In Defence of Rhetoric* (Oxford, 1988), chs I and V. For Italian humanism see J. E. Seigel, *Rhetoric and Philosophy in Renaissance Humanism* (Princeton, 1968), with an introductory chapter on Cicero, and C. Trinkaus, *The Scope of Renaissance Humanism* (Ann Arbor, 1983). For the political thought of the Northern humanists see Q. Skinner, *The Foundations of Modern Political Thought* (Cambridge, 1978), vol. I, Pt 3. J. W. Binns, *Intellectual Culture in Elizabethan and Jacobean England: The Latin Writings of the Age* (Leeds, 1990), emphasises the importance of the forgotten products of humanism. The relation between humanism and vernacular literatures is explored by A. F. Kinney, *Humanist Poetics: Thought, Rhetoric, and Fiction in Sixteenth-Century England* (Amherst, 1986), and *Continental Humanist Poetics: Studies in Erasmus, Castiglione, Marguerite de Navarre, Rabelais, and Cervantes* (Amherst, 1989). J. Martindale, ed., *English Humanism: Wyatt to Cowley** (London, 1985), is a useful anthology.

10 BIBLICAL EXEGESIS AND TYPOLOGY

For a general introduction see R. M. Grant, *A Short History of the Interpretation of the Bible** (rev. edn, London, 1965), and the excellent essay by E. Auerbach, 'Figura', in *Scenes from the Drama of European Literature* (New York, 1959). For biblical interpretation in the early Church see P. R. Ackroyd and C. F. Evans, eds, *The Cambridge History of the Bible,** vol. I (Cambridge, 1970), chs XII and XIII; J. Daniélou, *From Shadows to Reality: Studies in the Biblical Typology of the Fathers*, trans. W. Hibberd (London, 1960); R. M. Grant, *The Letter and the Spirit* (London, 1957), on the relation between Greek and Christian allegory; G. W. H. Lampe and K. J. Woollcombe, *Essays on Typology*

(London, 1957). For the influence of exegesis on medieval literature see D. W. Robertson, Jr, *A Preface to Chaucer* (Princeton, 1962), ch. IV. Two books on Dante which are more generally useful are A. C. Charity, *Events and their Afterlife: The Dialectics of Christian Typology in the Bible and Dante* (Cambridge, 1966), and R. Hollander, *Allegory in Dante's Commedia* (Princeton, 1969). On typology in medieval church architecture and drama see M. O. Anderson, *Drama and Imagery in English Medieval Churches* (Cambridge, 1963). For Luther's methods of exegesis see J. Pelikan, *Luther the Expositor* (Saint Louis, 1959). T. M. Davis, 'The Traditions of Puritan Typology',* in S. Bercovitch, ed., *Typology and Early American Literature* (Northampton, Mass., 1972), is a useful survey. Studies of typology and poetry include H. R. MacCallum, 'Milton and Figurative Interpretation of the Bible', *University of Toronto Quarterly*, XXXI (1962), 397–415; W. G. Madsen, *From Shadowy Types to Truth: Studies in Milton's Symbolism* (New Haven, 1968); R. Tuve, *A Reading of George Herbert* (London, 1952), an important work.

D. L. Jeffrey, ed., *A Dictionary of Biblical Tradition in English Literature** (Grand Rapids, 1992), is a very useful guide with bibliographies. See also R. Alter and F. Kermode, eds, *The Literary Guide to the Bible** (London, 1987). For medieval and Reformation biblical interpretation see the continuing series by G. R. Evans, *The Language and Logic of the Bible: The Earlier Middle Ages* (Cambridge, 1984) and *The Road to Reformation* (Cambridge, 1985). On literary aspects see E. Miner, ed., *Literary Uses of Typology from the Late Middle Ages to the Present* (Princeton, 1977), and P. J. Korshin, *Typologies in England 1650–1820* (Princeton, 1982), a very detailed account which is also relevant for the earlier seventeenth century. Studies of biblical interpretation by specific poets include M. A. Radzinowicz, *Milton's Epics and the Book of Psalms* (Princeton, 1989), J. H. Sims and L. Ryken, eds, *Milton and Scriptural Tradition* (Columbia, Mo., 1984), and D. R. Dickson, *The Fountain of Living Waters: The Typology of the Waters of Life in Herbert, Vaughan, and Traherne* (Columbia, Mo., 1987).

11 THEORIES OF POETRY

A. H. Gilbert, *Literary Criticism: Plato to Dryden* (Detroit, 1962, first pub. 1940), is a very useful general anthology. Detailed anthologies covering the English Renaissance are G. G. Smith, ed., *Elizabethan Critical Essays* (2 vols, Oxford, 1904), and J. E. Spingarn, ed., *Critical Essays of the Seventeenth Century* (2 vols, Oxford, 1908). Sir Philip Sidney, *An Apology for Poetry*, ed. G. Shepherd* (London, 1965), is very usefully annotated. A good general introduction to critical theory is D. Daiches, *Critical Approaches to Literature** (London, 1956). For detailed histories of literary criticism see J. W. H. Atkins, *Literary Criticism in Antiquity* (2 vols, Cambridge, 1934), and *English Literary Criticism: The Renascence* (London, 1947). On the poet as creator see E. R. Curtius, *European Literature and the Latin Middle Ages*, trans. W. R. Trask (London, 1953, first pub. 1948), and S. K. Heninger, *Touches of Sweet*

Harmony: Pythagorean Cosmology and Renaissance Poetics (San Marino, 1974), Pt 3.

For classical theories see D. A. Russell, *Criticism in Antiquity** (London, 1981), and *The Cambridge History of Literary Criticism*, vol. I, *Classical Criticism*, ed. G. A. Kennedy (Cambridge, 1989). D. A. Russell and M. Winterbottom, eds, *Ancient Literary Criticism: The Principal Texts in New Translations* (Oxford, 1972), is a very useful and wide ranging anthology. W. Trimpi, *Muses of One Mind* (Princeton, 1983), is a detailed, difficult analysis of classical principles. The last part of D. Daiches, *Critical Approaches to Literature,** has been expanded (2nd edn, 1981), but it is recommended for its treatment of earlier approaches in Pt 1. For Renaissance theories see B. Vickers, 'Rhetoric and Poetics', *The Cambridge History of Renaissance Philosophy*, ed. C. B. Schmitt *et al.* (Cambridge, 1988), and R. L. Montgomery, *The Reader's Eye: Studies in Didactic Literary Theory from Dante to Tasso* (Berkeley, 1979). T. M. Greene, *The Light in Troy: Imitation and Discovery in Renaissance Poetry* (New Haven, 1982), is a careful study of the application of theories of imitation.

12 ALLEGORY

Two introductory works, not especially concerned with the problems of Renaissance allegory, are G. Clifford, *The Transformations of Allegory** (London, 1974), and J. MacQueen, *Allegory** (London, 1970). A difficult, comprehensive theoretical work is A. Fletcher, *Allegory: The Theory of a Symbolic Mode* (Ithaca, 1964). The best book on Renaissance allegory is M. Murrin, *The Veil of Allegory: Some Notes Toward a Theory of Allegorical Rhetoric in the English Renaissance* (Chicago, 1969). On the antecedents of Renaissance allegory see C. S. Lewis, *The Allegory of Love* (New York, 1958, first pub. 1936), and two more scholarly, difficult books: D. C. Allen, *Mysteriously Meant: The Rediscovery of Pagan Symbolism and Allegorical Interpretation in the Renaissance* (Baltimore, 1970), and R. Tuve, *Allegorical Imagery: Some Mediaeval Books and their Posterity* (Princeton, 1966). Most books on Spenser include discussions of allegory; a good example is T. P. Roche, Jr, *The Kindly Flame: A Study of the Third and Fourth Books of Spenser's Faerie Queene* (Princeton, 1964). S. C. Chew, *The Pilgrimage of Life* (New Haven, 1962), is a comprehensive survey of literary and visual allegorical motifs. On emblems see R. Freeman, *English Emblem Books* (London, 1948), and M. Praz, *Studies in Seventeenth-Century Imagery* (2nd edn, Rome, 1964).

For ancient allegory and its Christian development see P. Rollinson, *Classical Theories of Allegory and Christian Culture* (Pittsburgh, 1981), and J. Whitman, *Allegory: The Dynamics of an Ancient and Medieval Technique* (Oxford, 1987). M. Murrin, *The Allegorical Epic* (Chicago, 1980), is a companion to *The Veil of Allegory* (see above). On Spenser see also I. G. MacCaffrey, *Spenser's Allegory* (Princeton, 1976).

13 NUMEROLOGY

There is a general introduction to the subject by C. Butler, *Number Symbolism**
(London, 1970). For medieval numerology and its background see E. R.
Curtius, *European Literature and the Latin Middle Ages*, trans. W. R. Trask
(London, 1953, first pub. 1948), Excursus XV, and V. F. Hopper, *Medieval
Number Symbolism* (New York, 1938). On numerology in Renaissance
architecture see R. Wittkower, *Architectural Principles in the Age of Humanism*
(3rd edn rev., London, 1962, first pub. 1949). On the Renaissance interpretation
of Pythagoreanism see S. K. Heninger, Jr, *Touches of Sweet Harmony:
Pythagorean Cosmology and Renaissance Poetics* (San Marino, 1974).
Numerological critiques of Renaissance poetry include A. K. Hieatt, *Short
Time's Endless Monument: The Symbolism of the Numbers in Edmund
Spenser's 'Epithalamion'* (New York, 1960); A. Fowler, *Spenser and the
Numbers of Time* (London, 1964), with a useful chapter on 'Numerological
Criticism', and *Triumphal Forms* (Cambridge, 1970); M. -S. Røstvig, *The
Hidden Sense* (Oslo, 1963).

See also K. G. Frost, *Holy Delight: Typology, Numerology, and Autobi-
ography in Donne's 'Devotions upon Emergent Occasions'* (Princeton, 1990).

Bibliographical Appendix

A ENGLISH RENAISSANCE AUTHORS

I have not provided biographical or bibliographical guides for these authors, since such information is easily accessible. The chief sources are:

The New Cambridge Bibliography of English Literature, ed. G. Watson, vol. I, 600–1660 (Cambridge, 1974) (abbreviated as *NCBEL*)
The Shorter New Cambridge Bibliography of English Literature, ed. G. Watson (Cambridge, 1981)
Great Writers Student Library, ed. J. Vinson, vol. II, *The Renaissance Excluding Drama*, ed. E. S. Donno (London, 1983)
Longman Literature in English Series, ed. D. Carroll and M. Wheeler: G. Waller, *English Poetry of the Sixteenth Century* (London, 1986); G. Parfitt, *English Poetry of the Seventeenth Century* (2nd edn, London, 1992)
A New History of French Literature, ed. D. Hollier (Cambridge, Mass., 1989)
The Oxford Companion to English Literature, ed. M. Drabble (5th edn, Oxford, 1985)
The Oxford History of English Literature: vol. III, C. S. Lewis, *English Literature in the Sixteenth Century Excluding Drama* (Oxford, 1954); vol. V, D. Bush, *English Literature in the Earlier Seventeenth Century* (2nd edn, Oxford, 1962)
The New Pelican Guide to English Literature, ed. B. Ford, *A Guide for Readers* (Harmondsworth, 1984)
Reference Guide to English Literature, ed. D. L. Kirkpatrick (3 vols, 2nd edn, Chicago, 1991)

For details of new editions and secondary works, students should consult the following annual bibliographies:

The Year's Work in English Studies (The English Association)
Annual Bibliography of English Language and Literature (Modern Humanities Research Association)
and the lists and annual review published in the following journal:
Studies in English Literature 1500–1900

The following are the most useful series containing editions of English Renaissance authors (where a series is now out of print it is marked o.p.):

Doubleday Anchor Seventeenth-Century Series o.p.
Everyman's Library (London)
Longman's Annotated English Poets (London)
Muses' Library o.p.
Norton Critical Editions (New York and London)
Penguin Classics (incorporating editions formerly designated as Penguin
　　English Library and Penguin English Poets) (Harmondsworth)
Oxford Authors (Oxford)
Oxford English Texts (Oxford)
Oxford Standard Authors o.p.
The World's Classics (Oxford)

B CLASSICAL, MEDIEVAL AND CONTINENTAL RENAISSANCE AUTHORS

Only the more important authors relevant to this book are included (hence the exclusion of e.g. the Greek tragedians). These brief guides, which are not intended to be complete, provide the following information: some biographical notes; a list of the author's chief works; any important Renaissance English translations, and modern editions of these; the most useful modern translations (where these exist, I have indicated Loeb and Penguin Classics editions); suggestions for further reading, biographical and critical (with easier works asterisked).

The chief reference works are:

Ancient Writers: Greece and Rome, ed. T. J. Luce (2 vols, New York, 1982)
　R. R. Bolgar, *The Classical Heritage and its Beneficiaries* (Cambridge, 1958)
　NCBEL (see above)
　The Cambridge History of Classical Literature: vol. I, *Greek Literature*, ed. P. E. Easterling and B. M. W. Knox (Cambridge, 1985); vol. II, *Latin Literature*, ed. E. J. Kenney and W. V. Clausen (Cambridge, 1982)
　The Cambridge History of Later Greek and Early Medieval Philosophy, ed. A. H. Armstrong (Cambridge, 1967)
　The Cambridge History of Later Medieval Philosophy, ed. N. Kretzmann *et al.* (Cambridge, 1982)
　The Cambridge History of Renaissance Philosophy, ed. C. B. Schmitt *et al.* (Cambridge, 1988)
　A. J. Krailsheimer, ed., *The Continental Renaissance 1500–1600* (Harmondsworth, 1971)
　H. B. Lathrop, *Translations from the Classics into English from Caxton to Chapman* (Madison, 1933)
　The Macmillan Dictionary of Italian Literature, ed. P. and J. C. Bondanella (London, 1979)
　The Oxford Classical Dictionary, ed. N. G. L. Hammond and H. H. Scullard (2nd edn, London, 1970)

The Oxford Dictionary of the Christian Church, ed. F. L. Cross and E. A. Livingstone (2nd edn, London, 1974)
The Oxford History of the Classical World, ed. J. Boardman *et al.* (Oxford, 1986)
R. Pfeiffer, *History of Classical Scholarship from 1300 to 1850* (Oxford, 1976)
L. D. Reynolds and N. G. Wilson, *Scribes and Scholars: A Guide to the Transmission of Greek and Latin Literature* (3rd edn, Oxford, 1991)
E. H. Wilkins, rev. T. G. Bergin, *A History of Italian Literature* (2nd edn, Cambridge, Mass., 1974)

In addition, two series of short monographs are very useful:

Greece and Rome: New Surveys in the Classics (Oxford)
Past Masters (Oxford)

ALCIATI, ANDREA 1492–1550. *Emblemata* (1531, many edns), Latin emblem book. G. Whitney, *A Choice of Emblems* (1586), contains several trans. from Alciati.
    H. Green, *Andrea Alciati and his Books of Emblems* (London, 1872), bibliography; J. Seznec, *The Survival of the Pagan Gods* (New York, 1961, first pub. in French 1940); R. Freeman, *English Emblem Books* (London, 1948); M. Praz, *Studies in Seventeenth-Century Imagery* (2nd edn, Rome, 1964; first pub. 1939).

ANAXAGORAS *c.* 500–*c.* 428 BC. Greek philosopher and cosmologist, charged at Athens with impiety. Said to have taught that the heavenly bodies are red-hot stones torn from earth. Fragments in G. S. Kirk and J. E. Raven, *The Presocratic Philosophers* (rev. edn, Cambridge, 1962).
    J. L. E. Dreyer, *A History of Astronomy from Thales to Kepler* (rev. edn, New York, 1953); S. Sambursky, *The Physical World of the Greeks** (London, 1956).

APULEIUS 2C AD. Roman novelist. Known in the Middle Ages for work on Plato and adaptation of the magical work *Asclepius* from the body of Hermetic writing – and for the attack on them by Augustine in the *City of God*. From the 14C, his novel *Metamorphoses* was widely read; trans. into English by W. Adlington as *The Golden Asse* (1566, modern edn in TT, 1893): this forms the basis of the old Loeb trans., rev. S. Gaselee (1915). Modern trans. in PC, by R. Graves, rev. M. Grant (1990); by J. Lindsay (Bloomington, Ind., 1960); and Loeb – 2 versions (2nd by J. A. Hanson (1989) in 2 vols).
    T. Hägg, *The Novel in Antiquity* (Oxford, 1983); J. Tatum, *Apuleius and the Golden Ass* (Ithaca, N.Y., 1979); P. G. Walsh, *The Roman Novel* (Cambridge, 1970).

AQUINAS, ST THOMAS *c.* 1225–74. Medieval philosopher and theologian;

Dominican friar; known as the Angelic Doctor. Italian by birth, taught principally at Paris. Attempted to harmonise Aristotelian philosophy and Christianity. His system, Thomism or scholasticism, attacked by humanists and Protestant reformers, but upheld by the Council of Trent. Chief work *Summa Theologiae* or *Theologica* (1265–74); modern trans. by Blackfriars (60 vols, London and New York, 1964–6); selections ed. T. Gilby, *Philosophical Texts* (London, 1951). Also *Summa contra Gentiles* (1258–63), modern trans. by A. C. Pégis *et al.* as *On the Truth of the Catholic Faith* (London, 1955).

F. C. Copleston, *Aquinas* (Harmondsworth, 1955); D. Knowles, *The Evolution of Medieval Thought** (London, 1962). M. D. Chenu, *Toward Understanding Saint Thomas*, trans. A. -M. Landry and D. Hughes (Chicago, 1964); PM* by A. Kenny (1980).

ARIOSTO, LUDOVICO 1474–1533. Italian poet, in the service of the court of Ferrara. Romantic epic *Orlando Furioso* (final version 1532), continuation of Boiardo's *Orlando Innamorato* (1495). Important influence on structure and meaning of Spenser's *Faerie Queene*. Trans. by Sir J. Harington with preface (1591, modern eds by G. Hough, London, 1962, and R. McNulty, Oxford, 1972). Modern trans.: prose by G. Waldman (Oxford, 1974), in WC (1983); verse, in PC by B. Reynolds (2 vols, 1975–7).

C. P. Brand, *Ariosto** (Edinburgh, 1974); R. M. Durling, *The Figure of the Poet in Renaissance Epic* (Cambridge, Mass., 1965); G. Hough, *A Preface to 'The Faerie Queene'** (London, 1962).

ARISTARCHUS 3C BC. Greek astronomer. Originated heliocentric theory, i.e. that earth moves round stationary sun and rotates on its own axis. Knowledge of his theory comes from Archimedes and Plutarch.

J. L. E. Dreyer, *A History of Astronomy from Thales to Kepler* (rev. edn, New York, 1953).

ARISTOTLE 384–322 BC. Greek philosopher and scientist. Born Stagira, hence sometimes referred to as 'the Stagirite'. Pupil of Plato at his Academy, tutor of Alexander the Great, founder of research institute called the Lyceum and Peripatetic school of philosophy. Worked in many fields: biology, physics, cosmology, logic, metaphysics, politics, ethics, literary theory. Logical and scientific works basis of medieval education; ethical and critical more valued in Renaissance. *Poetics* virtually rediscovered in 16C, especially influential in Italy. Majority of corpus available in Latin trans. from 13C; largely read in variety of Latin trans. in Renaissance, though Greek text printed. No significant English trans. in Renaissance. Modern trans. in Loeb (23 vols): see especially *On the Heavens, Metaphysics, Nicomachean Ethics, Physics, Poetics, Politics, Rhetoric, On the Soul, On Coming-To-Be and Passing-Away* (otherwise *On Generation and Corruption*). Modern trans, in PC: *Ethics* (1953); *Poetics*, in *Classical Literary Criticism* (1965); *Politics* (1962). *Complete Works* in 2 vols, rev. J. Barnes (Oxford, 1984). *Nicomachean Ethics* in WC (1992).

G. E. R. Lloyd, *Aristotle: The Growth and Structure of his Thought** (Cambridge, 1968); J. H. Randall, Jr, *Aristotle* (New York, 1960). PM* by J. Barnes (1982); C. B. Schmitt, *Aristotle and the Renaissance* (1983).

ARMINIUS, JACOBUS 1560–1609. Dutch anti-Calvinist theologian. Views summarised after his death in the Remonstrance (1610), condemned at Synod of Dort (1618–19). Some influence on 17C Anglicans and on Milton.

A. W. Harrison, *The Beginnings of Arminianism to the Synod of Dort* (London, 1926); *Arminianism** (London 1937). C. Bangs, *Arminius: A Study in the Dutch Reformation* (Nashville, 1971); N. Tyacke, *Anti-Calvinists: The Rise of English Arminianism c. 1590–1640* (Oxford, 1987).

AUGUSTINE, ST 354–430. Theologian, bishop of Hippo in North Africa, one of the four 'Doctors of the Church'. Voluminous works, many provoked by controversies with pagans and heretics, notably Pelagians. After Paul, chief formulator of Christian theology. Influence in abeyance 13–14C, but revived 15C and particularly strong in Reformation. Chief works: *Confessions* (397–401); *On The Trinity* (399–419); *The City of God* (413–27). Some important minor works: *On Music* (387); *On the Spirit and the Letter* (412); *Enchiridion* (421–3); *On Grace and Free Will* (426–7); *Christian Instruction* (396–426). Several Renaissance English trans.: *The City of God*, by J. Healey (1610, modern edn in EL, 1945); *Confessions*, by Sir T. Matthew (1620); by W. Watts (1631, modern edn in Loeb, 2 vols, 1912). Modern trans. in FC, 21 vols; in LCC vols VI, VII, VIII; in Loeb, *The City of God*, 6 vols (1957–60); in PC, *The City of God* (1972); *Confessions* (1961).

R. W. Battenhouse, ed., *A Companion to the Study of St Augustine* (New York, 1955); P. Brown, *Augustine of Hippo* (London, 1967); H. Marrou, *St Augustine and his Influence through the Ages,** trans. P. Hepburne-Scott (New York, 1957). PM* by H. Chadwick (1986).

AVERROES (Ibn Rushd) 1126–98. Arab philosopher. Commented on Plato's *Republic*, and on many works of Aristotle: known in the Middle Ages as 'the Commentator', as Aristotle was known as 'the Philosopher'. Important in the development of philosophy in the West. Modern trans.: *Averroes' Three Short Commentaries on Aristotle's 'Topics', 'Rhetoric' and 'Poetics'*, by C. E. Butterworth (Albany, N.Y., 1979); *Averroes on the Harmony of Religion and Philosophy*, by G. Hourani (London, 1978, first pub. 1961); *Averroes on Plato's 'Republic'*, by R. Lerner (Ithaca, 1974).

M. Fakhry, *A History of Islamic Philosophy* (New York, 1970); O. Leaman, *Averroes and his Philosophy* (Oxford, 1978).

BEMBO, PIETRO 1470–1547. Italian humanist, Neoplatonist poet, admirer of Petrarch, and cardinal. *Asolani* (1505), dialogue on love. Known in England chiefly through portrait in Castiglione's *Book of the Courtier*. Modern trans. of *Asolani* (Bloomington, 1954). J. C. Nelson, *Renaissance Theory of Love* (New York, 1958); N. A. Robb, *Neoplatonism of the Italian Renaissance* (London, 1935).

BOCCACCIO, GIOVANNI 1313–75. Italian humanist, author of romance and realistic fiction. Friend of Petrarch, admirer of Dante. Earlier works principally narrative in Italian. *Teseida* and *Filostrato* basis of Chaucer's *Knight's Tale* and *Troilus and Criseyde* respectively. Chief work *Decameron*, containing a hundred stories; very influential in England as source of plots; complete English trans. by E. Hutton (1620, modern edn in TT, 4 vols, 1909). Later works scholarly, many in Latin. *Life of Dante*; *Genealogy of the Pagan Gods*, mythological handbook with defence of poetry (first printed 1472; widely used until displaced by handbooks of Gyraldus and Comes). Modern trans.: *Decameron* in PC (1972); *Life of Dante* (New York, 1901); C. G. Osgood, *Boccaccio on Poetry*, in LLA (1956), contains Bks XIV–XV of *Genealogy*.

V. Branca, *Boccaccio: The Man and his Works*, trans. R. Monges (New York, 1976); J. Seznec, *The Survival of the Pagan Gods*, trans. B. Sessions (New York, 1961, first pub. in French 1940); H. G. Wright, *Boccaccio in England* (London, 1957).

BOETHIUS, ANICIUS MANLIUS SEVERINUS *c*. 480–*c*. 524. Roman statesman, scholar, philosopher. Translated much of Aristotle into Latin. Treatises on music, arithmetic and theology. Chief work: *The Consolation of Philosophy*, written while Boethius awaiting execution; important source of Neoplatonism for Middle Ages. Several English trans.: by King Alfred, Chaucer, Queen Elizabeth. Some of metres trans. by H. Vaughan. Loeb (1918) contains (modified) version of 1609 by I.T. Modern trans.: *The Consolation of Philosophy* in new Loeb (1973), in PC (1969); *The Principles of Music*, by C. M. Bower (George Peabody College Ph.D., 1966; contains ch. I of *The Principles of Arithmetic*).

H. R. Patch, *The Tradition of Boethius* (New York, 1935). M. Gibson, ed., *Boethius: His Life, Thought and Influence* (Oxford, 1981).

BRUNO, GIORDANO 1548–1600. Italian philosopher; supporter of Copernicanism, pantheism, theory of infinite universe; burnt for heresy by Inquisition. In England 1583–5; friendship with Sidney and Greville. Philosophical dialogues include *On the Infinite Universe and Worlds* (1584); *The Heroic Frenzies* (1585). Modern trans.: *On the Infinite Universe* in D. W. Singer, *Giordano Bruno: His Life and Thought* (New York, 1950); *Concerning the Cause, Principle, and One* in S. Greenberg, *The Infinite in Giordano Bruno* (New York, 1950); *The Heroic Frenzies*, trans. P. Memmo, Jr (Chapel Hill, 1964). *The Ash-Wednesday Supper*, trans. E. A. Gosselin and L. S. Lerner (Hamden, Conn., 1977); *The Expulsion of the Triumphant Beast*, trans. A. D. Imerti (New Brunswick, N.J., 1963).

J. C. Nelson, *Renaissance Theory of Love* (New York, 1958). H. Gatti, *The Renaissance Drama of Knowledge: Giordano Bruno in England* (London, 1989).

CALVIN, JEAN 1509–64. French Protestant theologian, spent most of life at Geneva. His doctrine and system of church government model for Scottish, English and New England Presbyterianism. Large corpus of treatises and biblical commentaries, many trans. into English 16C. Chief work: *Institutes of the Christian Religion*, in Latin and French (1536–60). English trans. by T. Norton (1561, many 16C and 17C edns). Modern trans. in LCC (2 vols) by F. L. Battles, ed. J. T. McNeill.

F. Wendel, *Calvin: The Origins and Development of his Religious Thought*, trans. P. Mairet (London, 1965, first pub. France, 1950). W. J. Bouwsma, *John Calvin: A Sixteenth-Century Portrait* (New York, 1988); R. T. Kendall, *Calvin and English Calvinism to 1649* (Oxford, 1979); A. E. McGrath, *A Life of John Calvin* (Oxford, 1990); M. Prestwich, ed., *International Calvinism 1541–1715* (Oxford, 1985).

CARTARI, VINCENZO 16C (dates uncertain). Italian mythographer. *The Images of the Gods* (1556), in Italian. Latin trans. by A. du Verdier (1581); abbreviated English trans. by R. Linche as *The Fountain of Ancient Fiction* (1599).

J. Seznec, *The Survival of the Pagan Gods*, trans. B. Sessions (New York, 1961, first pub. in French 1940); D. T. Starnes and E. W. Talbert, *Classical Myth and Legend in Renaissance Dictionaries* (Westport, Conn., 1973, first pub. 1955).

CASTIGLIONE, BALDASSARE 1478–1529. Italian diplomat in service of court of Urbino. *The Book of the Courtier* (1528), very influential dialogue on education, manners and Neoplatonic philosophy. English trans. by Sir T. Hoby (1561, modern edn in EL). Modern trans. in PC (1968).

W. A. Rebhorn, *Courtly Performances: Masking and Festivity in Castiglione's 'Book of the Courtier'* (Detroit, 1978).

CICERO, MARCUS TULLIUS 106–43 BC. Roman orator, statesman, moralist. Principal transmitter of Greek philosophy to Romans. Republican, opponent of Caesar, put to death by Mark Antony. Writings include orations, philosophical works, rhetorical treatises, letters. Chief philosophical works: *The Republic* (fragments, including *The Dream of Scipio*, 54–51); *Views of Good and Evil* (45); *Tusculan Disputations*, *The Nature of the Gods*, *Of Old Age*, *Of Friendship*, *Of Duties* (all in 44). Chief rhetorical works: *On the Orator* (55); *The Orator: to Brutus* (46); texts of these recovered early 15C. Enormously popular and influential in Renaissance; many trans. into English. Modern trans. in Loeb (28 vols); in PC *The Nature of the Gods* (1972); *On the Good Life* (1971), extracts from several works. Also in PC: *Selected Letters* (1982); *Murder Trials* (rev. edn, 1990). *On Duties*, trans. with commentary by E. M. Atkins and M. T. Griffin (Cambridge, 1991).

T. A. Dorey, ed., *Cicero* (London, 1965); H. A. K. Hunt, *The Humanism of Cicero* (Melbourne, 1954); E. Rawson, *Cicero: A Portrait* (London, 1975; rev. edn, Bristol, 1983); C. B. Schmitt, *Cicero Scepticus: A Study of the Influence of the Academica in the Renaissance* (The Hague, 1972).

COMES, NATALIS (otherwise NATALE CONTI) 16C (dates uncertain). Italian mythographer. *Ten Books of Mythology* (1568, many 16C and 17C edns); handbook with Neoplatonic interpretations. Very influential in England in Latin and French edns. See secondary works for CARTARI.

COPERNICUS, NICOLAUS 1473–1543. Polish astronomer; initiator of Copernican, heliocentric theory of planetary motion; regarded himself not as revolutionary but as returning to early Greek science. *On the Revolutions of the Celestial Spheres* (1543), in Latin. English trans. of Bk I, *Perfect Description of the Celestial Orbs*, by T. Digges (1576, part in M. Boas Hall, ed., *Nature and Nature's Laws*, London, 1970). T. S. Kuhn, *The Copernican Revolution* (Cambridge, Mass., 1975, first pub. 1957), contains modern trans. of Bk I.

M. Boas (Hall), *The Scientific Renaissance** (London, 1962); F. R. Johnson, *Astronomical Thought in Renaissance England* (New York, 1968, first pub. 1927), for Digges.

DANTE ALIGHIERI 1265–1321. Italian poet. Chief works: *The New Life* (*c.* 1293), on love for Beatrice; *Convivio*, or *Banquet* (*c.* 1307), didactic philosophical work, influenced by Boethius' *Consolation*; *Divine Comedy* in 3 parts, *Hell (Inferno), Purgatory, Paradise* (*c.* 1307–21). Boccaccio lectured on works and wrote eulogistic *Life of Dante*. Reputation declined in Italy later in Renaissance; read and assimilated by Milton, otherwise little read in England. Modern trans.: complete works in prose trans., Temple Classics edn, by J. A. Carlyle, T. Okey and P. H. Wicksteed (London, 1899–1906, many reprints); in PC, *Divine Comedy* (verse trans.) by D. L. Sayers and B. Reynolds (1949–62). *The New Life* by B. Reynolds (1969); *Divine Comedy* (prose trans.) by C. S. Singleton (Princeton 1970–5). In WC, *Vita Nuova* by M. Musa (1992); *Divine Comedy* (verse trans.) by C. H. Sisson (Manchester, 1980).

T. G. Bergin, *An Approach to Dante** (New York, 1965); F. Fergusson, *Dante** (London, 1966); I. Samuel, *Dante and Milton* (Ithaca, 1966); C. S. Singleton, *Dante Studies* I (Cambridge, Mass., 1954) and II (1958). *The Cambridge Companion to Dante**, ed. R. Jacoff (Cambridge, 1993); PM* by G. Holmes (1980).

DEMOCRITUS *see* EPICURUS *and* LUCRETIUS

(PSEUDO) DIONYSIUS THE AREOPAGITE *c.* 500. Greek Neoplatonic mystical theologian, wrongly identified in Middle Ages and Renaissance with Athenian of IC converted by St Paul. Works: *Celestial Hierarchy* (on nine orders of angels), *Ecclesiastical Hierarchy, Divine Names, Mystical Theology*. Great influence on medieval mysticism and Florentine Neoplatonism; Latin trans. by Scotus Erigena 9C, by Ficino 15C. Modern trans.: *On the Divine Names and Mystical Theology* by C. E. Rolt (London, 1920). *The Complete Works* by C. Luibheid (London, 1987); *The Mystical Theology* by J. D. Jones (Wisconsin, 1980).

C. S. Lewis, *The Discarded Image** (Cambridge, 1964); D. Rutledge, *Cosmic Theology* (London, 1964).

DU BARTAS, GUILLAUME DE SALLUSTE 1544–90. French Huguenot (Protestant) poet. Two-part epic on creation (1578 and 1584), trans. by J. Sylvester as *Du Bartas His Divine Weeks and Works* (1605 and 1608, many 17C edns). Modern facsimile edn (Gainesville, 1965). Modern edn of Sylvester by S. Snyder (Oxford, 1979).
   G. C. Taylor, *Milton's Use of Du Bartas* (Cambridge, Mass., 1934).

EMPEDOCLES 5C BC. Greek philosopher. Only fragments of two long poems survive. Originator of theory of four elements and conflict of Love and Strife.
   G. S. Kirk and J. E. Raven, *The Presocratic Philosophers* (rev. edn, Cambridge, 1962).

EPICTETUS *c*. 55–*c*. 135. Stoic philosopher, one-time slave, taught at Rome. *Discourses* and *Manual* of selections (in Greek) collected posthumously by historian Arrian. English trans. of *Manual* by J. Healey (1610). Modern trans. in Loeb (2 vols. 1925–8). Selected trans. in A. A. Long and D. N. Sedley, *The Hellenistic Philosophers* (Cambridge, 1987).
   F. H. Sandbach, *The Stoics** (London, 1975; 2nd edn, Bristol, 1989).

EPICURUS 341–270 BC. Greek philosopher; his school known as 'the Garden'. Almost all his works are lost; some letters and sayings survive. Taught that philosophy is means to happy life, free from pain and disturbance, whether intellectual, political or emotional. Scientific ideas, totally opposed to those of Aristotle, derived from Democritus and Leucippus: man is mortal, the universe is infinite, there is no divine providence, atoms form the basis of matter. Important influence on Lucretius. Growth of interest in all aspects of Epicureanism 17C. The popular interpretation of Epicureanism as hedonism is false. Modern trans. of surviving works in G. K. Strodach, *The Philosophy of Epicurus* (Evanston, 1963). Also in A. A. Long and D. N. Sedley, *The Hellenistic Philosophers* (Cambridge, 1987).
   J. M. Rist, *Epicurus: An Introduction* (Cambridge, 1972). H. Jones, *The Epicurean Tradition* (London, 1989).

ERASMUS, DESIDERIUS *c*. 1466–1536. Dutch humanist, one-time monk; travelled widely in Europe, chief link between Italian and northern humanism; three visits to England, friend of Colet and More; voluminous letter-writer. Favoured reform in Church, but opposed Lutheran Reformation. Numerous works (all in Latin) include *Adagia* or proverbs (1500, many enlarged edns); *Enchiridion* or *Handbook of the Militant Christian* (1503), source of 'philosophy of Christ'; *The Praise of Folly* (1509), satire on Church, dedicated to More; *Colloquies* (1516, many edns); *The Education of a Christian Prince* (1516); ed. and trans. of New Testament (1516); edns of Church Fathers and Seneca. Very widely read and trans. in England; *The Praise of Folly* by T. Chaloner (1549, modern edn, London, 1965). Modern trans.: *Adages*, selection by M. M. Phillips (Cambridge, 1964); *Colloquies*, by C. R. Thompson (Chicago, 1965), selections in LLA (1957); *Enchiridion*, by R. Himelick (Bloomington, 1963); *The Praise of Folly*, by B. Radice in PC (1971); several works in *The Essential Erasmus*, by

J. P. Dolan (New York, 1964); also in *Christian Humanism and the Reformation*, by J. C. Olin (3rd edn, New York, 1987); *The Erasmus Reader*, ed. E. Rummel (Toronto, 1990). Multi-volume trans. in progress, *The Collected Works of Erasmus* (Toronto, 1974–).

M. M. Phillips, *Erasmus and the Northern Renaissance** (London, 1949; rev. edn, Woodbridge, 1981). T. A. Dorey, ed., *Erasmus* (London, 1970); W. H. Woodward, *Erasmus Concerning the Aim and Method of Education* (New York, 1964, first pub. 1904).L. -E. Halkin, *Erasmus: A Critical Biography*, trans. J. Tonkin (Oxford, 1993); PM* by J. McConica (1991); B. Mansfield, *Phoenix of his Age: Interpretations of Erasmus c. 1550–1750* (Toronto, 1979).

EUSEBIUS *c.* 260–340. Church historian. Chief work: *Ecclesiastical History*, culminating with Emperor Constantine. Modern trans. in Loeb (2 vols, 1926–32); in PC (1965).

R. Lane Fox, *Pagans and Christians* (Harmondsworth, 1988, first pub. 1986).

FICINO, MARSILIO 1433–99. Italian humanist and Neoplatonic philosopher. Trans. whole Platonic corpus into Latin (1484), also Plotinus. Chief works: *Platonic Theology* (1482); *Commentary on Plato's Symposium* (1484, both Latin and Italian), very influential in Italy. Not much direct influence in England; English Neoplatonism derived from Pico, Bembo and Castiglione. Modern trans. of *Commentary on Symposium*, by S. R. Jayne (Columbia, Mo., 1955; 2nd edn, Dallas, 1985); trans. of two other commentaries by M. J. B. Allen, *Marsilio Ficino: The Philebus Commentary* (rev. edn, Berkeley, 1979); *Marsilio Ficino and the Phaedran Charioteer* (Berkeley, 1981).

P. O. Kristeller, *Eight Philosophers of the Italian Renaissance** (London, 1965); *The Philosophy of Marsilio Ficino*, trans. V. Conant (New York, 1943); S. R. Jayne, 'Ficino and the Platonism of the English Renaissance', *Comparative Literature*, IV (1952), 214–38. M. J. B. Allen, *The Platonism of Marsilio Ficino* (Berkeley, 1984); J. Hankins, *Plato in the Italian Renaissance* (Leiden, 1990), vol. I, Pt 4.

GALEN 2C BC. Doctor, philosopher, rhetorician. Works of practical medicine very influential in the Middle Ages; theoretical and philosophical works recovered in 16C. Views on circulation attacked by Vesalius and Servetus in 16C, and finally disproved by William Harvey in 17C. *Methodus Medendi* trans. by T. Gale (1586). Modern trans. in Loeb, *On the Natural Faculties* (2 vols, 1916); *Three Treatises on the Nature of Science*, trans. R. Walzer and M. Frede (Indianapolis, 1985).

V. Nutton, ed. *Galen: Problems and Prospects* (London, 1981); O. Temkin, *Galenism* (Ithaca, N.Y., 1973).

GALILEO GALILEI 1564–1642. Italian astronomer, defender of Copernican system, used telescope to observe new phenomena in heavens; ideas condemned by Inquisition (1633), placed under house arrest; visited by Milton (1638). Wrote in Italian as well as Latin to reach non-learned public. Chief works: *The Starry Messenger* (1610); *Letters on Sunspots* (1613); *Dialogue*

Concerning the Two Chief World Systems (1632). Modern trans.: *Discoveries and Opinions of Galileo*, by S. Drake (New York, 1957); *Dialogue Concerning the Two Chief World Systems*, by S. Drake (Berkeley, 1962, first pub. 1953).

A Koestler, *The Sleepwalkers** (London, 1959); G. de Santillana, *The Crime of Galileo* (Chicago, 1955). PM* by S. Drake (1980).

GELLIUS, AULUS *c.* AD 130–*c.* 180. Roman author, studied at Athens. *Attic Nights*, literary and philosophical compendium and commonplace book. Modern trans. in Loeb (3 vols, 1927).

L. Holford-Strevens, *Aulus Gellius* (London, 1988).

GYRALDUS, LILIUS GREGORIUS (otherwise GIRALDI) 1479–1552. Italian mythographer. *On the Pagan Gods* (1548), Latin handbook; widely used by humanists and poets. *See* secondary works for CARTARI.

HERACLITUS 6–5C BC. Greek philosopher. Only fragments survive. Taught that the universe is in constant process of flux; it is a unity through the reconciliation of opposites. Some influence on Florentine Neoplatonism. Modern trans. in Loeb (1931). Trans. and commentary by C. H. Kahn, *The Art and Thought of Heraclitus* (Cambridge, 1979).

G. S. Kirk and J. E. Raven, *The Presocratic Philosophers* (rev. edn, Cambridge, 1962); E. Wind, *Pagan Mysteries in the Renaissance* (London, 1958).

HERMES TRISMEGISTUS Mythical theologian and philosopher. Believed in the Renaissance to be author of a body of supposedly ancient philosophical and magical dialogues: these aimed to teach man to become divine through knowledge, and seemed to indicate the fundamental unity of Platonism and Christianity. They were trans. into Latin by Ficino in the 1460s, and became widely known. In 1614, the scholar Isaac Casaubon proved that they were not older but later than Plato and Christ, but it took some time for the reputation of Hermes to die entirely. English trans. by J. Everard (1650). Modern trans. by B. P. Copenhaver (Cambridge, 1992) (the older trans. by Scott is not very reliable).

W. Shumaker, *The Occult Sciences in the Renaissance* (Berkeley, 1972), ch. V; D. P. Walker, *The Ancient Theology* (London, 1972); R. S. Westman and J. E. McGuire, *Hermeticism and the Scientific Revolution* (Los Angeles, 1977); F. A. Yates, *The Occult Philosophy in the Elizabethan Age* (London, 1979).

HERODOTUS 5C BC. Greek historian of war of Greece with Persia. English trans. of first 2 bks of *Histories* by B. R. (1584, modern edn in TT, 1924). Modern trans.: Loeb (4 vols, 1920–4); PC (1954); by D. Grene (Chicago, 1987); Norton (1992).

J. Gould, *Herodotus* (London, 1989); D. Lateiner, *The Historical Method of Herodotus* (Toronto, 1989).

HESIOD 8–7C BC. One of the earliest Greek poets. Chief works: *Theogony* (genealogy of gods); *Works and Days* (didactic poem, dealing with cosmology, practical ethics, farming; influenced Virgil). English trans. of *Works and Days* by G. Chapman as *Georgics* (1618). Modern trans.: Loeb (1914); PC (1973); WC (1988).

R. Lamberton, *Hesiod* (New Haven, 1988); O. Murray, *Early Greece* (2nd edn, London, 1993).

HIPPOCRATES 5C BC. Greek physician. The collection of surviving Hippocratic writings is probably not by him. Modern trans. in Loeb (4 vols, 1931).

HOMER Dates unknown; before 700 BC. Greek oral epic poet (or poets, as some scholars maintain), traditionally believed to be blind. *Iliad*, on Trojan war, anger of Achilles and death of Hector; *Odyssey*, on wanderings of Odysseus and his return to Ithaca. Important influence on Virgil. Known only in Latin trans. in Middle Ages; Greek text published 15C. English trans. by G. Chapman: *Iliad* (1598–1612), *Odyssey* (1614–15); modern edn by A. Nicoll (2 vols, New York, 1956). Many modern trans.: prose by E. V. Rieu in PC (1946 and 1950); verse by R. Lattimore, *Iliad* (Chicago, 1961), *Odyssey* (New York, 1967). Two more versions of *Iliad* in PC, prose by M. Hammond (1987), verse by R. Fagles (1991); WC *Iliad* verse by R. Fitzgerald (1984); *Odyssey* by W. Shewring (1980); PC *Odyssey* rev. D. C. H. Rieu (1991).

C. M. Bowra, *Homer** (London, 1972); G. S. Kirk, *The Songs of Homer* (Cambridge, 1962); E. M. W. Tillyard, *The English Epic and its Background* (London, 1954). PM* by J. Griffin (1980); J. Griffin, *Homer on Life and Death* (Oxford, 1980).

HORACE (QUINTUS HORATIUS FLACCUS) 65–8 BC. Roman poet, satirist, critical theorist, celebrator of Augustus. Patron Maecenas gave him Sabine farm. Works: *Epodes, Satires, Odes, Epistles* (including *The Art of Poetry*). Very widely read, translated and imitated in England, especially in 17C; see e.g. epistles of Daniel and Jonson. *Art of Poetry* trans. by Jonson (1640). Modern trans.: Loeb (2 vols, 1914 and 1926); PC *Odes* (1967); *Satires* (1973).

S. Commager, *The Odes of Horace* (New Haven, 1962); L. P. Wilkinson, *Horace and his Lyric Poetry* (2nd edn, Cambridge, 1951); M. -S. Røstvig. *The Happy Man* vol. I (rev. edn, Oslo, 1962), for Horatian influence on 17C retirement poetry. H. Erskine-Hill, *The Augustan Idea in English Literature* (London, 1983); R. O. A. M. Lyne, *The Latin Love Poets* (Oxford, 1980).

IGNATIUS LOYOLA, ST *c.* 1491–1556. Spanish founder of Society of Jesus or Jesuits, based in Rome; concerned with education of priests, spiritual life, missionary work, combatting Protestantism. *Spiritual Exercises* (1548) teaches method of self-discipline and meditation. (1618). Several modern trans. e.g. by W. H. Longridge (rev. edn, London, 1930).

H.O. Evennett, *The Spirit of the Counter-Reformation* (Cambridge, 1968); L. Martz, *The Poetry of Meditation* (rev. edn, New Haven, 1962).

ISIDORE (ISIDORUS) d. 636. Bishop of Seville. Important transmitter of classical learning to Middle Ages. Chief work: *Etymologies*, influential encyclopedia.

E. Brehaut, *An Encyclopedist of the Dark Ages: Isidore of Seville* (New York, 1964, first pub. 1912).

ISOCRATES 436–338 BC. Greek orator and teacher of rhetoric. Orations written to be read, not recited. Influential in development of Hellenistic education, and in 16C humanism. Various English trans.: *To Nicocles* (*c.* 372) by Sir T. Elyot as *The Doctrinal of Princes* (1534). Form of Milton's *Areopagitica* (1644), as written oration, follows *Areopagiticus* (*c.* 354). Modern trans. in Loeb (3 vols, 1954); in PC *Greek Political Oratory* (1970).

H. I. Marrou, *A History of Education in Antiquity*, trans. G. Lamb (New York, 1964, first English edn 1956).

JEROME, ST (EUSEBIUS HIERONYMUS) *c.* 342–420. Roman biblical and classical scholar and controversialist; spent much of life in Near East. One of the four 'Doctors of the Church'. Struggled to reconcile love of classics with Christianity. Revised existing Latin versions of Scriptures in light of Hebrew and Greek originals; this translation, the Vulgate, became standard in Church until Reformation and was made official by Catholic Church at Council of Trent. Voluminous letter-writer; Augustine among his correspondents. Collected works ed. by Erasmus (1516). Modern trans. of *Select Letters* in Loeb (1933).

E. H. Harbison, *The Christian Scholar in the Age of the Reformation* (New York, 1956); J. N. D. Kelly, *Jerome: His Life, Writings, and Controversies* (London, 1975). E. F. Rice, Jr, *Saint Jerome in the Renaissance* (Baltimore, 1985).

JUVENAL (DECIUS JUNIUS JUVENALIS) AD 55–130. Roman satirist. Nothing known for certain about his life. His work, fiercer than that of Horace, was influential in the Renaissance; see e.g. satires of Donne and Marston. First complete English trans. pub. by Sir. R. Stapylton (1647); contemporary trans. by B. Holyday pub. posthumously (1673). Individual satires pub. earlier, e.g. Satire X by H. Vaughan (1646). Modern trans. in Loeb (1918); PC (rev. edn, 1974); WC (1992); EL (1992).

M. Coffey, *Roman Satire* (2nd edn, Bristol, 1989, first pub. 1976); R. Jenkyns, *Three Classical Poets* (London, 1982), ch. 3.

KEPLER, JOHANNES 1571–1630. German astronomer, Neoplatonist mathematician, developer of Copernican system, assistant to Tycho Brahe. Chief works: *Cosmographic Mystery* (1596); *Harmony of the World* (1619). Trans. of *New Astronomy* (1609) by W. H. Donahue (Cambridge, 1992); of *Defence of Tycho* in N. Jardine, *The Birth of History and the Philosophy of Science* (Cambridge, 1984).

M. Boas, *The Scientific Renaissance** (London, 1962); J. L. E. Dreyer, *A History of Astronomy from Thales to Kepler* (rev. edn, New York, 1953); A. Koestler, *The Sleepwalkers** (London, 1959).

LACTANTIUS, LUCIUS COELIUS FIRMIANUS *c.* 240–*c.* 320. Latin Christian apologist, tutor to son of emperor Constantine. His theology optimistic, drawing heavily on classical writers; known in Renaissance as the Christian Cicero. Chief work *Divine Institutes*; modern trans. in FC, vol. XLIX (1964).

C. N. Cochrane, *Christianity and Classical Culture* (Oxford, 1940).

LIPSIUS, JUSTUS 1547–1606. Belgian humanist and Neostoic philosopher;

attempted reconciliation of Stoicism and Christianity. Works (in Latin) include *On Constancy* (1584); *Guide to Stoic Philosophy, Physics of the Stoics* (1604); edn of Seneca (1605). *Two Books of Constancy* trans. by Sir J. Stradling (1595, modern edn with introduction by R. Kirk, New Brunswick, 1939).

J. L. Saunders, *Justus Lipsius* (New York, 1955). G. Oestreich, *Neostoicism and the Early Modern State*, trans. D. McLintock (Cambridge, 1982), Pt 1.

LIVY (LIVIUS), TITUS *c.* 59 BC–*c.* AD 17. Roman historian. *History of Rome* in 142 books; only 35 survive. MSS scattered in Middle Ages; some put together by Petrarch in 14C, some discovered early 16C. Popular among humanist historians; Machiavelli, *Discourses on Livy* (written *c.* 1513–18), draws on Livy to illustrate contemporary political problems. English trans. by P. Holland (1600). Modern trans. in Loeb (14 vols, 1919–59); in PC (3 vols, 1960–76).

T. A. Dorey, ed., *Livy* (London, 1971); M. L. W. Laistner, *The Greater Roman Historians* (Berkeley, 1947). P. G. Walsh, *Livy* in GR (1974); *Livy: His Historical Aims and Methods* (2nd edn, Bristol, 1989).

LUCAN (MARCUS ANNAEUS LUCANUS) AD 39–65. Roman Poet. Nephew of Seneca. Former friend to Nero, who forbade him to pub. his work. Joined unsuccessful conspiracy against Nero, committed suicide. Only extant work epic of Civil War (sometimes called *Pharsalia*). Bk I trans. by Marlowe (pub. 1600); complete trans. by Sir A. Gorges (1614), and T. May (1627). Modern trans. in Loeb (1928, rep. 1969); by R. Graves (London, 1961); by S. H. Braund (Oxford, 1992).

F. M. Ahl, *Lucan: An Introduction* (Ithaca, 1976); M. P. O. Morford, *The Poet Lucan* (Oxford, 1967).

LUCIAN 2C AD. Greek satirist. A favourite author of More and Erasmus, who imitated and translated him into Latin; but shunned by some Renaissance writers for his anti-Christian satire. J. Rastell, More's brother-in-law, trans. *Menippus* (*c.* 1530); *Select Dialogues* trans. by F. Hickes (1634). Modern trans. in Loeb (8 vols, 1913–67); PC (1961).

J. Hall, *Lucian's Satire* (New York, 1981); C. Robinson, *Lucian and his Influence in Europe* (London, 1979).

LUCRETIUS (TITUS LUCRETIUS CARUS) *c.* 94–55 BC. Roman poet and Epicurean philosopher. *On the Nature of the Universe* expounds for Roman audience theories of Greek materialist philosophers (*see* EPICURUS). Not read in Middle Ages, text recovered early 15C. Influence on Bruno. English trans. by L. Hutchinson (1640s, unpub., ms in British Library); Bk I by J. Evelyn (1656); complete by T. Creech (1682). Modern trans.: prose in Leob (1924); in PC (1951); verse by C. H. Sisson (Manchester, 1976).

D. P. and P. G. Fowler, *A Companion to Lucretius* (Oxford, 1993); E. J. Kenney, *Lucretius* in GR (1977).

LUTHER, MARTIN 1483–1546. Protestant reformer and theologian. Formulated ideas *c.* 1515–20; condemned at Diet of Worms (1521). Enormous and varied body of work in Latin and German: biblical commentaries, controversial and didactic works, catechisms, hymns. Three important manifestoes (1520): *To the*

Christian Nobility of the German Nation; *On the Babylonian Captivity of the Church*; *The Freedom of A Christian*. Trans. Bible into German (1522 and 1534). Many English trans.: W. Tyndale, *Prologue to Romans* (1526, modern edn Cambridge, 1848). Modern trans.: *Selected Writings*, ed. T. G. Tappert (4 vols, Philadelphia, 1967); *Luther's Works*, ed. J. Pelican and H. T. Lehmann (55 vols, Saint Louis and Philadelphia, 1958–67); Luther and Erasmus, *Free Will and Salvation*, ed. E. G. Rupp and B. Drewery (London, 1696). Extracts in *A Compend of Luther's Theology*, ed. H. T. Kerr (Philadelphia, 1943), and in E. G. Rupp and B. Drewery, *Martin Luther** (London, 1970).

R. H. Bainton, *Here I Stand: A Life of Martin Luther** (New York, 1950); P. S. Watson, *Let God be God!* (London, 1947). A. E. McGrath, *Luther's Theology of the Cross* (Oxford, 1985); D. C. Steinmetz, *Luther in Context* (Bloomington, Ind., 1986).

MACHIAVELLI, NICCOLO 1469–1527. Italian political theorist; Florentine historian and civil servant. Chief works: *The Prince* (1532, written 1514); *Discourses* (1531, written 1513–18). Popularly misinterpreted in England 16C; more sympathetic approach 17C. English trans. by E. Dacres, *Discourses* (1636). *The Prince* (1640, modern edn in TT, 1905). Modern trans. in PC: *The Prince* (1961); *Discourses* (1970); in EL *The Prince* (1981); in WC *The Prince* (1984).

F. Raab, *The English Face of Machiavelli* (London, 1964). J. G. A. Pocock, *The Machiavellian Moment* (Princeton, 1975); PM* by Q. Skinner (1981); Skinner, *The Foundations of Modern Political Thought* (1978), vol. I, Pt 2.

MACROBIUS 4–5C AD. Roman Neoplatonist; nothing known of his life. *Commentary on the Dream of Scipio* preserved this part of Cicero's *Republic*; popular source of Neoplatonism for Middle Ages. *Saturnalia* includes important criticism of Virgil. Modern trans.: *Commentary on the Dream of Scipio* by W. H. Stahl (New York, 1952); *Saturnalia* by P. V. Davies (New York, 1969).

MARCUS AURELIUS ANTONINUS AD 121–80. Roman emperor and Stoic philosopher. *Meditations*, in Greek. English trans. by M. Casaubon (1634, modern edn London, 1900). *The Golden Book of Marcus Aurelius*, by Lord Berners (from French version of Guevara's Spanish fiction, 1534, many 16C edns), is not a translation. Modern trans. in Loeb (1916); in PC (1964); in WC (1989).

F. H. Sandbach, *The Stoics** (London, 1975, 2nd edn, Bristol, 1989); R. B. Rutherford, *The Meditations of Marcus Aurelius* (Oxford, 1989).

MARTIANUS CAPELLA 5C AD. Roman author of *The Marriage of Mercury and Philology*, allegorical encyclopedia much used in medieval education. Modern trans.: W. H. Stahl and R. Johnson, *Martianus Capella and the Seven Liberal Arts* (2 vols, New York, 1971–7).

MONTAIGNE, MICHEL DE 1533–92. French essayist. Early interest in Stoicism, later in scepticism. *Essays* rev. and enlarged between edns (1580, 1588, 1595). English trans. by J. Florio (1603, several modern edns, 2 vols, London, 1931). Modern trans. by D. M. Frame (Stanford, 1958); in PC by M. A. Screech (1991).

D. M. Frame, *Montaigne's Discovery of Man* (New York, 1955). PM* by P. Burke (1981); R. A. Sayce, *The Essays of Montaigne* (Oxford, 1972); M. A. Screech, *Montaigne and Melancholy* (London, 1983).

NICHOLAS OF CUSA (OR CUSANUS) *c*. 1400–64. German Neoplatonic philosopher, cardinal. Chief work *On Learned Ignorance* (1440); truth unknowable except by intuition. Rejected Aristotelian cosmos; influenced Bruno. Modern trans. by G. Heron (London, 1954); J. P. Dolan, ed., *Unity and Reform: Selected Writings of Nicholas de Cusa* (Notre Dame, Ind., 1962).

E. Cassirer, *The Individual and the Cosmos in Renaissance Philosophy*, trans. M. Domandi (Oxford, 1963); A. Koyré, *From the Closed World to the Infinite Universe* (Baltimore, 1957). P. M. Watts, *Nicolaus Cusanus: A Fifteenth-Century Vision of Man* (Leiden, 1982).

ORIGEN(ES), ADAMANTIUS *c*. 185–*c*. 254. Alexandrian Greek biblical commentator and theologian; student of Clement of Alexandria. Some works survive only in fragments or Latin trans. Developed tradition of biblical allegory initiated by Philo. Modern trans. of *Commentary on The Song of Songs* by R. P. Lawson (Westminster, Md, 1957). *Contra Celsum* (Against Celsus), trans. H. Chadwick (Cambridge, 1980, first pub. 1953); selections in Ante-Nicene Christian Library, ed. F. Crombie (Edinburgh, 1869–72), vols X, XXIII.

J. Daniélou, *Origen* (New York, 1955, first pub. France, 1948); R. P. C. Hanson, *Allegory and Event* (London, 1959); J. W. Trigg, *Origen* (London, 1985).

OVID (PUBLIUS OVIDIUS NASO) 43 BC–AD 17. Roman poet. Chief works: *Amores* (love poems); *Heroides* (letters of famous lovers); *Metamorphoses* (collection of mythological stories, linked by idea of continuity in change and order in variety). Very widely read, trans. and imitated in Renaissance. English trans. of *Metamorphoses* by A. Golding (1567, many edns, modern edn New York, 1965); by G. Sandys (1626, 1632 with allegorical annotation, modern edn Lincoln, Neb., 1970). Much Ovidian narrative poetry in 1590s by Marlowe, Chapman, Shakespeare, Drayton, etc: see E. S. Donno, ed., *Elizabethan Minor Epics* (London, 1963); N. Alexander, ed., *Elizabethan Narrative Verse* (London, 1967). Modern trans.: complete poems in Loeb (6 vols); *Metamorphoses* in PC (1955); in WC *The Love Poems* (1990), *Metamorphoses* (1987); in PC *Erotic Poems* (1982); *Heroides*, trans. D. Hine (New Haven, 1991); *Tristia*, trans. A. D. Melville (Oxford, 1992).

F. S. Boas, *Ovid and the Elizabethans* (London, 1947); D. P. Harding, *Milton and the Renaissance Ovid* (Urbana, 1946); B. Otis, *Ovid as an Epic Poet* (2nd edn, Cambridge, 1970); L. P. Wilkinson, *Ovid Recalled* (Cambridge, 1955). L. Barkan, *The Gods Made Flesh: Metamorphosis and the Pursuit of Paganism* (New Haven, 1986); G. Braden, *The Classics and English Renaissance Poetry* (New Haven, 1978), ch. I, 'Golding's Ovid'; C. Martindale, ed., *Ovid Renewed* (Cambridge, 1988); C. and M. Martindale, *Shakespeare and the Uses of Antiquity* (London, 1990); L. Martz, *Poet of Exile: A Study of Milton's Poetry* (New Haven, 1980), Pt 3; J. B. Solodow, *The World of Ovid's 'Metamorphoses'* (Chapel Hill, 1988).

PARACELSUS (THEOPHRAST BOMBAST VON HOHENHEIM) 1493–1541. Swiss physician and alchemist. Rejected theories of Aristotle and Galen, and stressed importance of observation and chemical investigation; his medicine was also mystical, and he believed the Creation to be a work of divine alchemy. Modern trans.: selections in N. Goodrick-Clarke, ed, *Paracelsus* (Wellingborough, 1990).

A. G. Debus, *The English Paracelsians* (London, 1965); W. Pagel, *Paracelsus: An Introduction to Philosophical Medicine in the Era of the Renaissance* (2nd edn rev., Basle, 1982); C. Webster, *From Paracelsus to Newton: Magic and the Making of Modern Science* (Cambridge, 1982).

PELAGIUS 4–5C AD. British monk, opponent of Jerome and Augustine, excommunicated by Church for heresy (417). Very few works survive. Theological system known as Pelagianism stresses man's reason, free will and ability to act independently of God's grace, and rejects original sin. Pelagius attacked Augustine's *Confessions* X xl for undermining moral responsibility; several of Augustine's later works are attacks on Pelagianism.

R. F. Evans, *Pelagius* (London, 1968); J. Ferguson, *Pelagius* (Cambridge, 1956, rep. N.Y., 1978); B. R. Rees, *Pelagius: A Reluctant Heretic* (Woodbridge, 1988).

PETRARCH (PETRARCA), FRANCESCO 1304–74. Italian poet and humanist. Lived part of life in France, near Avignon. Largely responsible for stimulating humanist interest in classical antiquity, and search for classical MSS, though himself unable to read Greek. Excellent private library; favourite authors included Cicero, Seneca, Livy, Virgil, Horace, Ovid, Augustine and Boethius. Crowned as Laureate at Rome (1341) for Latin poem *Africa* on Scipio Africanus; sometimes regarded as symbolic beginning of Renaissance. Chief works: in Italian, *Canzoniere* (love poems to Laura); *Triumphs* (allegorical processions; very popular in Renaissance); in Latin (valued more highly by Petrarch), *Secret* (dialogues with Augustine); *On the Remedies of Good and Bad Fortune*; *On His Own Ignorance and That of Many Others*. *Canzoniere* much imitated by sonneteers in 1590s e.g. Sidney, Daniel, Drayton, Spenser. A. Mortimer, ed., *Petrarch's Canzoniere in the English Renaissance* (Bergamo, 1975), anthology of trans. *Triumphs* trans. Lord Morley (1555?, modern edn Cambridge, Mass., 1971). Modern trans.: *Petrarch's Secret*, by W. H. Draper (London, 1911); selections in *Petrarch: A Humanist among Princes*, ed. D. Thomas (New York, 1971); short prose pieces in *The Renaissance Philosophy of Man*, ed. E. Cassirer *et al.* (Chicago, 1948). *Africa*, trans. T. G. Bergin and A. S. Wilson (New Haven, 1977); *Bucolicum Carmen*, trans. T. G. Bergin (New Haven, 1974); *Lyric Poems* trans. R. M. Durling (Cambridge, Mass., 1976); in WC *Selections from the Canzoniere* (1985).

T. G. Bergin, *Petrarch** (New York, 1970); P. O. Kristeller, *Eight Philosophers of the Italian Renaissance** (London, 1965); G. Watson, *The English Petrarchans* (London, 1967, critical bibliography). K. Foster, *Petrarch, Poet and Humanist* (Edinburgh, 1984); P. Hainsworth, *Petrarch the Poet* (London, 1988); PM* by N. Mann (1984); S. Minta, ed., *Petrarch and Petrarchism: The*

English and French Traditions* (Manchester, 1980).

PHILO JUDAEUS *c*. 20 BC–*c*. AD 50. Alexandrian Jewish biblical commentator. Read Old Testament in light of Greek especially Platonic philosophy. Developed allegorical interpretation; strongly influenced Origen and later Christian biblical exegetes. Works (in Greek) include *Life of Moses, On the Creation of the World*. Modern trans. in Loeb (10 vols, 1929–53); selections in *The Essential Philo*, ed N. Glatzer (New York, 1971). *The Contemplative Life, The Giants, and Selections*, trans. D. Winston (New York, 1981).

E. R. Goodenough, *An Introduction to Philo Judaeus* (2nd edn, Oxford, 1962). J. Dillon, *The Middle Platonists* (London, 1977); S. Sandmel, *Philo of Alexandria: An Introduction* (New York, 1979).

PICO DELLA MIRANDOLA, GIOVANNI 1463–94. Italian humanist, friend of Ficino. Attempted to create syncretic philosophy by fusing Jewish Cabala with Christian theology and Platonic and Aristotelian philosophy. Chief works (in Latin): *On the Dignity of Man, On Being and the One, Heptaplus*. Life of Pico by his nephew trans. by Sir T. More (*c*. 1510). Passages from *Dignity of Man* in H. Reynolds, *Mythomystes* (1632, modern edn in J. E. Spingarn, ed., *Critical Essays of the Seventeenth Century*, London, 1908). *Commentary* (in Italian) on Benivieni's *Canzone on Divine* Love trans. by T. Stanley as *A Platonic Discourse upon Love* (1651, modern edn Boston, 1914); included by Stanley in *The History of Philosophy* (3 vols. 1655–62), under 'Plato'. Modern trans. of *On the Dignity of Man, On Being and the One, Heptaplus* in LLA (1965). *Commentary on a Canzone of Benivieni*, trans. S. R. Jayne (New York, 1984).

J. L. Blau, *The Christian Interpretation of the Cabala in the Renaissance* (New York, 1944); P. O. Kristeller, *Eight Philosophers of the Italian Renaissance** (London, 1965). D. P. Walker, *The Ancient Theology* (London, 1972).

PLATO *c*. 429–347 BC. Greek philosopher, disciple of Socrates (executed by Athenians for impiety), founder of Academy (philosophic school). Derived some ideas from Pythagoreans. Approx. 26 works, mostly in dialogue form with Socrates as chief speaker; early works based on Socrates' teachings, later with Socrates as mouthpiece for Plato's ideas. *Apology* (Socrates' speech at his trial); *Symposium* (or drinking-party; on theory of love); *Phaedo* (on the immortality of the soul, and the death of Socrates); *Republic* (on justice, the ideal state, the education of the ruling class); *Phaedrus* (on rhetoric and the love of truth); *Timaeus* (on cosmology). Complete corpus available in 16C in Latin trans. (by Ficino 1484; by Serranus 1578) and in Greek (1513). No dialogues trans. into English till 1675. Platonic political theory influenced humanists; dialogue form rarely imitated (e.g. More's *Utopia*). Modern trans.: complete in Loeb (9 vols); several in PC, including *Apology* and *Phaedo* in *The Last Days of Socrates* (1954); *Symposium* (1951); *Timaeus* (1965). For *Republic* see trans. by F. M. Cornford (Oxford, 1941); in EL by A. D. Lindsay (rep. 1992); by R. Waterfield (Oxford, 1993).

J. E. Raven, *Plato's Thought in the Making* (Cambridge, 1965); A. E. Taylor, *Plato: The Man and his Work* (5th edn, London, 1948). PM* by R. M. Hare

(1982); R. Kraut, ed., *The Cambridge Companion to Plato* (Cambridge, 1992).

PLINY THE ELDER (GAIUS PLINIUS SECUNDUS) AD 23/4–79. Roman historian and encyclopedist. Ended successful military and administrative career by incautious investigation of the eruption of Vesuvius. Only surviving work the enormous *Natural History* (37 books), compendium of ancient science. Distinguished from his nephew Pliny the Younger (famous for his letters) only in 14C, when commentaries on *Natural History* began to be produced. Remained standard work of reference, rivalling Aristotle in some universities, until well into 17C. English trans. by I. A. (1566) and P. Holland (1601). Modern trans. in Loeb, 10 vols (rev. edn 1949); selections in PC (1991).

M. Beagon, *Roman nature: The Thought of Pliny the Elder* (Oxford, 1992).

PLOTINUS 205–70. Neoplatonic philosopher. Studied at Alexandria, taught at Rome. Works (in Greek) collected posthumously as *Enneads* ('groups of nine') by Porphyry. Influence largely indirect, through Augustine and Dionysius. Trans. into Latin by Ficino (1492); Greek not printed till 1580. Modern trans. by S. Mackenna, rev. B. S. Page (London, 1969, first pub. 1917–30); selections by A. H. Armstrong (London, 1953); complete in Loeb (7 vols, 1966–88); Mackenna trans. in PC (1991).

A. H. Armstrong, *An Introduction to Ancient Philosophy* (London, 1947). J. M. Rist, *Plotinus* (London, 1980, first pub. 1967); R. T. Wallis, *Neoplatonism* (London, 1972).

PLUTARCH(US), MESTRIUS Before AD 50–after 120. Greek moralist, biographer, essayist. Philosophical bias Platonic and anti-Stoic. Works in two large groups, *Moralia* (ethical and miscellaneous pieces) and *Lives*. Very popular as historian, moralist and educator in Renaissance; *The Education of Children* wrongly attributed to him. Various English trans.: *Quiet of Mind* by Sir T. Wyatt (1528); *The Education of Children* by Sir T. Elyot (1535?); *The Lives of the Noble Grecians and Romans* by Sir T. North (1579, several edns, from the French of J. Amyot; modern edn 8 vols, Oxford, 1928; selections in *Shakespeare's Plutarch*, ed. T. J. B. Spencer, Harmondsworth, 1964); *The Morals* by P. Holland (1603, modern selections in EL, 1911). Modern trans. in Loeb, *Moralia* (14 vols, 1927–67); *Lives* (11 vols, 1914–26). *Moral Essays* (selections) in PC (1971). Many *Lives* in PC, including *Makers of Rome* (1965), *The Fall of the Roman Republic* (1972), *The Age of Alexander* (1973), *On Sparta* (1988). *Selected Essays and Dialogues* in WC (1993).

D. A. Russell, *Plutarch** (London, 1973).

POLYBIUS *c.* 200–after 118 BC. Greek historian of Rome, and theorist of rise and fall of states. *Histories* in 40 books, of which only I–V and parts of others survive. Part trans. into Latin late 15C. Influence on Machiavelli. English trans. by E. Grimstone (1633). Drawn on by Ralegh for *History of the World* (1614). Modern trans. in Loeb (6 vols, 1922–7). *The Rise of the Roman Empire* in PC (1979).

F. W. Walbank, *Polybius* (Berkeley, 1972). K. Sacks, *Polybius on the Writing of History* (Berkeley, 1981).

PTOLEMY (PTOLEMAEUS), CLAUDIUS 2C AD. Alexandrian Greek astronomer and mathematician. Chief work: *Great Syntaxis* (or *Mathematical Syntaxis*), known as *Almagest* from Arabic title; provides detailed mathematical account of movement of celestial bodies, based on Aristotelian cosmology. Known in Middle Ages in Latin trans. from Arabic; in 16C Latin trans. from Greek and Greek text published. Copernicus' work began as attempt to modify Ptolemy's calculations.

    J. L. E. Dreyer, *A History of Astronomy from Thales to Kepler* (rev. edn, New York, 1953); T. S. Kuhn, *The Copernican Revolution* (Cambridge, Mass., 1975, first pub. 1957).

PYTHAGORAS 6C BC. Greek mathematician and philosopher, founded religious community in southern Italy. Very little definitely known about him, though many legends persisted. Information about Pythagoreanism derives from Plato, Aristotle, Diogenes Laertius (3C AD; historian of philosophy) and Porphyry (3C AD; Neoplatonist). *Carmina aurea* (Golden Verses), containing ethical precepts, attributed to Pythagoras; widely read in Renaissance; English trans. by T. Stanley in *History of Philosophy* (1655–62).

    G. S. Kirk and J. E. Raven, *The Presocratic Philosophers* (rev. edn, Cambridge, 1962); S. K. Heninger, *Touches of Sweet Harmony: Pythagorean Cosmology and Renaissance Poetics* (San Marino, 1974).

QUINTILIAN(US), MARCUS FABIUS 1C AD. Roman teacher of rhetoric. Chief work *Institutio oratoria (Education of an Orator)*, *c*. 95. Complete text recovered early 15C. Important influence on humanist educational theory. Passages included in Jonson's *Discoveries* (1640). Modern trans. in Loeb (4 vols, 1921–2); Bks I–II in LLA (1965).

    H. I. Marrou, *A History of Education in Antiquity*, trans. G. Lamb (New York, 1964, first English edn 1956); W. H. Woodward, *Studies in Education during the Age of the Renaissance* (Cambridge, 1906).

RABELAIS, FRANÇOIS *c*. 1492–1553. French writer of satiric and philosophic fantasy; monk, doctor of medicine, humanist. Works: *Pantagruel* (1532); *Gargantua* (1534); *Third Book (1546); Fourth Book* (1548–52); *Fifth Book* (1564, partly by Rabelais). English trans. of first 3 bks by T. Urquhart (1653–4, 1693); completed by P. Motteux (1694, modern edn London, 1970). Modern trans. in PC (1955).

    M. A. Screech, *The Rabelaisian Marriage: Aspects of Rabelais's Religion, Ethics, and Comic Philosophy* (London, 1958). T. Cave, *The Cornucopian Text* (Oxford, 1979); L. Febvre, *The Problem of Unbelief in the Sixteenth Century: The Religion of Rabelais*, trans. B. Gottlieb (Cambridge, Mass., 1982, first French edn 1942); M. A. Screech, *Rabelais* (London, 1979).

RIPA, CESARE 16C Italian iconographer. *Iconologia* (1593, illustrated edn 1603), dictionary of classical symbols and images for use by painters and sculptors. No English trans. till 1709, but used by masque writers, esp. Jonson.

    D. J. Gordon, *The Renaissance Imagination*, ed. S. Orgel (Berkeley, 1975). J. Aptekar, *Icons of Justice: Iconography and Thematic Imagery in Book V of*

'*The Faerie Queene*' (New York, 1969).

SALLUST (GAIUS SALLUSTIUS CRISPUS) *c*. 86–35 BC. Roman historian. Chief works: *The Conspiracy of Catiline*; *The Jugurthine War*. English trans. by T. Heywood (1608, modern edn in TT, 1924). Modern trans. in Loeb (rev. edn, 1931); in PC (1963).
    M. L. W. Laistner, *The Greater Roman Historians* (Berkeley, 1947); R. Syme, *Sallust* (Berkeley, 1964). D. C. Earl, *The Political Thought of Sallust* (Cambridge, 1961).

SALLUSTIUS 4C AD. Roman Neoplatonist, friend of the Emperor Julian. *On the Gods and the World*. Modern trans. by G. Murray in *Five Stages of Greek Religion* (Oxford, 1925).

SENECA, LUCIUS ANNAEUS *c*. AD 1–65. Roman Stoic Philosopher, tragedian and politician; Nero's tutor and minister; last years in retirement, forced to commit suicide. Works comprise 9 tragedies, letters and treatises, including *On Providence, On the Firmness of the Wise Man, On the Happy Life, On Tranquillity of Mind, To Helvia on Consolation, Moral Letters* (to Lucilius). Prose edited by Erasmus (1515, 1529) and Lipsius (1605). Tragedies much read and trans. 16C; prose more popular 17C. Moral writings trans. T. Lodge (1614). Much paraphrase in Jonson's poems; passages trans. in *Discoveries* (1640). Modern trans. in Loeb: *Epistulae Morales* (3 vols, 1917–25); *Moral Essays* (3 vols, 1928–35); selections in PC: *Letters from a Stoic* (1969).
    C. D. N. Costa, ed., *Seneca* (London, 1974); F. H. Sandbach, *The Stoics** (London, 1975, 2nd edn, Bristol, 1989); M. T. Griffin, *Seneca: A Philosopher in Politics* (Oxford, 1992, first pub. 1976).

SEXTUS EMPIRICUS 2C AD. Greek philosopher; main exponent of radical scepticism or pyrrhonism (so called after Pyrrho of Elis, whose works are lost). Principal work *Outlines of Pyrrhonism* available in Latin in Middle Ages but ignored. Latin text pub. 1562, major influence on Montaigne, *Apology for Raymond Sebond*. Greek text pub. 1621. Modern trans.: Loeb (4 vols, 1933); selections by S. G. Etheridge (Indianapolis, 1985), and A. A. Long and D. N. Sedley, *The Hellenistic Philosophers* (Cambridge, 1987).
    M. F. Burnyeat, ed., *The Skeptical Tradition* (Berkeley, 1983); R. H. Popkin, *The History of Scepticism from Erasmus to Spinoza* (rev. edn, Berkeley, 1979); C. L. Stough, *Greek Skepticism* (Berkeley, 1969).

SOCRATES *see* PLATO *and* XENOPHON

STATIUS AD 45–96. Roman Poet. Regarded in Middle Ages as crypto-Christian: Dante puts him in Purgatory. Chief work *Thebaid*, epic on the Seven Against Thebes; also *Silvae*, collection of occasional pieces. Jonson's titles *Forest, Underwood*, and *Timber* are versions of 'silvae'. Bks 1–5 of *Thebaid* trans. by T. Stephens (1648). Modern trans. in Loeb (2 vols, 1928); by A. D. Melville (Oxford, 1992).
    D. Vessey, *Statius and the Thebaid* (Cambridge, 1973); G. Williams, *Change and Decline: Roman Literature in the Early Empire* (Berkeley, 1978).

SUETONIUS (GAIUS SUETONIUS TRANQUILLUS) *c.* 69–*c.* 122. Roman writer of historical biography. Most famous work *Lives of the Twelve Caesars*. English trans. by P. Holland (1606; in TT, 2 vols, 1899). Modern trans. in Loeb (2 vols, rev. 1951); PC by R. Graves rev. M. Grant (1989).

T. A. Dorey, ed., *Latin Biography* (London, 1967); A. Wallace-Hadrill, *Suetonius: The Scholar and his Caesars* (London, 1983).

TACITUS, CORNELIUS 1C AD. Roman historian, castigator of vices of Rome under emperors, admirer of primitive virtues of Republic and German tribes. Largely unknown in Middle Ages; surviving MSS recovered 15C and early 16C. Much admired late 16C and early 17C. Ed. by Lipsius (1574). English trans. of *Histories* and *Agricola* by Sir H. Savile (1591). Modern trans. of complete works in Loeb (4 vols. 1914–37); in PC *Agricola* and *Germania* (rev. edn, 1970); *Annals* (rev. edn, 1971); *Histories* (rev. edn, 1968).

T. A. Dorey, ed., *Tacitus* (London, 1969). R. Martin, *Tacitus* (London, 1981).

TASSO, TORQUATO 1544–95. Italian poet and critical theorist. Chief works: *Jerusalem Delivered* (1581), epic on First Crusade, with allegory attached; recast and moralised as *Jerusalem Conquered* (1593); *Discourses on the Heroic Poem* (1594, revision of earlier *Discourses on the Art of Poetry*). Some episodes from *Jerusalem Delivered* imitated by Spenser in *Faerie Queene*; English trans. as *Godfrey of Boulogne* by E. Fairfax (1600, modern edn by J. C. Nelson, New York, 1963; K, M. Lea and T. M. Gang, Oxford, 1981). English trans. of *Aminta* by H. Reynolds (1628; modern edn by G. Pursglove, Salzburg, 1991). Modern trans. of *Discourses on Heroic Poem* by M. Cavalchini and I. Samuel (Oxford, 1973).

C. P. Brand, *Tasso* (Cambridge, 1965), esp. Pt 2, 'Tasso in England'. J. A. Kates, *Tasso and Milton: The Problem of Christian Epic* (Lewisburg, 1983).

TERESA OF AVILA, ST 1515–82. Spanish mystic and reformer of Carmelite order of nuns. Works include *The Way of Perfection* (1583, English trans. by T. Matthew as *The Flaming Heart*, 1623); *Life* (1588). 3 poems addressed to her by Crashaw (1646, 1652). Modern trans. of *Works* by E. A. Peers (3 vols, London, 1946; *Life* reprinted New York, 1960). *Life* in PC (1987, first pub. 1957).

R. T. Petersson, *The Art of Ecstasy: Teresa, Bernini, and Crashaw* (London, 1970).

TERTULLIAN(US), QUINTUS SEPTIMIUS FLORENS *c.* AD 160–*c.* 220. First Christian Latin apologist and controversialist; ascetic, strongly opposed to Christian assimilation of pagan culture. Large collection of controversial and doctrinal works. Modern trans.: *Apology* and *On Spectacles* in Loeb (rev. edn, 1953) and in FC vols X and XL (1950, 1959); *The Prescriptions against the Heretics* and *On Idolatry* in *Early Latin Theology*, LCC, vol. V (1956).

T. D. Barnes, *Tertullian* (Oxford, 1971). R. Lane Fox, *Pagans and Christians* (Harmondsworth, 1988, first pub. 1986).

THUCYDIDES *c.* 460–*c.* 400 BC. Greek historian of war between Athens and Sparta. *History of the Peloponnesian War* gives idealised portrait of Pericles'

Athens and traces stages of Athenian defeat. Much read by humanists; Latin trans. by L. Valla (1450–2); English trans. by T. Hobbes (1629, modern edn 2 vols, Ann Arbor, 1959). Modern trans. in Loeb (4 vols, 1919–23) and PC (rev. edn, 1972).

J. H. Finley, Jr, *Thucydides* (Cambridge, Mass., 1942). K. J. Dover, *Thucydides* in GR (1973); S. Hornblower, *Thucydides* (London, 1987).

VIRGIL (PUBLIUS VERGILIUS MARO) 70–19 BC. Roman poet. Works: *Eclogues* or *Bucolics* (pastoral poems, based on Greek poet Theocritus); *Georgics* (on farming and natural philosophy, indebted to Lucretius); *Aeneid* (epic based on Homer, on Aeneas' translation of empire from Troy to Italy; prophecy of Rome's greatness, celebration of Augustus). Works became bible of late pagans in conflict with Christians (in e.g. Macrobius' *Saturnalia*). *Aeneid* widely read as allegory of Christian life, e.g. by Fulgentius in 6C, by Landino in 15C. In *The Divine Comedy* Virgil is Dante's guide, but as pagan he cannot take Dante further than the Earthly Paradise. English trans. of *Aeneid* by G. Douglas (1553, modern edn 4 vols, Edinburgh, 1957–64), and J. Dryden (1697, modern edn Oxford, 1958); several trans. of individual books. Important Virgilian echoes in *Paradise Lost*. Many modern trans.: prose in Loeb (2 vols, rev. edn, 1934); in PC *The Aeneid* (1956) and *The Pastoral Poems* (1949); verse by C. Day Lewis, *Eclogues* (London, 1963); *Georgics* (London, 1940); *Aeneid* (London, 1952). Two further trans. of *Aeneid* in PC: verse by R. Fitzgerald (1985), prose by D. West (1991). *Georgics* also in PC (1982). Day Lewis trans. in WC in 2 vols: *Eclogues and Georgics* (1983), *Aeneid* (1986). *Eclogues* trans. G. Lee (Liverpool, 1980); *Georgics* trans. R. Wells (Manchester, 1982).

C. M. Bowra, *From Virgil to Milton* (London, 1945); D. P. Harding, *The Club of Hercules: Studies in the Classical Background of Paradise Lost* (Urbana, 1962); M. Y. Hughes, *Virgil and Spenser* (Port Washington, N. Y., 1969, first pub. 1929). P. Alpers, *The Singer of the Eclogues* (Berkeley, 1979); W. A. Camps, *An Introduction to Virgil's 'Aeneid'* * (Oxford, 1969); PM* by J. Griffin (1986); R. D. Williams and T. S. Pattie, *Virgil: His Poetry through the Ages* * (London, 1982).

VITRUVIUS, POLLIO 1C BC. Roman architect; author of treatise *On Architecture*. Influence on Renaissance architects, Alberti and Palladio in Italy, Inigo Jones in England. Modern trans. in Loeb (2 vols, 1931).

R. Wittkower, *Architectural Principles in the Age of Humanism* (3rd edn, London, 1962).

VIVES, JUAN LUIS 1492–1540. Spanish humanist, pupil and friend of Erasmus, taught at Louvain and Oxford, tutor to Princess Mary. Influenced humanist teaching methods. Chief work: *The Transmission of Knowledge* (1531, extracts trans. by Jonson in *Discoveries*, 1640). Modern trans. by F. Watson, *Vives: On Education* (Cambridge, 1913).

R. P. Adams, *The Better Part of Valor: More, Erasmus, Colet, and Vives, on Humanism, War, and Peace* (Seattle, 1962). C. G. Norena, *Juan Luis Vives* (The Hague, 1970).

WYCLIFFE, JOHN *c.* 1329–84. English theologian and philosopher. Questioned doctrine of transubstantiation and papal authority; favoured reading Bible in vernacular, and encouraged translation. Condemned posthumously by Church. Followers known as Lollards. Regarded after Reformation as one of its founders; celebrated in Foxe's *Acts and Monuments*. Selection of English works by his followers in A. Hudson, ed., *Selections from English Wycliffite Writings* (Cambridge, 1978).

PM* by A. Kenny (1985); A. Kenny, ed., *Wyclif in his Times* (Oxford, 1986).

XENOPHON *c.* 428–*c.* 354 BC. Greek soldier, historian, moralist, educational theorist, friend of Socrates. Chief works: *Anabasis* (the march up country; account of Persian revolt in which Xenophon took part); *Cyropaedia* (historical romance on education of Persian king Cyrus the Great). English trans. of *Cyropaedia* by P. Holland (1632, modern edn Newtown, 1936). Modern trans. in Loeb (7 vols, 1914–25), in PC *The Persian Expedition (Anabasis)* (1949); *History of my Times (Hellenica)* (1966); *Memoirs of Socrates* and *Symposium* (1970); in EL *The Education of Cyrus* (1992, first pub. 1914).

J. K. Anderson, *Xenophon* (London, 1974).

Author Index

This is an index to authors and works named in the introductory sections of each chapter. For an index to the extracts see References; for further details of authors see Bibliographical Appendix.